POPULATION AND HEALTH

POPULATION AND HEALTH

Edited by

Dr. Aditya Kumar Patra

Deptt. of Economics
Kalinga Mahavidyalaya
Berhampur University
G.Udayagiri, Kandhamal Distt.
(Orissa)

&

Mr. Rajib Lochan Panigrahy

Faculty of Information Technology & Management
Ambedkar College of Management & Technology
Berhampur
(Orissa)

DPH

DISCOVERY PUBLISHING HOUSE PVT. LTD.
NEW DELHI-110 002

Published by:

DISCOVERY PUBLISHING HOUSE PVT. LTD.
4383/4B, Ansari Road, Darya Ganj
New Delhi-110 002 (India)
Phone : +91-11-23279245; 23253475; 43596065
E-mail : discoverybooksindia@gmail.com
discoverypublishinghouse@gmail.com
namitwasan9@gmail.com
web : www.discoverypublishinggroup.com

***First Edition:* 2010**

ISBN: 978-81-8356-584-4

Population and Health

Printed at:
Infinity Imaging Systems
Delhi

Preface

"Health is Wealth", it is a very popular notation in the society between common men. In any economy, the population is the best national property which is called as human resources. If the human resources are healthy, the economy will be healthy. So, the nation has its duty to maintain the healthy society in the nation. It implies for economic development of the nation, for Human Resource Development (HRD), public health is more crucial. Giving weightage to the health of the public, Government have assignments on health and sanitation matters. In the highly populated country such as India, most of the people are living in villages and many are living in slums, etc. Though who are living in urban areas, they are also living in less hygienic conditions, polluted environments. So, Government is providing many facilities on health and sanitation matters.

Of mostly health matters of India in such an over crowdedness and rapid population growth, the researchers has been contributed their valuable unique research articles to this book which compiles it a healthier one. So, we congratulate for their article(s) and owe out sense of gratitude for their timely contribution. Again we are very much thankful to the publisher to make it success to see the limelight.

Hope, it will be helpful to the authors, researchers, readers, libraries.

—Editors

Contents

Contributors/Author's Profile

1. **Arabinda Acharya** Compelted Master in Population Studies at International Institute for Population Science, Mumbai. At present he is working as Research Scholar at Gokhale Institute of Politics and Economics; and Demographer INDEPTH fellow at Vadu, HDSS site, Pune.
2. **Anand Singh**, Diploma in Population Studies from IIPS, Mumbai and presently working as a Senior Research Officer under the Global Adult Tobacco Survey Project under WHO at IIPS, Mumbai.
3. **Dr. H. Lhungdim**, Reader in Mortality, Morbidity and Public Health Department in IIPS, Mumbai.
4. **Uma Shankar Majhi** Compelted Master in Population Studies at International Institute for Population Science, Mumbai and currently Junior Research Fellow at the institute.
5. **Hrusikesh Tripathy** Compelted Master in Economics from Utkal University, Vani Vihar, Bhubaneswar at present Research Officer at International Institute for Population Science, Mumbai in National Rural Health Mission Evaluation Project, Mumbai.
6. **Manas Ranjan Pradhan** Completed PhD at IIPS at present associating with MAMATA Mother and Child Health Organization, New Delhi as Senior Programme Manager.

7. **Hiralal Nayak** Completed Master in Population Studies from International Institute for Population Science; currently pursuing PhD at Gokhale Institute of Politics and Economics, Pune and Research Associate at International Center for Research on Women, New Delhi.

8. **Sabyasachi Behera**, Completed Master in Population Studies from International Institute for Population Science at present Research Officer at Institute in District level Household Survey—Reproductive and Child Health Survey-III project.

9. **Sangram Kishore Patel** Completed PhD at IIPS and at present associating with World Health Organisation-Global Adult Tobacco Survey project as Information Technology (IT) consultant at institute. And he is Consultant, GATS—India Project, International Institute for Population Sciences K(IIPS), Govandi Station Road, Deonar, Mumbai.

10. **Dilip Tarai**, Completed Master in Population Studies at IIPS, Mumbai. Presently working as Epidemiologist in NRHM Project under Government of Orissa.

11. **M Guruswami** is Professor and Head in Development Studies, IIPS, Mumbai.

12. **Sandhya Mahapatro**, Research Scholar (PRC), Institute for Social and Economic Change(ISEC), Bangalore.

13. **Anadi Charan Sethi** completed Master in Population Studies at IIPS, Mumbai.

14. **Dr. M Siva Kami** is Working as Associate Professor in Institute for Social and Economic Change (ISEC), Bangalore.

15. **Dr. Rajiva Prasad** , Reader in Department of Migration and Urbanization, IIPS, Mumbai

16. **Hari Hara Sahu**, Lecturer Dept. of Sociology, Dr. Baba Saheb Ambedkar Marathwada University, Aurangabad, Maharasthra.

17. **Dr. Sudhansu Sekhar Nayak** is a Senior Faculty Member of Commerce, Rama Narayan Mahavidyalaya, Dura, Berhampur, Ganjam, Orissa under Berhampur University.

18. **Dr. Aditya Kumar Patra** is Faculty of Economics in Kalinga Mahavidyalaya, G.Udayagiri, Kandhamal Distt. of Orissa.

19. **Rajib Lochan Panigrahy** is Faculty of Information Technology and Management in Ambedkar College of Management & Technology, Berhampur.

20. **Satyaban Sahu** Compelted Master in Population Studies from International Institute for Population Science, Mumbai at present Monitoring and Evaluation Officer in *RAKSHYA*—Project of Postpartum Hemorrhage at Pathfinder International, New Delhi.

1

Knowledge and Awareness About HIV/AIDS among Married Women of 15-44 Years of Age in Maharashtra

With Reference to High and Low Prevalence Areas

Mr. Anand Singh
Dr. H. Lhungdim

INTRODUCTION

Since the first case of HIV was detected in Chennai and Mumbai in 1986, the infection has been on the rise and reported in every State of India. Within a short period it has emerged as one of the most serious public health problem in the country. India is now second only to South Africa in terms of number of people infected with HIV/AIDS, and within India Maharashtra has the largest number of infected persons. Though the rate of HIV infection is not alarmingly high but keeping in the view larger population base the number of HIV infection person in India has been estimated to be highest in the world. By the year 2003, it was estimated that India has over 5 million HIV-infected individuals and over one million persons with the Acquired Immuno-Deficiency Syndrome, AIDS (NACO). However, estimates at the national level conceal wide variations across the States. Maharashtra and Tamil Nadu account for a major share of the AIDS cases in India. Maharashtra State is no stranger to HIV/AIDS risk. Already more than one per cent women in Maharashtra are infected with HIV, showing that the epidemic has reached the general population. And in high risk group such as sex workers the rate is much higher (about 60 per cent).

The initial cases of HIV/AIDS were reported among commercial sex workers in Mumbai and Chennai and injecting drug users in the north-eastern State of Manipur. The disease spread rapidly in the areas adjoining these epicentres and by 1996 Maharashtra, Tamil Nadu and Manipur together accounted for 77 per cent of the total AIDS cases with Maharashtra reporting almost half the number of cases in the country. About 75 per cent of the infections occur from the sexual route (both heterosexual and homosexual), about 8 per cent through blood transfusion, another 8% through injecting drug use. About 89% of the reported cases are occurring in sexually active and economically productive age group of 18-40 years. One in every 4 HIV cases reported is a woman.

Table 1.1: Estimation of infection of HIV/AIDS in India

Year	*Persons infected (in million)*
1998	1.80
1999	3.70
2000	3.86
2001	3.97
2002	4.58
2003	5.106
2004	5.134

Sources: NACO.

The range of population segments already affected by the epidemic and the transmission modes suggest that most adult population is at the risk. Therefore, the epidemic has the potential of gaining alarming dimension in the country and in States like Maharashtra in the next few decades. Current statistics imply possibility of a devastating epidemic, particularly for women, who are at higher risk of HIV/AIDS due to biological and social vulnerabilities. In addition, the high prevalence of RTIs, STDs among women than their counterparts makes them more vulnerable to HIV infection. Women are also at more risk for HIV infection due to their lower status, stigmatization and other cultural taboos. Socio-economic and gender based inequalities have resulted in higher illiteracy, poor access to health care and other social services and nutritional deficiencies among women, which further compound the extent of risk of HIV infections.

Government Response to HIV/AIDS Epidemic

In 1986, the Government of India established National AIDS Control Programme (NACP) with in the Ministry of Health and Family Welfare. The programme's principal activity was then limited to monitoring HIV infection rates among risk populations in select urban areas. Later in 1991, the strategy was revised to focus on blood safety, prevention among high-risk populations, raising awareness in the general population, and improving surveillance. A semi-autonomous body, the National AIDS Control Organization (NACO), was established to implement this programme. This "first phase" of the National AIDS Control Programme lasted from 1992 -1999. It focused on initiating a national commitment, increasing awareness and addressing blood safety. It achieved some of its objectives, notably an increased awareness. Law banned professional blood donations and screening of donated blood became almost universal by the end of this phase.

The second phase of the NACP began in 1999 (until March 2006). During this phase, the programme expands at the state level and greater emphasis placed on targeted interventions for high-risk groups, preventive interventions among the general population, and involvement of NGOs and other sectors and line departments, such as education, transport and police. The Government of India is currently preparing for the third phase of the National AIDS Control Programme (NACP 3). The design of NACP 3 envisages a complex consultative process including nationwide consultations with various national stakeholders, as well as international development partners.

State AIDS Control Societies

State AIDS Cells were created in all the 32 States and UTs of the country for the effective implementation and management of National AIDS Control Programme.

Non-Governmental Organizations (NGOs)

Since 1986, numerous NGOs are working on HIV/AIDS issues in India at the local, State, and national levels. Most programmes include targeted interventions with high-risk groups; direct care of people living with HIV/AIDS; general awareness campaigns; and care for AIDS orphans. Most NGOs could implement their programmes with support from a variety of sources such as the ministry or state governments, international donors, and local contributions.

HIV/AIDS Scenario in Maharashtra

As of 2006 there are 14,325 AIDS cases in Maharashtra (NACO, 2006). Based on NACO sentinel sites, HIV prevalence in Maharashtra was 16 per cent (9 STD sites) and 2 per cent (35 ANC sites) in 1998, which declines to 10.40 per cent and 1.25 per cent respectively in 2004. Accordingly, Maharashtra is categorized as a 'high prevalence State' along with the States of Tamil Nadu, Manipur, Andhra Pradesh, Karnataka and Nagaland.

Besides the creation of Maharashtra State AIDS Control Society (MSACS), Mumbai Districts AIDS Control Society (MDACS) was also established in 1998 by Municipal Corporation of Greater Mumbai (MCGM) for control & prevention of HIV/AIDS in Mumbai. MDACS plays a role to catalyse, strengthen and orchestrate the expertise and resources of the various organizations working in this field under a single banner, with one overarching goal, i.e. AIDS control. The MDACS works closely with other General Health Sector, NGOs, CBOs, People Living with HIV/AIDS, Corporate Houses and Media etc. (MDACS, 1998). The Mumbai Districts AIDS Control Society has reached out to approximately1350 secondary schools till date and supported the training of teachers and implementation of the programme in all zones in Mumbai till 2005.

Some of the major activities initiated by the Government of Maharashtra through the Maharashtra State AIDS Control Society (MSACS) are: (1) STD Control Programme (to reduce STD cases and thereby control HIV transmission); (2) Information, Education and Communication programmes (to generate awareness, modify attitudes and change behaviour through various means such as theatre groups, folk artists, publishing pamphlets, posters, banners, television spots, radio jingles, exhibition sets, newspaper advertisements, etc.); (3) Organizing Mahothsavs for creating awareness amongst the general population; (4) Youth awareness programmes; and (5) Primary teachers conventions.

NEED FOR THE STUDY

HIV/AIDS is now a major public health problem in India, which gradually affects only high risk groups or urban population. The infection has spread to rural area and the general population and the epidemic continues to shift towards younger women and young men.

Even in spite of increasing realization that the adult population is vulnerable to HIV/AIDS in Maharashtra, most of HIV/AIDS studies and programme interventions are focus either on 'high risk groups' such as commercial sex workers (CSWs), truckers and eunuchs (*hijras*), or in and around Mumbai areas and other selected high prevalent districts of the state. There is no focus on district-wise picture of awareness or infection, particularly of low prevalent areas of the state. Besides, as HIV/AIDS has no cure so far, prevention through awareness programmes has been the most essential medicine. Therefore, awareness level has to be high and consistent in all the districts and sub-populations to prevent further spread of HIV.

The gap in KAP of HIV/AIDS is widening due to more attention given to some districts. In this paper the focus has been to examine and highlight the pattern and gaps in HIV/AIDS awareness among married women in both high as well as low prevalent areas. This study also highlight differentials with respect to selected socio-economic back ground characteristics like residence, religion, caste and standard of living, in the extent of knowledge and awareness about HIV/AIDS between two areas with different levels of prevalence. The results of such comparative studies are expected to be more useful in terms of programme implementations and to strengthen intervention programmes for women. The variations in the extent of knowledge will also strengthen programmes at grass root level for all segments.

DATA AND METHOD

The data used in this study is the DLHS-RCH–2 survey, conducted in 2002. In DLHS, information on awareness of HIV/AIDS sources of knowledge, mode of transmission, misconception and preventive measures of HIV/AIDS have been collected from ever married women age 15-44. Thus, this study is based on responses from 20,332 women only for the state of Maharashtra and two divisions, namely Pune and Aurangabad.

Besides understanding the extent and differentials in the overall level of knowledge and awareness of HIV/AIDS in the state among the women, it also intended to examine the issue among women in: (1) a high prevalence area; and (2) a low prevalence area. To do this, Pune Division and Aurangabad Division have been selected for analysis based on NACO's definition of prevalence. By this definition of NACO, Pune division is a high prevalence area (>5% among high risk groups and 1% from ANC sites) and Aurangabad Division is a low prevalence area (<5% among high risk groups and <1% in ANC sites). In Pune division there are five districts namely Pune, Solapur, Kolhapur, Sangli, and Satara, while Aurangabad division has eight districts namely Nanded, Hingoli, Parbhani, Jalna, Aurangabad, Bid, Latur and Osmanabad. The number of respondents is 3441 women and 5418 women respectively.

Of the several variables used in this study, two variables namely religion and education have been coded differently for this purpose. Besides cross tabulations, a regression analysis is also done to understand the factors influencing awareness in Maharashtra and in the two other divisions.

OBJECTIVES

The objectives of the study are:

- To know the level of knowledge and awareness of HIV/AIDS among married women age 15-44.
- Differentials in HIV/AIDS knowledge by related socio-demographic indicators
- To examine the differences in awareness and knowledge of HIV/AIDS between Pune division (high prevalence area) and Aurangabad division (low prevalence area) in Maharashtra.

RESULTS AND FINDINGS

1. Profile of the respondents by background characteristics

DLHS-2 covers 20,332 ever married women age 15-44 in Maharashtra. The survey interviewed larger proportion of women age 20-35 (63 per cent) compared to 35-44 (28 per cent) and 9 per cent women age 15-19. Eighty-two per cent women are Hindu and 42 per cent have education upto primary level. Majority of women are from rural areas (64 per cent) compared to urban areas. Twenty-eight per cent women are from the highest standard of living (SLI). Forty-one per cent belong to other caste category while OBC women accounted for 27 per cent.

In the case of Pune division and Aurangabad division also the background characteristics of women show a similar pattern.

2. Awareness and knowledge about HIV/AIDS among married women age 15-44 in Maharashtra and in Pune and Aurangabad divisions

Table 1.2 presents the percentage of ever married women who have ever heard of HIV/AIDS by their background characteristics, Maharashtra, Pune and Aurangabad division, (RCH_DLHS 2002-2004).

Table 1.2: Percentage of ever-married women who ever heard of HIV/AIDS by background characteristics in Maharashtra, Pune Division and Aurangabad Division(RCH-2002-2004)

Background characteristics	*Pune* %	*Division Number*	*Aurangabad* %	*Division Number*	*Maharashtra* %	*Division Number*
1	*2*	*3*	*4*	*5*	*6*	*7*
Age group						
15-19	91.0	334	78.1	830	73.9	1693
20-34	92.6	2200	77.5	3329	76.5	13083
35-44	88.7	907	72.7	1259	72.6	5556
Education						
Upto primary	93.0	1072	83.4	1511	78.9	5831
Middle	97.9	1003	95.0	1124	92.4	5960
Secondary and Higher	99.1	533	100.0	574	99.2	3713
Religion						
Hindu	91.3	3005	76.1	4095	73.8	16327
Muslim	91.5	247	78.4	757	80.9	2057
Others	94.1	191	76.5	566	81.4	1949
Residence						
Rural	90.8	2219	71.1	3434	67.3	11564
Urban	92.4	1223	87.7	1984	89.0	8768

(Contd…)

1	2	3	4	5	6	7
Caste						
SC	90.4	499	77.1	975	78.2	2965
ST	89.3	241	63.3	692	48.0	2258
OBC	87.9	729	77.3	1221	74.7	5514
Others	93.2	1954	80.3	2505	86.2	9467
SLI						
Low	84.8	932	65.3	2205	54.7	5434
Medium	92.5	1262	82.6	2068	80.5	7600
High	95.9	1248	94.9	1145	95.1	7298
Total	**91.4**	**3441**	**76.4**	**5418**	**75.2**	**20332**

The Table 1.2 indicates that 75 percent of ever married women in Maharashtra heard about HIV/AIDS. However, by age the awareness level is highest among women age 20-34 (77 percent) and lowest among women age 35-44 (73 percent). Among married adolescent women the awareness level is 74 percent. Awareness level is highest among married women who had secondary and above education (99 percent) and women in the highest standard of living (95 percent). Therefore, data indicate that education, urban and economic parameters have positive relation with awareness in Maharashtra.

When comparing the two divisions (areas of high and low prevalence), it is found that overall awareness level is higher by 15 percent point in Pune division (91 percent) compared to Aurangabad division (76 percent). Overall, awareness level for each background characteristic is much higher in Pune division. However, in Pune division variation in awareness is found to be sharper when considering standard of living. For instance, the difference in the level is about 11 percent point between the low and high SLI groups. There is not much variation even by residence. However, OBC women reported lower awareness (88 percent) compared to other caste groups.

In the case of Aurangabad division (low prevalence area), more variation in awareness is indicated, particularly with education, residence and standard of living. For instance, 65 percent of women in the low SLI have heard of HIV/AIDS compared to 95 percent women in the high SLI. Similarly, a large gap in awareness level is also indicated by education. While all (100 percent) married women who studied upto secondary and above levels have heard of HIV/AIDS, it is only about 83 percent among those who had upto primary level education. Awareness level is also much lower among ST women (63 percent) than among other groups.

Besides the overall awareness, knowledge about prevention is also examined by state and divisions. It can be seen from the graph (Fig 1.1) that in all the five modes of transmission of HIV/AIDS, women in Pune have better/higher knowledge compared with women in Aurangabad division. The proportion of married women is the highest in both the divisions (77 percent in Aurangabad division and 81 percent in Pune division) who consider heterosexual intercourse as one of the most important factor of HIV/AIDS transmission, followed by sharing needles/ syringes (36 percent and 51 percent respectively). Among the modes, very few women (less than one percent in Aurangabad division and 6 percent in Pune division) knew that homosexual intercourse could transmit HIV/AIDS.

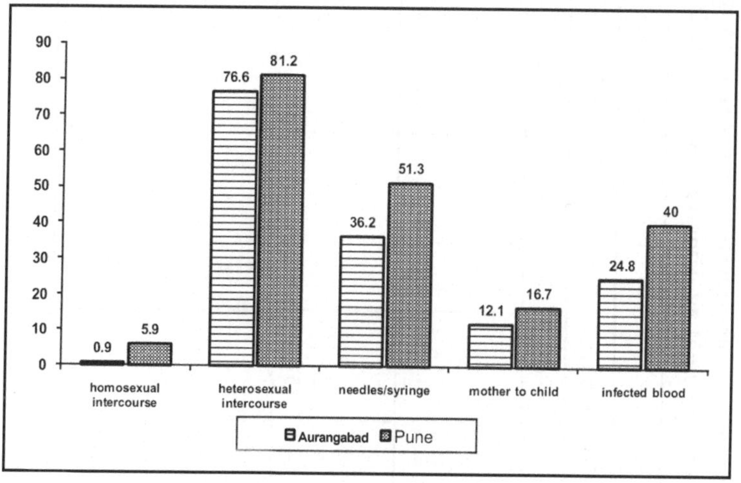

Fig. 1.1: **Per cent of ever married women who are aware about HIV/AIDS models of Transmission**

3. Sources of HIV/AIDS

Table 1.3 shows the distribution of ever-married women by sources of knowledge of HIV/AIDS with their background characteristics for Pune and Aurangabad divisions (RCH_DLHS 2002-2004).

Source of knowledge is an important indication of household economic status of women, which reflects the awareness level of HIV/AIDS. The table shows that relative and friends are the most prominent source of knowledge in both the divisions (66 percent in Pune division and 64 percent in

Table 1.3: Percentage distribution of ever married women basis of sources of knowledge by background characteristics Pune division and Aurangabag division, (RCH-2002-2004)

Background characteristics	*Radio*		*Television*		*News*		*Doctor*		*Health worker*		*Relative & friends*	
	Aurangabad	*Pune*	*Aurangabad*	*Pune*	*Aurangabad*	*Pune*	*Aurangabad*	*Pune*	*Aurangabad*	*Pune*	*Aurangabad*	*Pune*
1	*2*	*3*	*4*	*5*	*6*	*7*	*8*	*9*	*10*	*11*	*12*	*13*
Age group												
15-19	4.5	18.6	54.5	58.8	9.0	23.7	1.7	9.6	1.8	4.5	62.9	66.3
20-34	5.9	16.0	53.7	64.3	14.1	22.1	2.5	7.2	2.6	3.9	62.4	64.5
35-44	3.5	16.1	42.6	56.8	10.2	20.0	2.3	5.1	1.4	5.6	69.6	67.7
Education												
Up to primary	4.4	15.7	54.1	55.8	8.1	11.0	1.3	5.4	2.3	3.7	62.9	72.3
Middle	7.9	19.7	73.7	76.8	21.9	30.6	3.1	8.3	2.2	5.7	53.7	57.3
Secondary & Higher	14.3	23.3	93.0	91.6	51.2	58.9	9.1	15.0	3.8	7.3	39.0	43.7
Religion		97.7		74.8		17.6		6.3		35.1		
Hindu	5.4	17.0	48.1	60.8	12.8	22.0	2.3	6.6	2.3	4.5	66.5	66.3
Muslim	3.6	11.7	66.2	67.2	9.8	17.4	1.8	6.9	1.2	3.7	53.6	56.1
Others	5.0	11.5	54.1	70.2	13.1	23.6	3.5	12.1	3.2	4.7	61.0	64.4
Residence												
Rural	4.5	16.9	37.0	54.1	7.0	17.2	1.9	5.9	2.5	5.4	73.4	71.8
Urban	6.3	15.4	75.9	75.7	21.7	29.9	3.1	8.6	1.7	2.7	48.0	54.0

(Contd…)

1	2	3	4	5	6	7	8	9	10	11	12	13
Caste												
SC	5.7	13.3	48.9	59.5	10.4	16.2	2.6	7.0	3.3	3.4	64.5	70.1
ST	4.2	5.4	35.0	52.5	6.9	16.6	2.0	6.2	3.0	3.3	72.7	82.9
OBC	4.5	12.3	50.9	61.2	11.6	21.4	2.9	7.1	2.5	3.0	67.1	66.0
Others	5.5	19.6	56.8	63.6	15.2	23.7	2.2	6.8	1.5	5.3	60.4	62.1
SLI												
Low	3.2	14.4	21.7	28.1	3.3	7.7	1.5	5.5	2.6	4.4	79.6	82.0
Medium	5.2	15.4	63.0	67.0	10.3	16.3	1.8	5.8	2.0	5.2	60.0	66.6
High	8.8	18.7	86.8	81.7	33.8	37.6	5.0	9.1	1.9	3.8	41.8	52.1
Total	**5.2**	**16.3**	**51.2**	**61.8**	**12.4**	**21.7**	**2.4**	**6.9**	**2.2**	**4.4**	**64.1**	**65.5**

Aurangabad division), followed by TV (62 percent in Pune and 51 percent in Aurangabad). The least popular source in both the divisions is the health worker (4 percent in Pune and 2 percent in Aurangabad). Doctors also do not fare well as a source in both the divisions (7 percent in Pune areas and 2 percent in Aurangabad areas).

The sources of knowledge for HIV/AIDS differ greatly by education and SLI. Women who live in urban areas, most educated (secondary and above) and those in high SLI learnt about HIV/AIDS mainly from TV. TV as a source is mentioned by 93 percent in Aurangabad areas and 92 in Pune areas. Newspaper/pamphlet/slogan are other important sources for those women who had secondary and above education and high SLI (51 percent in Aurangabad and 59 percent in Pune).

In Aurangabad division, relatives and friends are the most important sources of HIV/AIDS for married women living in rural areas (73 percent), belonging to scheduled caste (73 percent) and from lowest SLI (80 percent). A similar pattern is seen in Pune division also but the proportions are much higher (83 percent for ST women, 82 percent for low SLI women and 72 percent for women with education up to primary).

4. Misconceptions about HIV/AIDS transmission

Table 1.4 presents the percentage distribution of misconceptions about HIV/AIDS transmission among ever-married women age 15-44 by their background characteristics in Pune and Aurangabad divisions (RCH_DLHS 2002-2004).

People generally have misconception about ways in which HIV/AIDS is transmitted such as shaking hands with a person having AIDS, hugging and kissing with them, sharing their clothes or sharing eating utensils and bitten by mosquitoes. Understanding the level of misconceptions is crucial for effective prevention and implementation of programmes. Table 1.4 shows that overall majority of women have misconceptions about HIV/AIDS transmission with regard to mosquito bites and sharing utensils/clothes. Interestingly, women of all backgrounds have similar misconceptions in this regard.

Table 1.4: Percentage distribution of ever married women basis of misconception about HIV/AIDS by background characteristics Pune division and Aurangabag division, (RCH-2002-2004)

Background characteristics	*Handshaking*		*Hugging*		*Kissing*		*Sharing clothes*		*Sharing Utensils*		*Mosquito Bites*	
	ABD	*Pune*	*ABD*	*Pune*	*ABD*	*Pune*	*ABD*	*Pune*	*ABD*	*Pune*	*ABD*	*Pune*
1	*2*	*3*	*4*	*5*	*6*	*7*	*8*	*9*	*10*	*11*	*12*	*13*
Age group												
15-19	22.0	9.6	24.1	10.2	28.8	19.5	31.1	15.2	32.9	15.3	35.4	26.0
20-34	16.3	11.0	18.2	11.6	21.8	16.0	24.3	16.2	25.1	17.2	28.9	26.0
35-44	17.5	9.8	20.1	11.2	24.6	14.4	27.1	16.0	27.6	15.7	29.6	22.5
Education												
Primary	18.4	13.5	20.8	14.3	24.6	18.9	27.9	19.1	29.6	19.9	31.4	27.4
Middle	15.1	7.6	16.5	8.3	21.6	15.3	23.0	15.2	23.7	15.5	31.1	27.2
Secondary & Higher	5.2	2.8	5.9	4.3	9.8	6.8	9.8	6.0	9.4	6.4	22.6	21.4
Religion												
Hindu	18.3	10.7	20.8	11.4	24.8	16.0	27.5	16.2	28.5	16.8	30.5	25.4
Muslim	14.7	11.8	15.7	13.0	19.2	18.1	20.1	15.4	19.6	16.2	27.6	24.8
Others	15.2	7.3	15.5	8.4	20.3	12.6	22.6	13.7	24.8	14.2	30.2	20.0
Residence												
Rural	21.3	11.9	23.7	12.7	27.8	18.0	30.5	17.8	31.9	18.7	32.0	26.1
Urban	10.9	8.3	12.4	9.0	16.2	12.2	18.1	12.8	18.1	12.8	26.8	23.3

(Contd...)

1	2	3	4	5	6	7	8	9	10	11	12	13
Caste												
SC	18.7	10.6	20.1	11.2	25.2	17.2	27.3	18.3	28.8	18.6	31.9	24.4
ST	18.2	12.9	22.0	12.9	26.0	15.4	29.9	15.8	31.5	16.2	30.5	24.6
OBC	18.6	9.7	19.8	11.1	21.8	13.7	26.0	14.4	25.9	15.6	29.0	27.0
Others	16.3	10.5	18.5	11.3	23.1	16.2	24.5	16.1	25.4	16.5	29.8	24.4
SLI												
Low	22.3	15.0	25.2	16.3	29.0	22.2	33.2	21.0	33.7	22.6	32.0	26.0
Medium	17.4	11.2	19.0	11.3	22.5	15.6	25.0	16.8	26.5	17.3	30.2	26.3
High	8.4	6.7	9.7	7.8	14.9	11.5	14.1	11.6	14.3	11.3	26.1	23.2
Total	**17.5**	**10.6**	**19.6**	**11.4**	**23.5**	**15.9**	**26.0**	**16.1**	**26.9**	**15.2**	**30.1**	**25.1**

Between the two divisions, it is also indicated that women in Aurangabad divisions showed more misconceptions than in Pune division. In Aurangabad division, women have higher level of misconception particularly with mosquito bites (30 percent), sharing utensils (27 percent), sharing clothes (26 percent) and kissing (24 percent). Even the lowest percentage of misconceptions about HIV/AIDS in Aurangabad division is quite substantial. For instance, 18 percent women think HIV/AIDS can be acquired by shaking hands while 20 percent believe it can be transmitted by hugging someone. In the case of Pune divisions, the picture is slightly better. The proportions of women having misconceptions with various modes of HIV/AIDS are much lower.

5. Women's likelihood of awareness about HIV/AIDS by selected characteristics: Results of regression analyses.

Table 1.5 shows odds ratios from regression analyses assessing women's likelihood of awareness about HIV/AIDS by selected characteristics.

In multivariate analyses for Maharashtra, women age 35-44 had significantly low odds than 15-19 years old of being aware about HIV/AIDS. Similarly, compared with illiterate women, literate women had significantly greater odds of being aware about HIV/AIDS (3.75 odds ratios). The odds are also lower for Muslim and others women compared with Hindu women. However, the odds are significantly higher for urban women than rural women (1.23 odds ratios). In case of ethnicity also, women of scheduled tribe and OBC had significantly lower odds of awareness about HIV/AIDS compared with women of scheduled caste. As expected, women in medium and high SLI had significantly higher odds of being aware about HIV/AIDS (2.04 and 6.18 respectively).

Women in Pune and Aurangabad divisions reflect a different pattern of the likelihood of awareness than that of Maharashtra. In Aurangabad division, older women had significantly higher odds of awareness about HIV/AIDS than the younger women age 15-19. Also, literate women in both Pune and Aurangabad divisions had significantly higher odds compared

Table 1.5: Odds ratios from regression analyses assessing women's likelihood of being aware about HIV/AIDS by selected characteristics

Background characteristics	*Exp (B) (Aurangabad Div.)*	*Exp (B) (Pune Division)*	*Exp (B) (Maharashtra)*
1	2	3	4
Age group			
15-19@			
20-34	1.161*	1.485*	0.978
35-44	1.059	1.204	1.153**
Education			
Illiterate @			
Literate	.274***	.204***	3.754***
Religion			
Hindu@			
Muslim	.726***	0.852	1.517***
Others	.751**	1.741	
Residence			
Rural@			
Urban	1.500***	.751**	.813***

(Contd…)

1	2	3	4
Caste			
SC@			
ST	.492***	0.839	2.941***
OBC	.731***	.632**	1.727***
Others	.792**	1.005	0.911
Standard of living index			
Low@			
Medium	1.774***	1.721***	.489***
High	3.809***	2.545***	.162***

@ = reference category

*** At 1 % level of significance.

** At 5% level of significance.

* At 10 % level of significance.

with illiterate women of awareness (4.91 and 3.64 respectively). Similarly, compared with scheduled caste women other women in both the divisions had significantly higher odds of being aware about HIV/AIDS. In the case of SLI, women with medium and high SLI had significantly much higher odds of awareness.

SUMMARY AND CONCLUSIONS

In conclusion, the following points emerge from this study on knowledge and awareness about HIV/AIDS among ever married women age 15-44 in Maharashtra:

1. Maharashtra has almost half the number of HIV/AIDS cases in the country. As of 2006 there are 14,325 AIDS cases in Maharashtra (NACO, 2006). Based on NACO sentinel sites, HIV prevalence in Maharashtra was 16 percent (9 STD sites) and 2 percent (35 ANC sites) in 1998, which declines to 10.40 percent and 1.25 percent respectively in 2004.
2. Overall awareness and knowledge levels are much higher in the high prevalence area (Pune division) compared to low prevalence area (Aurangabad division). The level is higher by 15 percent point in Pune division (91 percent) compared to Aurangabad division (76 percent).
3. Relatives and friends are the most common sources of HIV/AIDS in Maharashtra, more so for women belonging to ST, low SLI and illiterate. TV and newspaper/pamphlets/slogan are more important sources for women in the high SLI, urban and higher education. Health worker and doctors are the least mentioned sources for HIV/AIDS by women.
4. The most common misconception women had about HIV/AIDS transmission is mosquito bites in Maharashtra (21 percent), followed by sharing utensils/clothes (16 percent).
5. Majority of women in Maharashtra (82 percent) mention heterosexual intercourse main mode of transmission of HIV/AIDS. The figure is 81 percent for Pune division and 77 percent in Aurangabad division.

6. Multivariate analyses clearly bring out the fact that the odds of awareness about HIV/AIDS is significantly higher with married women of higher age groups (20-44), educated women, and women from the medium and high SLI.

REFERENCES

Bhende, A (1995), *Evolving a Model for AIDS Prevention, Education Among Under –Privileged Adolescent Girls in Urban India,* Research Report, Series No. 5, Women and AIDS Research Programme.

Eleanor., M *et al.*, 1994 *Knowledge, Attitude and Beliefs About HIV/AIDS Among Women in Northern Thailand.* AIDS Education and Prevention, 6(3): 205-218.

Family Health International (2001) *What Drives HIV in Asia*? "A Summary of Trends in Sexual and Drug-taking Behaviour (Prepared by Elizabeth Pisani and Boonyaruk Winitthama)." Arlington: Family Health International.

HIV Patientd: Knowledge and Sexual Risk Patterns",T.S. Arunkumar, S. Irudaya Rajan, RAKEE, *EPW* MARCH 20, 2004.

Kulkarni, V. (1999), *Networks, Language and Sexual Behaviour of Men who have Sex with Men,* Report to Ford Foundation, New Delhi.

Kilmarx P *et al.* (2000) *Youth and HIV/AIDS: Can We Avoid Catastrophe?* Population Report, Series L, No. 12. Baltimore, The Johns Hopkins University Bloomberg School of Public Health, Population Information Programme.

National AIDS Control Organization (2001), *Behavioural Surveillance Survey, Report,* New Delhi.

Nag, M. (1994), "Sexual Behaviour and AIDS in India; State of the Art", *Indian Journal of Social Work,* Vol. 55, 4, pp. 503-547.

National AIDS Control Organization (NACO) (2004), *Annual Report of 2004,* New Delhi.

Nampanya, S. Namposya (2000), "Socialand Economic Risk Factors for HIV/AIDS Affected Families in Zambia" Paper Presented at the AIDS and Economic Symposium, Durban South Africa, July 7-8.

Parvi K, (1989) Epidemiological Features of AIDS : "A Global Public Health Problem." *Bulletin of CARC* (ICMR) : 2 (No. 2, 3, 4): 4-10.

Reproductive and Child Health (2002-04), *District Level Household Survey, Report,* International Institute for Population Sciences, (Deemed University) Mumbai - 400 088.

Row Kavi, A. (1993), "HIV/AIDS Awareness in the Self Identified Gay Community and Its Implication", Paper Presented at the Workshop on the Sexual Aspect of AIDS/STD Prevention in India, Tata Institute of Social Sciences, Mumbai.

Shalini, B. (1995), HIV/AIDS and the Family: Issues in Care and Support. Indian Journal of Social Work. 56 (2): 177-194.

United Nations Population Fund, India (1999), *Reproductive Tract Infections in India: The HIV/AIDS Connection*, November, UNFPA, New Delhi.

UNAIDS (2000), *Report on the Global HIV/AIDS Epidemic*, UNAIDS, Geneva.

WHO (1989), *Special Programme on AIDS: Statement from the Consultation on STD as a Risk Factor for Transmission*, HO/SPA/INF/89.6.

UNESCO (2001) Strategic Resource Guide: Strategies for Action to Combat HIV/AIDS with in the Education Sector Ghana.

UNAIDS (2000) Enhancing the Greater Involvement of People Living with or Affected by HIV/AIDS (GIPA) in sub-Saharan Africa. A UN Response: How Far have we gone? G ENEVA: UNAIDS.

2

Antenatal Care
A Contributing Factor for Enhancing Child Immunization

Hiralal Nayak

INTRODUCTION

Health and wellbeing of mother and children is an important indicator of human development. Thus the Government of India has accorded high priority to the programs aimed at improving the health of mother and children. As a part of over-all strategy, for improving the child survival rate, the Universal Immunization Programme (UIP) was launched in November 1985. The objective of it is to accelerate the coverage of immunization and to protect all infants from the devastating, but vaccine preventable diseases like, Neo-natal tetanus, Poliomyelitis, Diphtheria, Pertussis (Whooping cough), Measles, and Tuberculosis. As neonatal tetanus is one of the major causes of infant deaths, vaccinating the pregnant woman with Tetanus Toxoid is very important. It not only protects the pregnant woman but also protects the newborn from tetanus infection. Besides this after live birth vaccinating the child with BCG, DPT, and Measles is equally important for child survival.

Over time the growing concern remained on promotion of maternal and child health. Looking into this concern, the Reproductive and Child Health (RCH) programme was launched with a focus on improvement of women's health by providing better quality of care, promoting interaction between providers and beneficiaries and increasing the availability of female health care providers at the grass root level. Thus at least three antenatal checkups for a pregnant women and complete immunization of the children is considered as an important aspect for safe motherhood and child survival. However these services are provided to community through Dispensaries, Sub-Centres, Primary Health Centres and Community Health Centres. Similarly the National Rural Health Mission also aims at reducing maternal and child mortality. It has a intense focus on universal access and optimum utilization of public health care services by the community. The mission emphasizes on the services, which are addressing women's and children's health needs. Even various schemes have been launched for promoting a healthier motherhood and baby.

Experiences in studying the issues around antenatal care clearly depicts that, ANC has a strong influence on mother and her newborn's health, which has potential for child survival. Research has shown that a narrower range of antenatal services during visits to health care providers can also improve maternal and newborn *health* (Population Reference Bureau, 2003). A study in central Uttar Pradesh shows that, provision of health care services to mothers during the antenatal period promotes the acceptance of immunization programmes (Srivastava, and Saksena, 1998). The National Family Health Survey-II results show that medical care for mothers has an important effect on child survival. Infant mortality rates are more than twice as high for children whose did not receive any maternity related care as for children whose mothers received such care (Asia Pacific Population and Policy, 2001). As nearly two thirds of infant deaths are neonatal deaths and of those, almost two thirds of these on these on the first day after birth (CARE, 2005), it has been estimated that up to 70 per cent of newborn deaths could be prevented by interventions for mother during pregnancy and childbirth and by simple, low technical newborn care such as cleanliness, breast feeding and warmth (Maternal and Neonatal Health, 2005).

OBJECTIVE

Though significant improvements have been made in many spheres of health, we still have a long way to go in improving the health of children. Thus maternal and child health has been the priority area of intervention for past many years. Since child health is an important indicator of development, this paper has attempted to examine the influence of antenatal care on child immunization.

DATA AND METHODOLOGY

The data from National Family Health Survey- II, India has been used for this study. Here information on antenatal care and child immunization has been collected from the mothers of 15 to 49 years who had given birth to a child during past three years preceding the survey.

In this paper, BCG and DPT vaccination is considered as the important component of child immunization. BCG vaccination is the first vaccination for children and it is given only once, where as DPT has three doses with regular interval. Antenatal checkups during pregnancy is important for the health of mother and child. But it is effective only when women receive necessary tests and measurements for safe motherhood. In this analysis Tetanus Toxoid vaccination of the mother is considered, as it is effective in preventing tetanus infection in growing foetus and mother. Here immunization of the last pregnancy and child is taken into consideration.

To examine the linkages between antenatal care and child immunization, bivariate relationship and logistic regression analysis has been carried out separately by controlling the socio-economic variables. Here BCG vaccination of children is used as dependent variables, which is dichotomous as 0 = Not given and 1= Given. For independent variables, modern family planning methods like condom and male sterilization is considered as male methods where as OCP, IUD, and female sterilization is considered as female methods. In addition to it, demographic variables like sex of the child, number of living children, child loss, and socio-economic variables, religion, caste, standard of living, couple's educational status, inter spousal communication about family planning, mass media exposure and availability of health facilities are also taken as independent variables for the analysis. The same is carried out separately for *urban* and *rural* areas, as it is meaningful for comparison purpose.

ANALYSIS AND FINDINGS

Relationship Between Antenatal Care and Child Immunization

Association of antenatal care and child immunization is examined by carrying out bi-variate relationship. It is observed that BCG and DPT immunization for children is significantly high among those who are going for ANC during pregnancy (Table 2.1).

Table 2.1: Percentage of BCG and DPT immunization in urban and rural India by ANC taken during Pregnancy

ANC taken during pregnancy	*BCG*				*DPT*			
	Urban		*Rural*		*Urban*		*Rural*	
	Yes	*No*	*Yes*	*No*	*Yes*	*No*	*Yes*	*No*
Yes	87.7	12.3	73.9	26.1	84.8	15.2	72.2	27.8
No	43.6	56.4	30.0	70.0	42.5	57.5	30.5	69.5

Nearly 88 and 74 per cent of the children have been immunized with BCG vaccination among the mothers who have gone for ANC during pregnancy in urban and rural areas respectively. Similarly DPT immunization for the children is 85 per cent in urban and 72 per cent in rural areas among the mothers who have gone for ANC during pregnancy. Whereas both BCG and DPT immunization of children is comparatively low among the mothers who have not received ANC during pregnancy. From the bivariate relationship it is clear that ANC during pregnancy has a positive relationship with BCG and DPT immunization of children.

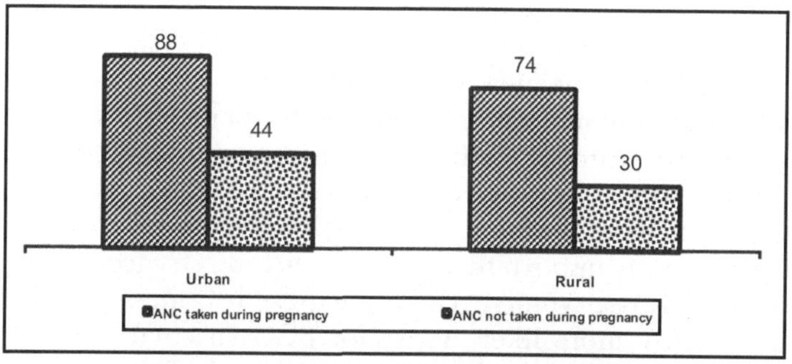

Fig. 2.1: **Percentage of BCG immunization of children by mothers ANC during pregnancy**

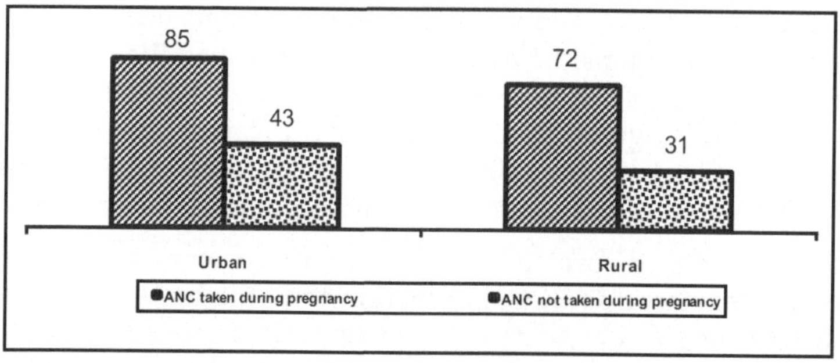

Fig. 2.2: **Percentage of DPT immunization of children by mothers ANC during pregnancy**

Variation in BCG Immunization

Further, an attempt has been made to find out the important correlates of BCG given to children (dichotomous as 0= not given, 1= given), by using logistic regression analysis (Table 2.2). Two programme components namely contraceptive use by male and female methods and ANC during pregnancy are used in this model along with other demographic and socio-economic variables. The odds ratio of BCG given to children among female family planning method users is 2.4 times higher than the same among the non-users of any family planning method in urban areas, but in case of male method users it is 3.4 times higher than the non-users. It has been seen that in case of rural areas, child immunization among the users of male and female method are almost same. The women who had gone for ANC during pregnancy are 2.8 times more likely to go for BCG immunization of her child than women who have not gone for the same. Here female child immunization is less than that of male. It is observed that as the number of living children increases the BCG immunization among children decreases significantly. Discussion about the family planning between husband and wife also plays an important role in giving BCG vaccination to children. Those women who are exposed to mass media are significantly more likely to go for BCG vaccination of their children than those who are not exposed. There is also a significant and positive relationship between BCG given to children and educational status of the couple. The odds ratio of immunizing BCG among the women of medium and high standard of living is 1.2 and 1.9 times higher than the women of low standard of living respectively. In case of non-Hindus the odds of BCG given to children is significantly less than the Hindus. Similarly the odds of BCG given to children in other categories are significantly higher than the SC/ST population.

In case of rural India contraceptive users are however more lean towards BCG vaccination than the non-users. ANC during pregnancy seems to be an important motivating factor for BCG vaccination of children. Here the odds ratio of BCG is 2.6 times higher than the non-receivers of ANC and vaccination of female child is less than male. The BCG vaccination for children decreases significantly with increase in number of living children. Mass media and inter spousal communication about family planning also plays a significant role in BCG immunization of children. There is a significant rise in BCG immunization with increasing educational level of couples. It is observed that among the non-Hindus BCG vaccination is significantly less than that of Hindus. Similarly, BCG vaccination in other caste people is higher than the SC/ST population. As the standard of living of women increases, BCG immunization among children also increases significantly. Availability of health facility near to the village has a positive impact on the BCG immunization. From this analysis it is very clear that ANC during pregnancy and family planning behaviour have a positive influence on the child immunization.

Table 2.2: Logistic regression results for BCG immunization *(0=Not given, 1=Given)* in India

Background Characteristics		*Exp* (β)	
		Urban	*Rural*
1	*2*	*3*	*4*
Contraceptive use	Not using ®		
	Female method	**2.385*****	**2.316*****
	Male method	**3.445*****	**2.259*****
	Others	**1.735**	**1.335**
ANC taken during pregnancy	No ®		
	Yes	**2.759*****	**2.573*****
Sex of the child	Male ®		
	Female	**0.893***	**0.936****
No. of living children	< 2 ®		
	> 3	**0.654*****	**0.773*****
Child loss	Not experienced ®		
	Experienced	**0.903**	**0.921****
Inter spousal communication about family planning methods	No ®		
	Yes	**1.216*****	**1.222*****

(Contd…)

1	*2*	*3*	*4*
Exposure to mass media	No ®		
	Yes	**1.400*****	**1.468*****
Educational status of the couple	Both are illiterate ®		
	One of them are literate	**1.397*****	**1.429*****
	Both are literate	**2.371*****	**2.230*****
Religion	Hindu ®		
	Non Hindu	**0.841****	**0.816*****
Caste	SC/ST ®		
	Others	**1.118**	**0.983**
Standard of living	Low ®		
	Medium	**1.228****	**1.106*****
	High	**1.860*****	**1.495*****
Availability of health facilities	Within 5 km ®		
	More than 5 km	–	**0.859*****

(Contd…)

1	2	3	4
Regions	North ®		
	Central	0.770***	0.767***
	East	0.834	0.623***
	North-east	0.652***	0.549***
	West	1.718***	1.891***
	South	2.517***	2.238***
Constant		3.810***	2.625***

Note: *indicates significant at 10% i.e. p<0.1 level, **indicates significant at 5% i.e. p<0.05, ***indicates significant at 1% i.e. p<0.01.

CONCLUSION

The obtained results depict that, antenatal care has a significant impact on enhancing child immunization. Thus an intense focus on antenatal care in the maternal and child health programmes seems to have an additional value in strengthening child survival.

REFERENCES

Anthony K. Mboney, (2003) *"Delivering Family Planning Messages Through Parantel Care Clinics In Kumi District, Uganda"*. The International Electronic Journal of Health Education, 6 : 34-40.

Asia-Pacific Population and Policy, 2001. *"Although the Situation is Improving, Women and Children Still Face Serious Health Problems in India"*156.

Audinarayana, N. (1997) *"Determinants of Maternal and Child Immunization and Family Planning Acceptance: An Inter State Analysis"*. *The Journal of Family Welfare*, 43(1): 30-36.

CARE-India, 2005. *"Newborn Care at the Community Level"*. Technical Guide, RACHNA Programme, New Delhi, India.

CARE-India, 2005. *"The Need for a Focus on a Child Health and Nutrition"*. Technical Guide, RACHNA Programme, New Delhi, India.

International Institute for Population Sciences. *"National Family Health Survey-II"*. Report, (1998-99), India.

Maternal and Neonatal Health, 2005. *"Newborn health"*. http://www.mnh.jhpiego.org.

Ministry of Health and Family Welfare. *"Family Welfare Programme In India"*. *Year Book*, (1997-98), New Delhi.

Ministry of Health and Family Welfare, 2006. *"National Rural Health Mission"*, Process manual, Government of India.

Mishra, U.S, Roy, T.K, Irudaya Rajan. (1998) "Antenatal Care And Contraceptive Behaviour In India: Some Evidences from The National Family Health Survey". *The Journal of Family Welfare*, 44(2): 1-14.

Roy, N.C, Mishra Bhaskar and Sharma Veena. (1988) "Immunization Knowledge of Acceptors And Practice of Family Planning". *The Journal of Family Welfare*, 35(2): 13-25.

Srivastava, J.N, and Sakesena, D.N. (1988) "Immunization of Children and It's Correlates in Rural Uttar Pradesh". *The Journal of Family Welfare*, 35(1): 22-33.

UNICEF, 2006. *"Integrated Management of Neonatal and Childhood Illness"*, Rajasthan, India.

Zulfiqar, A., Gary, L. and Elizabeth, I., 2003. *"Using Evidence to Save Newborn Lives - Policy Perspectives on Newborn Health"*. Population Reference Bureau, Save the Children.

3

Estimation of Infant and Child Mortality by Caste and Place of Residence in Districts of Orissa

Mr. Dillip Tarai
M. Guruswami

INTRODUCTION

That developing countries are experiencing wide disparities in various dimensions of economic status, child nutrition, and child mortality is well established, and in many developing countries, there are hardly any proper maternal and child health services available to take care of the needs of children. The result is that in most of the developing countries infant and child mortality rates are still very high. According to a WHO report (1995), of all the deaths in developing countries, 31 per cent is among children under age five. While the general mortality in India, i.e. the crude death rate has declined since the beginning of this century, infant and child deaths have not reduced significantly. In India, approximately 1.72 million children die each year prior to reaching their first birthday, which represents one of the greatest wastages of human potential in the country.

Mortality transition in India shows infant and child mortality declining over the years. In the 19th century it declined slowly and during the 20th century the decline accelerated and reached 66 per 1000 live births in 2001. Therefore, for monitoring and evaluating population and health programmes special emphasis is laid on infant and child mortality rates. The International Conference on Population and Development (ICPD, 1994) focused on reproductive health with the objective of ensuring safe pregnancy and childbirth. Reduction of infant and child mortality is one of the important Millennium Development Goals (MDGs) which envisages reducing infant and child mortality by two-thirds between 1990 and 2015. For India, this would imply reduction of the infant mortality rate (IMR) to 27 and under five mortality rate (U5MR) to 32 by 2015. The National Population Policy 2000 has set a goal of reducing infant mortality to 30 by 2010. Reduction in infant and child mortality is not only a major goal but also an important strategy to achieve health for all.

Orissa is one of the States in eastern India, which is neither industrially nor agriculturally developed. The population of Orissa is 36.7 million of which 18.6 million were males and 18.1 million were females (constituting 3.6 per cent of the nation's population). The sex ratio was 972 females per 1000 males which are higher than the national level and the density of population increased from 203 in 1991 to 236 persons per sq km in 2001. The literacy level was 64 per cent in 2001, with male literacy of 76 per cent and female literacy of 51 per cent, which was lower than the national average. Nearly 87 per cent of Orissa's population is living in rural areas and depends mostly on agriculture. In terms of the Human Development Index, the state ranks at 11th position, and in the Human Poverty Index its rank is 31st. The total fertility rate was three children per woman and the infant mortality rate was 88 per 1000 live births in 2001.

According to the 2001 census, the total number of districts in Orissa has increased from 13 to 30. Out of the erstwhile 13 districts, the jurisdiction of only three districts viz; Sundergarh, Kendujhar and Mayurbhanj remain in tact while the remaining 10 districts were divided into 27 districts. Orissa has the highest number of tribal (62) and primitive tribal (13) groups in the country. The tribal population in Orissa constitutes a significant proportion of 30 per cent of the state's population. In western Orissa, there is heavy concentration of tribal population and in the coastal districts, they constitute a low percentage. In the KBK (Kalahandi, Balangir and Koraput) districts, noted for their poor economic infrastructure, low spread of medical facilities and widespread poverty, IMR continues to be at a high level. Orissa is classified as a socio-economically and demographically backward state in India.

Infant mortality is considered to be sensitive indicator of socio-economic and health conditions prevailing in a community and is closely associated with national socio-economic development (Antonovsky and Bernestein 1977). Mosley and Chen (1984) provided an analytical framework to study determinants of child survival in developing countries, which considered five proximate determinants namely, maternal factors (Age, parity, birth interval), environmental contamination (air, food, water), nutrient deficiency; injury (accidental, intentional) and personal illness control (preventive measures and treatment). The inverse relationship between socio-economic indicators and child and infant mortality often reflects differences in parental knowledge and skill as well as family resource (Caldwell, 1979).

A number of studies have examined empirical evidence concerning the influence of socio-economic and demographic variables on child survival (Hobcraft, 1984; Cleland, 1988; Miller, 1981; Das Gupta, 1990). UNICEF in 1985 found that where female literacy is low, infant mortality rates tend to be very high. In the Indian context, Pandey *et al.* (1998) while analyzing the NFHS-I data considered sex of the child, birth order, year of birth, place of residence, mother's education status, work participation, religion, caste and exposure to mass media, availability of toilet facility, type of cooking fuel and standard of living as the core determinants of infant and child mortality. Several other studies have also focused on the analysis of determinants of infant and child mortality covering different States of India, Rajasthan, Uttar Pradesh and Gujarat (Kanitkar and Murthy, 1988; Koshy, 1992; Tiwari, 1989; Jain et al, 1985).

There have been studies undertaken to observe the influence of previous child loss with subsequent risk to know the neonatal, post neonatal and infant mortality among women going to family welfare clinics (Prakasam, 1980). Infant and child mortality rates are also greatly reduced if mothers receive antenatal and delivery care from trained professionals (IIPS, 1995, Govindasamy, 1997). Literate mothers usually give birth to healthier babies, as they themselves tend to be healthier than mothers who are illiterate. In addition, literate mothers are more likely to provide their children with a healthy environment and nutrious food than illiterate mothers, even when other conditions are similar. Lastly, literate mothers are likely to have more information about health care facilities and to have more influence within the family in deciding to take sick children for treatment. These traits are likely to result in lower mortality for children at all ages under five (Caldwell, 1994; Cleland and Kaufman, 1993; World Bank, 1993).

NEED FOR THE STUDY

In Orissa, there is considerable regional diversity in the distribution of population groups, availabity and quality of health services including maternal health services. The scheduled tribe population constitutes about 30 per cent of the State's population and is largely concentrated in the former KBK (Kalahandi, Balangir and Koraput) region. This region is not only economically and socially underdeveloped, but also has lower coverage of health services. Though there are estimates at the state level on the differentials on infant and child mortality, there are no estimates available for the districts of Orissa by caste groups. As resource available for health services are limited, it would be useful to provide the estimates of infant child mortality by caste groups in the districts of Orissa according to place of residence. Also, the correlates of infant mortality among scheduled castes and scheduled tribes have not been explored. Therefore, this study is a modest attempt to estimate the infant mortality and child mortality in the districts of Orissa by caste and place of residence.

OBJECTIVES

The specific objectives of the study are as follows:

1. To estimate the infant and child mortality rates by caste groups and place of residence in the districts of Orissa.
2. To understand the linkages of selected reproductive and child health indicators with infant and child mortality in Orissa.

DATA SOURCE

The estimates are arrived at by using the data on children ever born (CEB) and children surviving (CS) to the women aged 15-49 years from the Census of India, 2001. Apart from the Census of India, the district level household survey (DLHS-2) data conducted by RCH-II is used to examine the linkage between selected Reproductive and Child Health indictors with infant and child mortality rates. The focus of DLHS-RCH has been on the utilization of basic reproductive and child health services such as coverage of ANC, standard of living and immunization service indicators, which influence infant and child mortality.

CONCEPTUAL FRAMEWORK

Infant mortality and child mortality is determined by demographic and socio-economic factors as background variable. Infant mortality is considered as a summary indicator of a population's living standard, health status, and socio-economic development, sanitation, immunization etc.

Socio-economic variable as background variables

- Education
- Work participation
- Medical technology
- Immunization
- ANC
- Urbanization

- **IMR**
- **CMR**

Demographic variable

- Age of mother
- children ever born
- children survival

METHODOLOGY

There are a number of indirect methods to estimate infant and child mortality using CEB and CS data (Brass 1968, Sullivan 1972, Trussell 1975). Brass was the first to develop a procedure for converting proportions of children ever born reported by women in the age groups 15-19, 20-24 etc. into estimates of the probability of dying before attaining certain exact childhood ages by assuming fertility and childhood mortality to be constant in the recent past. If fertility has been changing, the ratios of average parities obtained from a cross-sectional survey will not replicate accurately the experience of any cohort of women. Brass found that the relation between the proportion of children dead (Di) and a life table mortality measure (qi) is primarily influenced by the age pattern of fertility, because it is this pattern that determines the distribution of the children of age group of women by length of exposure to the risk of dying. Brass estimated the (Ki) multipliers by using a third degree polynomial of fixed shape but variable age location to represent fertility the logit system generated by the general standard. Trussel modify and re-estimated by using multiplying factors for the Brass technique. In this paper, the Trussel method is used. MORTPACK (Mortality analysis package) is used to estimate the infant and child mortality data using the United Nations South Asian Pattern of model life table. The estimation of infant and child mortality requires data on the following:

(i) Total women (15-49);

(ii) Children ever born (the average number of children ever born per woman); and

(iii) Children surviving (the average number of children surviving per woman) in the same age group.

(iv) *Mean age of childbearing (M)* in the population was tabulated by age of mother.

The basic assumptions are:

(i) The reporting of CEB and CS is accurate, at least by younger women.

(ii) Mortality and Fertility have remained constant or have declined linearly and slowly.

(iii) There is no relation between IMR and CMR with the age of women.

The estimating equations are as follows:

$q_1 = K_1 * D_1$ *Where i=1 for* 15-19, 2 *for* 20-24, 3 *for* 25-29. . .

D_1 = Proportion of children dead = $CEB_i - CS_i / CEBi$

K_i = Multiplier (Constant) = $E_i + A_i * (P_1/P_2) + B_i * (P_2/P_3) + C_i * \ln(P_1/P_2) + D_i * \ln(P_2/P_3)$

The reference period is calculated using equation $t_i = a_i + b_i * (P_1/P_2) + ci * (P_2/P_3)$.

Mortality estimates based on the reports of women aged 15-19 are generally disregarded in part for this reason and part because the numbers of children born and dead are usually small.

An important assumption made in the development of this method is that the risk of dying of child is a function only of the age of the child and not of the other factors such as mother's age or the child's birth order. It generally appears that children of young mothers experience mortality risks well above average. For this reason, in the estimate of the IMR, q(1) the probability of dying before age one can be derived from reports of women aged 15-19, which frequently suggest heavier child mortality than estimates derived from reports of older women. Therefore, the average of IMR and CMR to the women aged 20-25, 25-30 30-35 age groups is used. These estimates are multiplied by 1000. In addition to this, a correlation matrix is constructed to understand the association among selected variables.

RESULTS AND DISCUSSION

Table 3.1 shows the socio-economic and demographic profile of Orissa and India for 1991 and 2001. The level of infant mortality rate in Orissa continued to be higher than the national average. The life expectancy at birth, the summary indicator of health status, is lower in the state compared to the country at both the periods. Female literacy, a key indicator of development, is also lower in Orissa than the national average. The work participation rate of males and females in the state is of a similar pattern as in the country.

Table 3.1: Socio-economic and Demographic Profile of Orissa and India

Variables	*ORISSA*		*INDIA*	
	1991	*2001*	*1991*	*2001*
Total Population	31659736	36706920	84638788	1027015247
Sex Ratio	971	972	927	933
IMR*	124	91	80	66
Life Expectancy at Birth	55.7	58.7	59	62.7
Density	211	236	267	324
Literacy				
Total	49.09	64	52.21	65.38
Male	63.09	76	64.13	75.85
Female	34.68	51	39.29	54.16
Work participation rate				
Total	37.53	38.88	37.67	39.26
Male	53.79	52.75	51.52	51.93
Female	20.74	24.62	22.69	25.68

Source: Census of India, 2001 and 1991;

Note: *Sample Registration System, 2001.

The estimated infant and child mortality rates by caste for the state by sex and place of residence is given in Table 3.2. It is observed that the infant mortality rate in the state is 88 compared to 98 for Scheduled tribes and 94 for Scheduled castes per 1000 live births. There is not much difference in the infant mortality rate by sex in the state. However, the differential in infant mortality rate between rural and urban areas is sharp. The estimated infant mortality rate in rural areas is 90 compared to 70 in urban areas. In rural areas, the infant mortality rate among Scheduled tribes is 99, for Scheduled castes is 96 and 90 for the state. Similarly, in urban areas, the estimated infant mortality rate for Schedule tribes is 81 for Schedule castes 78 and 70 for the state. The pattern is similar in the case of child mortality rate.

The child mortality rate for Scheduled tribes is 32, 51 for Scheduled castes and 46 in the State per 1000 live births for the State. The differences are wider by place of residence. In rural areas the child mortality rate of Scheduled tribes is 57 and for Scheduled castes 53, but in the urban areas it is 40 for Scheduled tribes and 41 for Scheduled castes per 1000 live births. There are a number of factors responsible such as education, medical facilities, safe drinking water facilities, immunization etc. A majority of the population of Orissa live in rural areas, but information about infrastructure facilities are not available. Table 3.3 shows the trends of infant mortality rate in Orissa from 1980 to 2005. The data used in the graph (Fig. 3.1.) is from the Sample Registration System (SRS) both for rural and urban areas. Infant mortality rate in Orissa declined very slowly from 143 in 1980 to 96 in 2000 per 1000 live births with some accelerated decline from 96 in 2000 to 75 in 2005. Since 1995, infant mortality in Orissa virtually remained stagnant at 103 per live births. After 2002 it declined from 96 to 75 in 2005. The trends for rural areas of Orissa are similar to those at the State level.

Table 3.2: Infant and Child mortality in Orissa by caste and place of residence

		Infant Mortality Rate			*Child Mortality Rate*		
		Total	*Male*	*Female*	*Total*	*Male*	*Female*
Total	**Total**	88	89	86	46	47	44
	Rural	90	92	88	48	50	46
	Urban	70	71	68	31	32	30
Schedule Caste	**Total**	94	96	91	51	54	49
	Rural	96	98	94	53	56	51
	Urban	78	83	74	38	41	34
ScheduleTribe	**Total**	98	101	95	32	59	53
	Rural	99	102	96	57	60	54
	Urban	81	81	80	39	40	40

Note: Estimated from CEB and CS in the age group 15-49.

Source: Census of India, 2001.

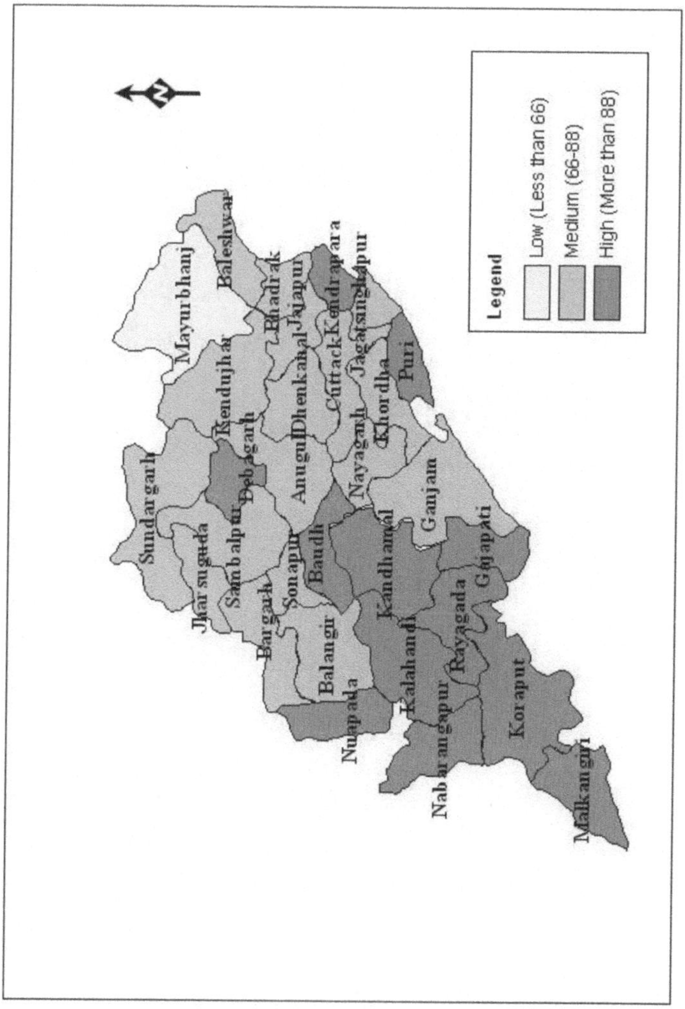

Fig. 3.1: **Infant Mortality Rate in District of Orissa (Total), 2001**

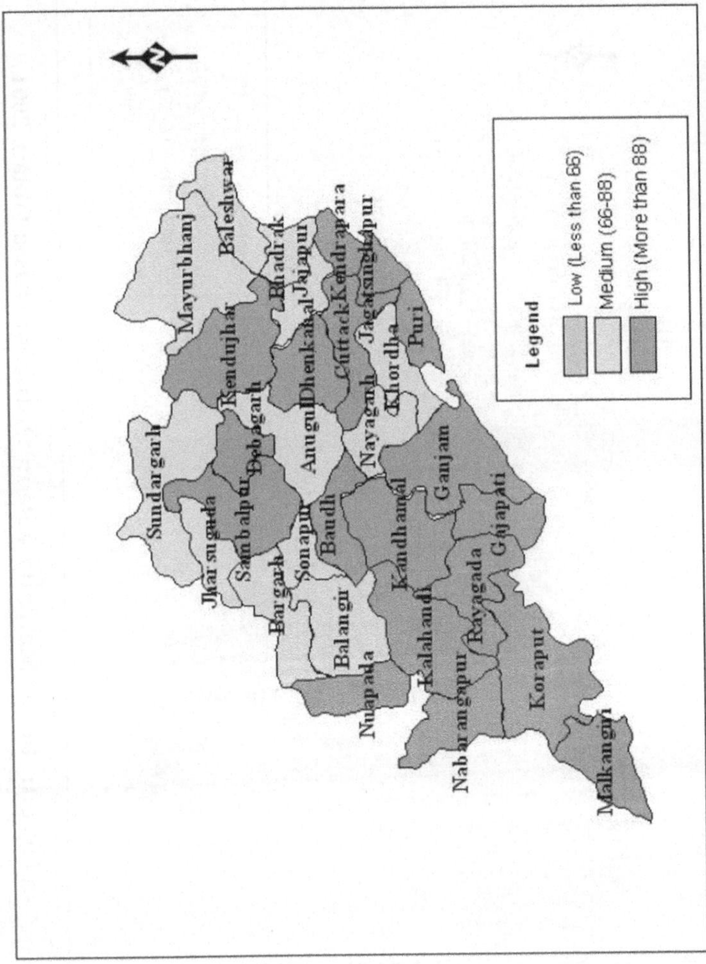

Fig. 3.2: **Infant Mortality Rate in Districts of Orissa (Rural), 2001**

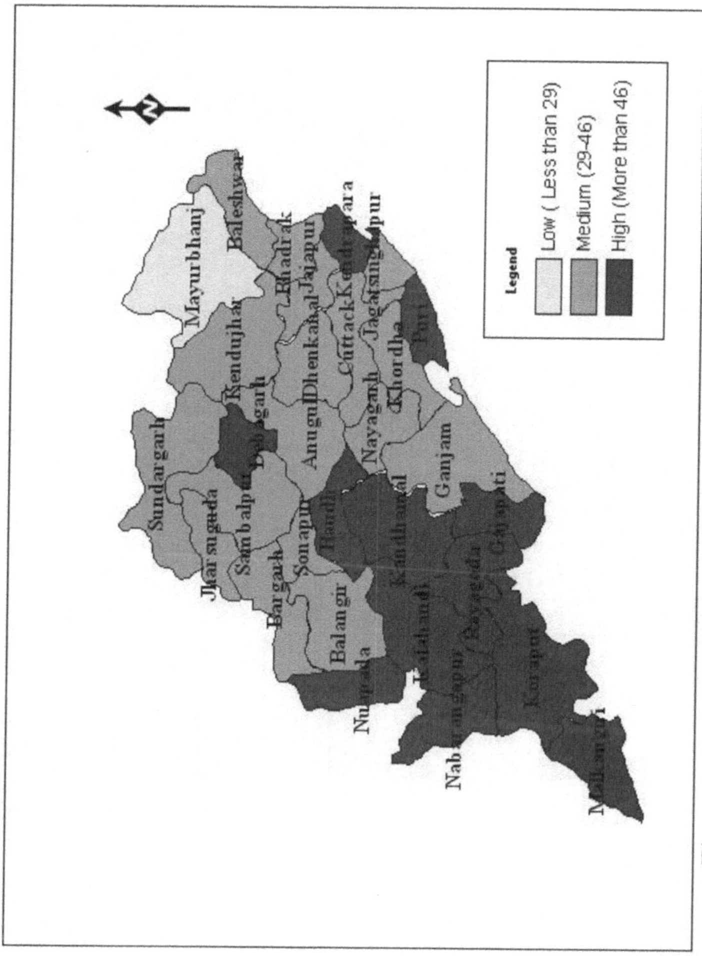

Fig. 3.3: **Child Mortality Rate in Districts of Orissa (Total), 2001**

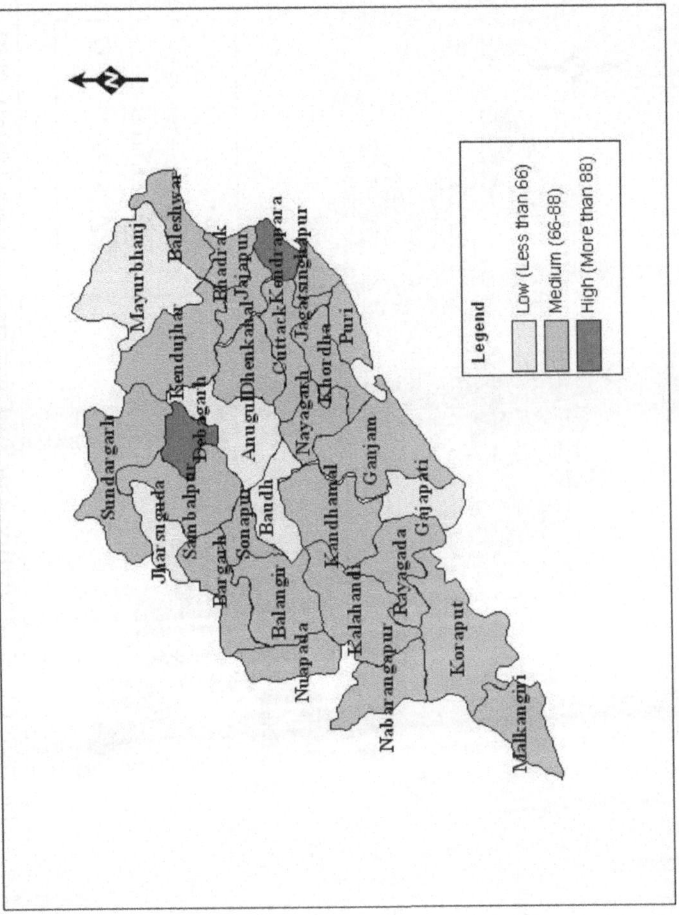

Fig. 3.4: **Infant Mortality Rate in Districts of Orissa (Urban), 2001**

Table 3.3: Levels and trends of infant mortality in Orissa

Year	*Total*	*Rural*	*Urban*
1980-1985	133	139	70
1985-1990	125	129	76
1990-1995	115	119	71
1995-2000	98	101	65
2000-2005	102	106	70

Source: Compendium of India's fertility and mortality, SRS.

Table 3.4(a) shows the estimates of infant mortality rate in the districts of Orissa. The districts have been arranged in ascending order of the infant mortality rate. It can be observed that the infant mortality rate is highest in the district of Kandhamal (119) followed by Gajapati (107) and Rayagada (106). The infant mortality rate is lowest in the district of Mayurbhanj (65) followed by Jharsuguda (68). There is a small variation in the infant mortality rate by sex. It shows the infant mortality rate of males is marginally higher than that of females in some of the districts. For a better understanding, the districts are classified into three groups on the basis of estimated infant mortality rate.

1. Infant mortality rate lower than national average (less than 66).
2. Infant mortality rate between state and national average (66-88).
3. Infant mortality rate more than state average (more than 88).

It is clear that all the districts of former KBK (Kalahandi, Balangir and Koraput) region fall under the higher range of infant mortality rate except Balangir. This region is also economically most backward. The incidence of poverty in this region is highest in the state. In addition to this, the reproductive health care utilization is lowest in this part of the State. However, only one of the 30 districts is having an infant mortality lower than the national average. The figure for the national average is obtained from the SRS (Sample Registration Sample) while that of State average is the estimated figure given in Table 3.2. It is found that only in one district (Mayurbhanj) is the infant mortality rate less than the national average. While 17 districts have an infant mortality between the state and national average, 12 districts have an infant mortality higher than the State average.

Table 3.4(a): Estimated Infant Mortality Rate by caste in Districts of Orissa (Total)

Rank	*State/ District*	*Total (IMR)*			*Schedule Caste (IMR)*			*Schedule Tribe (IMR)*		
		Total	*Male*	*Female*	*Total*	*Male*	*Female*	*Total*	*Male*	*Female*
1	*2*	*3*	*4*	*5*	*6*	*7*	*8*	*9*	*10*	*11*
01	Mayurbhanj	65	74	63	64	64	64	68	69	66
02	Jharsuguda	68	69	66	76	77	74	72	74	70
03	Bargarh	76	81	71	79	84	75	82	86	78
04	Sonapur	76	79	74	79	79	78	82	92	71
05	Khordha	79	78	79	91	93	89	93	93	93
06	Sundargarh	79	81	77	80	85	75	89	91	87
07	Baleshwar	80	92	80	90	91	89	76	77	75
08	Anugul	82	81	81	91	91	92	104	104	103
09	Balangir	82	87	76	72	87	72	93	101	84
10	Jagatsinghapur	83	85	97	88	89	88	81	82	81
11	Sambalpur	84	89	78	93	100	87	87	90	83
12	Jajapur	85	86	83	93	94	92	92	94	90
13	Ganjam	86	85	87	98	99	97	132	133	131
14	Cuttack	87	100	85	97	99	95	106	112	98
15	Kendujhar	87	90	85	85	89	82	97	99	95
	ORISSA	**88**	**89**	**86**	**94**	**96**	**91**	**98**	**101**	**95**
16	Dhenkanal	88	87	101	98	99	96	111	112	111
17	Nayagarh	88	88	88	105	109	102	121	128	116

(Contd...)

1	2	3	4	5	6	7	8	9	10	11
18	Bhadrak	88	102	87	96	97	95	85	84	86
19	Kendrapara	90	103	89	100	99	102	96	89	102
20	Puri	91	93	89	103	108	99	100	88	112
21	Nuapada	91	97	86	94	100	87	94	100	87
22	Baudh	95	100	91	98	101	96	132	135	129
23	Debagarh	98	99	105	110	114	105	113	115	112
24	Koraput	101	103	99	103	106	101	109	111	101
25	Nabarangapur	102	108	96	95	98	92	95	98	92
26	Kalahandi	103	110	96	105	114	96	119	126	112
27	Malkangiri	103	105	102	85	86	84	115	86	84
28	Rayagada	106	107	105	110	110	111	112	114	110
29	Gajapati	107	110	104	92	97	86	115	130	122
30	Kandhamal	119	122	115	114	120	107	128	132	124

Note: Estimated from CEB and CS in the age group 15-49.

Source: Census of India, 2001.

The differential in level of infant mortality rate by caste is sharp. It is found that the infant mortality rate is 132 per 1000 live births among Scheduled tribes in the district of Boudh followed by Kandhamal (128). The infant mortality rate of Scheduled castes in the districts of Kandhamal is 114 followed by Rayagada 110. The pattern is similar in many of the districts in the region. This indicates that programme efforts not been adequate to reduce the infant mortality of the Scheduled tribe population. In most of the districts, there are narrow differences in infant mortality rate between males and females. But in general, the infant mortality rate of males is higher than that of females. As females are biologically stronger than males, keeping other factors constant, the female infant mortality rate would be less than that of males.

Table 3.4(b) shows the infant mortality rate in rural Orissa. The districts have been arranged in ascending order of the infant mortality rate in rural Orissa. It may be observed that the infant mortality rate is highest in the district of Kandhamal (121) followed by Gajapati (111) and Rayagada (111). The infant mortality rate is lowest in the district of Mayurbhanj (66) followed by Jharsuguda (72). It is found that in none of the 30 districts is the infant mortality less than the national average. In 12 districts, the IMR was between the state and national average and in 18 districts; it was above the state average. It is observed that the estimated rural infant mortality rate is higher than State average in 18 out of 30 districts.

Table 3.4(b): Estimated Infant Mortality Rate by Caste in Districts of Orissa (Rural)

Rank	*State/ District*	*Total (IMR)*			*Scheduled Caste (IMR)*			*Scheduled Tribe (IMR)*		
		Total	*Male*	*Female*	*Total*	*Male*	*Female*	*Total*	*Male*	*Female*
1	*2*	*3*	*4*	*5*	*6*	*7*	*8*	*9*	*10*	*11*
01	Mayurbhanj	66	75	64	64	64	65	68	70	66
02	Jharsuguda	72	74	70	81	84	78	72	73	70
03	Bargarh	77	82	71	81	84	76	82	86	77
04	Baleshwar	77	79	76	90	91	89	77	79	76
05	Sonapur	77	88	75	78	80	76	84	75	94
06	Balangir	83	89	78	82	90	73	93	101	84
07	Anugul	84	96	82	93	92	93	104	105	103
08	Khordha	84	83	85	95	96	94	101	102	99
09	Jajapur	85	98	83	94	95	93	93	94	91
10	Bhadrak	86	85	86	97	97	97	86	85	86
11	Sundargarh	87	92	83	87	92	83	92	94	89
12	Nayagarh	88	88	88	105	107	102	121	127	116
13	Dhenkanal	89	103	87	98	99	97	111	112	110
14	Sambalpur	89	109	94	102	109	94	88	93	83
15	Jagatsinghapur	89	90	89	89	90	89	79	81	76

(Contd...)

1	2	3	4	5	6	7	8	9	10	11
16	Ganjam	89	104	87	100	101	100	133	135	132
17	Kendujhar	90	93	83	87	91	83	97	99	96
	ORISSA	**90**	**92**	**88**	**96**	**98**	**94**	**99**	**102**	**96**
18	Cuttack	91	91	91	101	102	99	106	115	98
19	Nuapada	93	98	88	96	101	90	96	101	90
20	Puri	94	96	111	105	110	102	106	95	116
21	Baudh	97	113	94	100	103	97	132	135	130
22	Debagarh	98	99	97	108	113	101	113	115	111
23	Kendrapara	100	98	102	100	98	102	99	98	101
24	Nabarangapur	103	109	98	96	99	93	96	99	93
25	Koraput	104	106	103	107	109	105	107	109	105
26	Kalahandi	105	112	97	107	116	99	104	116	99
27	Malkangiri	105	106	103	85	87	83	115	116	83
28	Rayagada	111	113	109	116	115	117	113	115	117
29	Gajapati	111	131	108	100	105	95	126	130	122
30	Kandhamal	121	142	118	115	120	110	129	133	124

Note: Estimated from CEB and CS in the age group 15-49.
Source: Census of India, 2001.

Table 3.4(c) shows the infant mortality rate in districts of urban Orissa. The pattern is relatively bettered compared to rural Orissa. It is observed that Kendrapara district ranks highest in total infant mortality rate (105) followed by Debagarh district (103). In case of schedule tribes the highest infant mortality is observed in the district of Dhenkanal (122) followed by Debagarh (114). In five districts the IMR in urban areas is found to be less than the national average, in 23 districts it is between the state and national average and in two districts it is higher than the state average This is because facilities such as water supply medical facilities, primary school, higher secondary school and immunization coverage etc are more easily available in urban than in rural areas. There is no significant sex differential in infant mortality in the urban areas. The infant mortality rate of Baudh, Puri and Nayagarh districts (urban) has not been estimated due to the small size of Schedule tribe population.

Table 3.4(c): Estimated Infant Mortality Rate by Caste in Districts of Orissa (Urban)

Rank	*State/District*	*Total (IMR)*			*Scheduled Caste (IMR)*			*Scheduled Tribe (IMR)*		
		Total	*Male*	*Female*	*Total*	*Male*	*Female*	*Total*	*Male*	*Female*
1	2	3	4	5	6	7	8	9	10	11
01	Baudh	55	56	54	48	46	51	NA	NA	NA
02	Jharsuguda	60	60	68	67	65	68	73	77	70
03	Gajapati	60	68	58	58	67	49	107	96	102
04	Mayurbhanj	63	63	60	63	63	60	54	56	51
05	Anugul	65	74	64	78	79	76	96	94	98
06	Baleshwar	67	65	70	82	83	81	67	65	70
07	Jagatsinghapur	67	69	64	67	69	64	89	88	90
08	Sambalpur	68	75	67	71	75	67	76	70	81
09	Jajapur	68	77	65	77	82	73	77	82	74
10	Sundargarh	68	72	64	68	72	64	69	72	66
11	Rayagada	68	70	67	74	77	71	90	77	71
12	Puri	69	78	67	72	85	59	NA	NA	NA
13	Ganjam	69	78	67	78	81	74	77	89	83
14	Balangir	69	72	66	66	64	67	66	64	67
15	Nuapada	69	84	54	74	89	61	74	89	61
	ORISSA	**70**	**71**	**68**	**78**	**83**	**74**	**81**	**81**	**80**
16	Bargarh	70	80	60	70	80	60	87	70	102
17	Khordha	71	80	69	81	84	78	77	73	80
18	Sonapur	71	81	69	84	75	94	75	80	76
19	Kendujhar	71	81	72	77	80	74	90	92	87

(Contd...)

1	2	3	4	5	6	7	8	9	10	11
20	Kalahandi	72	76	67	76	85	66	76	85	69
21	Cuttack	74	84	72	81	85	77	92	84	100
22	Dhenkanal	79	90	77	93	98	87	122	106	138
23	Koraput	79	83	74	87	94	79	87	94	79
24	Bhadrak	80	70	90	85	103	65	80	70	90
25	Kandhamal	80	92	78	101	116	84	94	90	96
26	Malkangiri	81	82	79	80	72	88	80	72	88
27	Nabarangapur	81	88	74	91	96	84	91	96	84
28	Nayagarh	83	95	69	116	139	84	NA	NA	NA
29	Debagarh	103	101	105	130	116	137	114	112	116
30	Kendrapara	105	111	96	105	111	96	67	59	113

Note: Estimated from CEB and CS in the age group 15-49.

Source: Census of India, 2001.

The estimated child mortality rate is given for all areas combined, rural and urban areas in Tables 3.5a, 3.5b and 3.5c respectively. The child mortality rates have been estimated using NFHS II data. The districts are classified into three groups on the basis of estimated child mortality rate:

(i) Child mortality rate lower than national average (Less than 29).

(ii) Child mortality rate between state and national average (29-46).

(iii) Child mortality rate more than state average (More than 46).

As in the case of infant mortality, it is only in Mayurbhanj district that the child mortality is less than the national average. In 17 districts the child mortality is between the State and national average and in 12 districts it is higher than the state average It is to be noted that child mortality rate is highest in Kandhamal (77) followed by Gajapati (65). The district with the lowest child mortality rate is Mayurbhanj (27) followed by Jharsuguda (30).

Table 3.5(a): Estimated Child Mortality Rate by Caste Districts of Orissa (Total)

Rank	*State/District*	*Total (CMR)*			*Scheduled Caste (CMR)*			*Scheduled Tribe (CMR)*		
		Total	*Male*	*Female*	*Total*	*Male*	*Female*	*Total*	*Male*	*Female*
1	*2*	*3*	*4*	*5*	*6*	*7*	*8*	*9*	*10*	*11*
01	Mayurbhanj	27	14	29	27	27	27	30	31	29
02	Jharsuguda	30	30	29	36	37	35	33	34	31
03	Bargarh	36	40	32	39	43	36	41	45	38
04	Sonapur	36	39	34	38	39	37	41	51	32
05	Khordha	38	38	39	49	50	47	51	50	51
06	Sundargarh	39	40	37	39	43	36	47	49	45
07	Baleshwar	39	21	39	48	49	47	36	37	35
08	Anugul	41	41	40	49	48	49	61	62	60
09	Balangir	41	45	36	33	45	33	51	59	43
10	Jagatsinghapur	41	43	23	47	47	46	40	41	40
11	Sambalpur	43	48	38	52	58	45	45	48	42

(Contd...)

1	2	3	4	5	6	7	8	*9*	*10*	*11*
12	Jajapur	44	44	43	52	53	50	50	52	48
13	Ganjam	45	44	45	55	56	54	92	94	91
14	Cuttack	45	24	48	54	57	53	63	70	56
	ORISSA	**46**	**47**	**44**	**51**	**54**	**49**	**32**	**59**	**53**
15	Kendujhar	46	48	43	44	47	41	55	56	53
16	Dhenkanal	46	46	25	55	57	54	69	69	69
17	Bhadrak	46	25	50	54	54	53	44	43	45
18	Nayagarh	46	46	46	63	66	59	80	87	74
19	Kendrapara	48	26	47	58	56	59	54	48	61
20	Puri	49	51	47	61	66	56	58	46	73
21	Nuapada	49	54	44	51	58	45	51	58	45
22	Baudh	53	57	49	55	59	53	93	97	89
23	Debagarh	55	56	62	67	72	62	71	73	69
24	Koraput	59	61	57	61	64	58	67	69	58

(Contd...)

1	2	3	4	5	6	7	8	9	10	11
25	Nabarangapur	60	66	54	53	56	50	53	56	50
26	Kalahandi	61	68	53	63	72	54	78	85	70
27	Malkangiri	61	62	60	43	45	43	73	45	43
28	Rayagada	64	65	62	68	68	69	70	72	68
29	Gajapati	65	68	62	49	54	45	73	90	81
30	Kandhamal	77	81	73	71	78	66	88	93	83

Note: Estimated from CEB and CS in the age group 15-49.

Source: Census of India, 2001.

Table 3.5(b): Estimated Child Mortality Rate by Caste in Districts of Orissa (Rural)

Rank	*State/District*	*Total (CMR)*			*Scheduled Caste (CMR)*			*Scheduled Tribe (CMR)*		
		Total	*Male*	*Female*	*Total*	*Male*	*Female*	*Total*	*Male*	*Female*
1	*2*	*3*	*4*	*5*	*6*	*7*	*8*	*9*	*10*	*11*
01	Mayurbhanj	28	15	30	27	27	27	30	31	29
02	Jharsuguda	34	35	32	41	43	39	33	34	32
03	Baleshwar	37	38	35	48	49	47	37	38	35
04	Bargarh	37	41	33	40	44	37	41	45	37
05	Sonapur	37	20	40	38	39	36	43	35	53
06	Balangir	42	47	37	40	48	33	51	59	43
07	Anugul	43	23	46	50	50	51	62	63	61
08	Khordha	43	42	44	53	54	52	58	59	57
09	Jajapur	44	24	47	52	53	51	50	52	49
10	Bhadrak	44	45	45	54	54	54	44	45	45
11	Sundargarh	46	51	42	46	51	42	50	52	48

(Contd...)

1	2	3	4	5	6	7	8	9	10	11
12	Nayagarh	46	46	46	62	65	60	80	86	75
13	Dhenkanal	47	26	50	55	57	54	69	69	68
14	Jagatsinghapur	47	48	47	47	48	47	38	40	36
15	Ganjam	47	26	51	58	59	57	95	96	93
16	Sambalpur	48	68	52	60	68	52	46	51	42
17	Kendujhar	48	50	42	45	49	42	55	57	53
	ORISSA	**48**	**50**	**46**	**53**	**56**	**51**	**57**	**60**	**54**
18	Cuttack	49	49	49	59	60	57	64	72	55
19	Nuapada	51	55	46	54	58	49	54	58	49
20	Puri	52	54	30	64	68	59	63	53	76
21	Baudh	54	31	58	58	61	55	94	97	90
22	Debagarh	55	56	54	65	71	59	71	74	69
23	Kendrapara	57	56	60	57	56	60	58	57	59
24	Nabarangapur	61	67	55	53	56	51	53	56	51

(Contd...)

1	2	3	4	5	6	7	8	9	10	11
25	Koraput	62	64	60	64	66	63	64	66	63
26	Malkangiri	63	64	62	44	46	43	74	75	43
27	Kalahandi	63	70	55	65	74	56	65	74	56
28	Gajapati	69	40	73	57	62	53	86	90	81
29	Rayagada	69	71	68	74	73	76	71	73	76
30	Kandhamal	79	46	84	73	78	68	89	94	84

Note: Estimated from CEB and CS in the age group 15-49.

Source: Census of India, 2001.

Table 3.5(c): Estimated Child Mortality Rate by Caste in Districts of ORISSA (Urban)

Rank	*State/District*	*Total (CMR)*			*Scheduled Caste (CMR)*			*Scheduled Tribe (CMR)*		
		Total	*Male*	*Female*	*Total*	*Male*	*Female*	*Total*	*Male*	*Female*
1	*2*	*3*	*4*	*5*	*6*	*7*	*8*	*9*	*10*	*11*
01	Baudh	21	22	20	17	15	18	NA	NA	NA
02	Gajapati	24	13	26	23	29	17	64	62	79
03	Jharsuguda	24	24	30	29	28	30	34	37	31
04	Mayurbhanj	26	27	24	26	27	24	20	22	18
05	Anugul	28	15	30	37	39	36	54	52	55
06	Baleshwar	29	27	31	41	42	40	29	27	31
07	Jagatsinghapur	29	31	29	29	31	29	48	49	48
08	Sambalpur	30	35	30	33	35	30	36	31	41
09	Sundargarh	30	33	27	30	33	27	31	33	29
10	Ganjam	30	16	33	37	40	35	39	51	54
11	Rayagada	30	32	29	35	37	33	48	37	33

(Contd...)

1	*2*	*3*	*4*	*5*	*6*	*7*	*8*	*9*	*10*	*11*
12	Nuapada	31	44	20	34	47	26	34	47	26
13	Jajapur	31	16	27	37	42	34	40	47	35
	ORISSA	**31**	**32**	**30**	**38**	**41**	**34**	**40**	**40**	**39**
14	Bargarh	31	39	24	31	39	24	47	34	59
15	Puri	31	16	33	33	44	24	NA	NA	NA
16	Balangir	31	33	28	28	27	29	28	27	29
17	Khordha	32	17	34	40	43	38	37	33	40
18	Sonapur	32	17	34	43	35	53	38	39	36
19	Kendujhar	33	17	31	38	40	36	47	50	46
20	Kalahandi	33	36	29	36	44	28	36	44	28
21	Cuttack	34	19	37	40	44	37	53	46	65
22	Dhenkanal	38	21	42	50	56	45	81	63	100
23	Bhadrak	39	33	49	44	61	28	39	33	49
24	Koraput	39	43	35	46	52	39	46	52	39

(Contd...)

1	2	3	4	5	6	7	8	9	10	11
25	Kandhamal	39	21	42	58	73	43	52	48	56
26	Nabarangapur	40	47	34	49	54	43	49	54	43
27	Malkangiri	40	40	40	40	33	47	40	33	47
28	Nayagarh	42	53	31	75	107	44	NA	NA	NA
29	Debagarh	62	60	64	90	78	102	72	71	75
30	Kendrapara	63	70	56	63	70	56	29	24	73

Note: Estimated from CEB and CS in the age group 15-49.

Source: Census of India, 2001.

The variation in child mortality rate among caste groups is very clear. Among the schedule tribes the highest child mortality rate is in Baudh (93) followed by Ganjam (92) but in the case of scheduled castes the highest child mortality rate is in the district of Kandhamal (71) followed by Rayagada (68). Sex differential among scheduled castes and scheduled tribes has shown almost a balanced picture between males and females. There is considerable variation in the child mortality rate between males and females. The pattern is similar in rural and urban child mortality in Orissa. In rural areas child mortality rate is highest in the district of Kandhamal (79) and in urban areas also child mortality is highest in Kandhamal (39). There is marginal difference in child mortality between rural and urban areas of Orissa. It is observed that children in rural areas of Orissa experience two times higher probability of dying before their fifth birthday than do urban children. Child mortality, however, is highest among children born to schedule caste and schedule tribe women. Variation in the child mortality rate among the scheduled castes and scheduled tribes indicates low education level of women, poverty and low nutritional status of children. Orissa is in a poor state of reproductive and child health where the percentage of population below poverty line is highest at 49 per cent and compared to 26 per cent at the national level. The state's domestic product per capita is also much lower than the national average.

Distribution of Districts according to Selected RCH Indicators

In order to understand the association of reproductive and child health with level of infant mortality rate and child mortality rate in districts of Orissa, a correlation matrix is constructed. The variables considered under reproductive and child health are: 1. Percentage of children received full immunization (PCIMM); 2. Percentage of women received full ANC (PRANC); and 3. Percentage of households with a low standard of living (PLSLI). The socio-economic indicators considered from the Census of India are female work participation rate (PWF), percentage of female literacy (PLF), percentage of urban population (PUF), percentage of having latrine (PHLT), percentage having safe drinking water (PSDWT), percentage of scheduled tribe (PSTP) and percentage of scheduled caste population (PSCP).

Table 3.6 presents the zero order correlation Matrix of the selected indicators in all 30 districts. It can be noted that infant mortality rate and child mortality rates are positively related with work participation rate (0.449). Similarly, the correlation coefficients of infant and child mortality with female literacy are found to be -0.563 and -0.591 respectively and statistically significant. This indicates that literacy is negatively associated with infant and child mortality. Higher literacy levels would improve child survival. Similarly, the correlation coefficients of infant and child mortality with percentage of urban are found to be -0.414 and -0.405 respectively. From the table it is clear that child immunization is negatively associated with infant and child mortality. The low standard of living also influences infant and child mortality and statistically significant. Similarly, antenatal services are negatively associated with infant and child mortality.

CONCLUSION AND POLICY IMPLICATIONS

The study reveals that the level of infant and child mortality is quite high in the district of Kandhamal followed by Gajapati and low in the district of Mayurbhanj. Seventeen districts have infant mortality higher than the national average and 12 districts have values higher than the state average. Infant and child mortality is high in those districts where schedule tribe population is high. For child mortality, only Mayurbhanj has levels lower than the national average, while for other districts similar pattern as for infant mortality can be observed. Among the scheduled castes and tribes also, a similar pattern is observed. Hence, it is clear that a majority of the districts in the state have high levels of infant and child mortality, equally prevalent among the different social groups. In most of the districts, levels of infant and child mortality are higher than the national average, which is definitely a cause of concern. Moreover, the differential is clear among SCs and STs. The reproductive health indicators also indicate very low coverage in districts of Orissa and these regions are not only economically and socially underdeveloped, but also have lower coverage of health services. There is significant variation in infant and child mortality rate among the districts of Orissa. The ranking of districts help us to identify the backward and most backward districts in reproductive and child health programme and to intensify the intervention strategies to reduce the infant and child mortality.

Table 3.6: Correlation Matrix of IMR, CMR and selected Reproductive and Child Health Indicators (N=30)

	PWF	*PLF*	*PUF*	*PHLT*	*PSDWT*	*PSTP*	*PSCP*	*PCIMM*	*PLSLI*	*PRANC*	*IMR*	*CMR*
1	*2*	*3*	*4*	*5*	*6*	*7*	*8*	*9*	*10*	*11*	*12*	*13*
PWF	1											
PLF	-0.888**	1										
PUF	-0.253	0.424*	1									
PHLT	-0.502**	0.607**	0.859**	1								
PSDWT	-0.008	-0.158	-0.107	-0.279	1							
PSTP	0.818**	-0.785**	-0.070	-0.331	-0.070	1						
PSCP	-0.415*	0.343	-0.201	-0.132	0.300	-0.632**	1					
PCIMM	-0.385*	0.515**	0.405*	0.416*	0.029	-0.482**	0.283	1				
PLSLI	0.751**	-0.816**	-0.459*	-0.723**	0.208	0.724**	-0.152	-0.594**	1			
PRANC	-0.018	0.138	0.230	0.145	-0.087	-0.078	-0.120	0.478**	-0.359	1		

(Contd...)

1	2	3	4	5	6	7	8	9	10	11	12	13
IMR	0.449*	-0.563**	-0.414*	-0.369*	0.004	0.387*	-0.048	-0.305	0.357	-0.038	1	
CMR	0.484**	-0.591**	-0.405*	-0.376*	-0.010	0.430*	-0.071	-0.313	0.383*	-0.052	0.998**	1

** Correlation is significant at the 0.01 level.

* Correlation is significant at the 0.05 level.

Description of Variables:

IMR- Probabilities of newborn child dying before age one (0q1)

CMR- Probabilities of dying between first and fifth birthday ((1q4)

PWF- Percentage of work participation Female

PLF- Percentage of literacy Female

PUF- Percentage of Urban Female

PCIMM- Percentage of Children received full immunization

PLSLI- Percentage of households with low standard of living

PRANC- Percentage of women received full ANC

PHLT- Percentage of having Latrine Total

PSDWT- Percentage of safe Drinking water

PSTP- Percentage of Scheduled Tribe Population

PSCT- Percentage of Scheduled Caste Population

APPENDIX of different variables

District	*PWF*	*PLF*	*PUF*	*PHLT*	*PSDWT*	*PSTP*	*PSCP*	*PCIMM*	*PLSLI*	*PRANC*	*IMR*	*CMR*
1	2	3	4	5	6	7	8	9	10	11	12	13
Bargarh	31.1	50.0	7.1	9	82	19.4	19.4	71.6	70.5	9.4	76	36
Jharsuguda	22.4	59.2	34.9	21	58	31.3	17.1	71.1	58.7	17.0	68	30
Sambalpur	35.6	54.8	24.3	19	63	34.5	17.0	65.7	64.6	22.8	84	43
Debagarh	38.6	47.6	6.0	8	57	33.6	15.4	46.5	70.5	17.5	98	55
Sundargarh	28.9	54.3	29.2	24	65	50.2	8.6	59.0	62.5	14.5	79	39
Kendujhar	28.0	46.7	12.3	10	55	44.5	11.6	34.0	77.1	13.7	87	46
Mayurbhanj	39.9	38.3	4.9	9	44	56.6	7.7	39.6	73.8	17.8	65	27
Baleshwar	11.4	59.6	9.5	15	87	11.3	18.8	69.2	52.4	16.4	80	39
Bhadrak	7.9	63.6	10.4	11	89	1.9	21.5	51.7	63.0	12.0	88	46
Kendrapara	9.9	67.3	5.3	9	73	0.5	20.5	55.5	60.2	15.5	90	48
Jagatsinghapur	11.4	69.9	9.8	13	79	0.8	21.1	46.6	54.7	19.6	83	41
Cuttack	13.6	66.2	23.5	26	56	3.6	19.1	82.8	44.5	33.0	87	45

(Contd...)

1	2	3	4	5	6	7	8	9	10	11	12	13
Jajapur	6.7	61.5	4.0	15	44	7.8	23.0	35.1	61.2	3.7	85	44
Dhenkanal	15.0	58.6	7.1	12	31	12.8	18.5	62.1	58.6	24.1	88	46
Anugul	26.5	56.0	11.7	18	44	11.7	17.2	50.8	56.3	14.2	82	41
Nayagarh	10.9	58.1	3.5	16	51	5.9	14.0	62.0	57.8	10.7	88	46
Khordha	8.6	71.1	38.6	38	52	5.2	13.5	63.4	48.7	13.4	79	38
Puri	7.5	67.8	11.8	18	78	0.3	18.2	69.5	48.1	19.1	91	49
Ganjam	31.1	47.7	13.1	19	59	2.9	18.6	51.5	56.7	11.2	86	45
Gajapati	49.8	28.9	6.7	10	45	50.8	7.5	46.3	65.9	19.6	107	65
Kandhamal	42.2	36.2	4.6	10	34	52.0	16.9	58.3	71.2	12.8	119	77
Baudh	35.5	39.8	3.5	5	65	12.5	21.9	66.8	67.3	20.0	95	53
Sonapur	32.9	47.3	6.3	7	76	9.8	23.6	58.4	71.3	13.8	76	36
Balangir	28.4	39.3	9.3	9	74	20.6	16.9	63.4	70.0	21.4	82	41
Nuapada	36.9	26.0	5.0	6	84	34.7	13.6	41.8	75.7	16.3	91	49
Kalahandi	35.8	29.6	6.1	8	81	28.6	17.7	50.1	72.9	15.1	103	61
Rayagada	41.3	24.3	9.8	10	79	55.8	13.9	45.0	71.1	19.7	106	64
Nabarangapur	42.3	21.0	4.3	7	79	55.0	14.1	46.2	73.9	14.3	102	60
Koraput	40.5	24.8	12.2	13	67	49.6	13.0	31.4	71.7	13.0	101	59
Malkangiri	44.1	21.3	5.9	7	82	57.4	21.4	39.7	91.5	7.5	103	61

Orissa is classified as an Empowered Action Group (EAG) State, and remains at the centre of policy efforts to ensure better maternal and child health outcomes. The findings of this paper suggest that at the district level risks of mortality continue to remain high among infants and children, which raises doubt about the efficacy of the child health programmes in these districts. The state needs to make concentrated efforts to improve the social and economic conditions of the schedule tribes by increasing level of literacy and improving technology to reach of the various services especially for the women and children.

It may be concluded that the most backward districts should be given special attention to improve child survival and maternal health in the state. Also, it is necessary to undertake carefully targeted sector specific interventions.

REFERENCES

Caldwell, John C. (1979), "Education As a Factor in Mortality Decline: An Examination of Nigerian Data" *Population Studies*, 23, 395-413.

Caldwell, John C. (1994). "How is Greater Maternal Education Translated into Lower Child Mortality?" *Health Transition Review*, 4, pp. 224-229.

Census of India, (2001), *Provisional Population Total-series*, F-series Registrar General of India.

Das Gupta, Monica (1990): "Death Clustering, Mother's Education and Determinants of Child Mortality in Rural Punjab, India" *Population Studies*, 44, 489-505.

Government of India (2000), National Population Policy.

Govindasamy, Pavalavalli and B.M Ramesh, (1997) "Maternal Education and Utilization of Maternal and Child Health Services in India, *NFHS Studies Reports* No. 5: IIPS.

Hobcraft, J.N; Mcdonald J.W and Rutstein S.O (1984) "Socio Economic Factors in Infant and Child Mortality Across Maternal Comparison" *Population Studies*, 37(2), 193-223.

IIPS (2004). *Reproductive and Child Health* RCH-2, 2002-04: Mumbai.

Jain, A.K (1985), "Determinants of Regional Infant Mortality in Rural India" *Population Studies*, 39(3), 407-424.

Mosley, W.H. and L.C Chen,(1984),"An Analytical Framework for the Study of Child Survival in Developing Countries" A Supplement to *Population and Development Review*, 10, pp. 24-45

National Family Health Survey-II (1998-99). IIPS, Mumbai.

Office of RGI, (1997), *Sample Registration System*: New Delhi.

Pandey, Arvind, Minjakim Choe, Norman Y. Luther, Damodar Sahu and Jagdish Chand (1998),"Infant and Child Mortality in India", *NFHS Reports* No 11, Mumbai.

Prakasam, C.P. (1980), "Infant Mortality in Relation with Woman's Reproductive Health", *Indian Journal of Public Health* Vol. XXIV No. 3 pp. 3.

Trussell, J. (1975), A Re-estimation of the Multiplying Factors for the Brass Technique for Demographic Childhood Survivorship Rates, *Population Studies* Vol. 29(1): 97-108.

William Brass, (1975), *Methods for Estimating Fertility and Mortality from limited and Defective Data* (Chapel Hill, North Carolina, Carolina population centre, laboratories for population statistics, 1975).

4

Factors Affecting Child Survival in Madhya Pradesh

Anand Singh

INTRODUCTION

Madhya Pradesh is the second largest State which lies in the central region of India. It has a population of about 60.38 million people (re: census 2001) in its forty eight district spread across an area of 308,000 square kilometres. About 20% of its population is tribal and majority of its population lives in rural areas. Human development indicators of the State point out urgency for the need of the State to bring intensive focus on survival of women and children and their care. It is said that first three years of life play a critical role, are a best start to a child's life, probably an area which needs attention in the state. As per the latest National Family Health Survey-3 Madhya Pradesh have highest rates of malnutrition among children. 60.3% of its children in the age group of 0-3 years are under nourished. Though steps to improve the systems and respond to the situation are being made but probably with an issue like this which impacts survival need to save lives is immediate.

State has 69,238 approved integrated child development centres but only 49,806 are functional. Integrated Child Development Centres, commonly known as *anganwadi* centres provide nutritional support to children, monitor its growth, provide immunization and others services to pregnant women and children including pre-school education to child and counselling on right care practices to pregnant mother. But when thousands of these child care centres are not even functional indicates that we have been missing on reaching out to thousands of children in the state. One of its districts Sheopur was called 'World's hotspots of malnutrition' by a Joint Commission of Enquiry which was set up by Supreme Court Commissioners on the ongoing public interest litigation on the issue of right to food and malnutrition in the country. State also has highest infant mortality rate in the country. At present infant mortality rate is 76 infant deaths per thousand live births - meaning out of every one thousand children born 76 die even before their first birth day. If we calculate on an indicative terms this means that approximately every four to five minutes a child dies in the state of Madhya Pradesh. Even deaths rate within first month (i.e. neo natal mortality rate) is also very high in the State and, which along with Uttar Pradesh and Bihar contributes 15% of global neo natal deaths. As per Lancet 'child survival series' titled as where and why are 10 million children dying every year? Prof. Robert E Black, Saul S Morris and Jennifer Bryce state, that more than 10 million children die each year, most from preventable causes and almost all in the poor countries. It has been observed that household and environmental factors are more influencing on a child's health. Better cooking facilities, availability of safe drinking water; better toilet facilities may lead to better health. Research study done in Mewat region of Haryana by Jatrana (2001) revealed that type of house and the presence of separate kitchen in the house affect infant survival. Further in this study presence of latrine, education of father and mother is showing a significant effect on infant survival. Another research study done in Nepal (Gubhaju *et.al,* 1991) examining fertility data show that probability of dying among infant was 44 per cent higher for those drinking lake or river water than those using piped or tube well water. In this study it has been observed that households not having toilet facilities had 64 per cent higher probability of infant dying than those with their own toilet facilities. Studies done in Bangladesh (Majumder; Islam 1993, Hoque *et, al.*, 1999) by using Matlab data show that household environmental facilities and mother's education affects infant survival. The NFHS-I data showed that persons living in households that primarily use biomass for cooking fuel have a considerably higher prevalence of active tuberculosis than persons living households that use clean fuels (Mishra *et. al,* 1997). This effect is reduced with availability of separate kitchen, pucca house type, lesser indoor crowding, etc. It is a fact, that measurement of household and environmental factors influencing child survival is a complex phenomenon. The variables differ by different societies, geographical areas and by caste affiliations.

NEED FOR THE STUDY

Infant and child mortality is now a major public health problem in India, which gradually affects not only uneducated groups or rural populations but also in the urban counterparts, especially in the urban slums. This type of health problem is also more prevalent among SC and ST population, particularly among those belonging to rural backgrounds.

Even in spite of increasing realization that the rural population is most suffering to infant and child deaths in Madhya Pradesh, most of the infant and child related studies and programme interventions have focused only on 'rural population' of the state. There is no focus on sub-regional or divisions-wise condition of child mortality, particularly by low environmental and household factors of the state. However, prevention through awareness programmes has been the most essential medicine. Therefore, awareness level has to be high and consistent in all the districts.

The gap in KAP (Knowledge, Awareness and Prevention) of this health problem is widening due to more attention given to some selected areas of the state only. In this paper the focus has been to examine and highlight the pattern and gaps in environmental and household factors among married women in rural areas, more specifically among the SC and ST populations. This study also highlights the differentials with respect to selected socio-economic and background characteristics like place of residence, caste and household standard of living, the extent of environmental and household factors between two areas with different levels of various household amenities. The results of such comparative studies are expected to be more useful in terms of programme implementations and to strengthen intervention programmes for women, and also targeting care of the children.

DATA AND METHOD

The data used in this study is the Census and DLHS-RCH–2, 2002-04. Utilizing DLHS, information on background and housing characteristics such as women's marital status, current age, education of women and husband, place of residence, and child survival ratios have been obtained. The study is based on responses from (27,052) women from the state of Madhya Pradesh and its five divisions, namely Bhopal, Ujjain, Jabalpur, Sagar and Chambal.

The list of variables considered for analysis has been listed in this paper. The set of variables have been divided into two categories such as indirect indicators and a second category is direct indicators. The dependent variable, child survival has been measured by considering the ratio of children ever born to children surviving. If this child survival index is equal to one, it indicates that the number of deliveries and surviving children are equal and if the index is less than one, it indicates that the women have experienced child loss in her reproductive period. A composite index has been calculated for environmental and household factors. The analysis has been done by SC, ST, OBC and women from other caste category to know the influence of environmental and household factors on child survival.

Further, Bhopal, Ujjain, Jabalpur, Sagar and Chambal Division have been selected for analysis based on Census data of all amenities. By the Census data it is found that Bhopal and

Ujjain division show better possession of household amenities whereas in the Jabalpur, Sagar and Chambal divisions, households possess lower number of amenities. In Bhopal division there are eight districts namely Betul, Bhopal, Harda, Hushangabad, Raisen, Rajgarh, Sehore, Vidisha; in Ujjain division there are six districts namely Dewas, Mandsaur Neemuch, Ratlam, Shajapur, Ujjain and in Jabalpur division there are eight districts namely Balaghat, Chhindwara, Dindori, Jabalpur, Katni, Mandla, Seoni, and Narsinghpur. While Sagar and Chambal division have eight and three districts respectively, namely Chhatarpur, Damoh, Panna, Sagar, Tikamgarh and in Chambal division Morena, Sheopur and Bhind. The number of respondents is (3766) women and (7089) women respectively.

Of the several variables used in this study, some variables have been coded differently for this purpose. Besides cross tabulations, a regression analysis is also done to understand the factors influencing on the child survival Madhya Pradesh and its divisions.

OBJECTIVES

To analyze the association between the household, socio-economic and environmental conditions with child survival in Madhya Pradesh and its district-wise divisions.

RESULTS AND FINDINGS

1. Profile of the respondents by background characteristics

Table 4.2 DLHS-2 covers 38024 currently married women age 15-44 in Madhya Pradesh. The survey interviewed larger proportion of women age 20-24 (22 per cent) compared to 15-19 (9.0 per cent). Literacy is lower among women (41.4) as compared to their husbands. Majority of women are from rural areas (69 per cent). Twenty-three per cent women are from the highest standard of living (SLI). Twenty-four per cent belong to other caste category while Other Backward Castes women accounted for 42 per cent and more than thirty-five per cent women belongs to the Scheduled Tribes.

Table 4.1: Households with basic amenities by divisions of Madhya Pradesh, Census-2001

Madhya Pradesh	*Total population*	*Total number of households*	*Electricity Available*	*Latrine Available*	*Drinking Water*	*Bathroom facility within the house*	*Separate kitchen within the house*	*Kerosene*	*LPG*	*Drainage*
1	*2*	*3*	*4*	*5*	*6*	*7*	*8*	*9*	*10*	*11*
Bhopal Division										
Betul	1394421	248131	74.79	20.22	68.98	21.67	88.57	3.68	8.38	26.14
Bhopal Division	1836784	335376	96.34	65.77	88.01	63.62	67.04	25.78	44.92	73.21
Harda	474174	81758	88.80	30.05	66.45	27.49	64.35	3.03	11.50	27.04
Hushangabad	1085011	198176	81.46	37.12	74.16	32.36	56.64	4.16	18.72	32.68
Raisen	1120159	197496	74.48	25.85	76.59	25.21	62.52	3.95	7.91	21.13
Rajgarh	1253246	218297	85.24	16.27	68.47	16.32	48.99	4.84	6.12	40.08
Sehore	1078769	183400	84.86	26.91	67.80	23.02	72.01	3.28	9.49	22.41
Vidisha	1214759	211320	68.45	21.04	71.53	29.99	56.34	3.66	10.75	42.38
Chambal Division										
Morena	1587264	238398	54.56	19.74	54.10	21.08	39.70	1.54	8.47	40.07
Sheopur	559715	98694	64.85	11.91	78.30	8.86	23.58	1.55	6.45	25.19
Bhind	1426951	218489	43.23	21.87	53.49	28.60	39.45	1.06	6.00	45.24

(Contd…)

1	2	3	4	5	6	7	8	9	10	11
Jabalpur Division										
Balaghat	1445760	316470	58.29	13.19	53.90	12.68	73.67	2.85	3.64	18.17
Chhindwara	1848882	356244	84.62	20.78	71.37	23.23	63.97	5.19	9.03	29.19
Jabalpur	2167469	421203	82.37	45.08	84.95	39.88	61.21	8.61	29.97	52.13
Katni	1063689	222551	63.18	17.09	65.27	15.21	57.33	3.93	8.59	23.99
Mandla	893908	191633	49.42	11.54	53.99	8.53	79.51	2.29	4.10	13.69
Seoni	1165893	234760	66.74	14.63	64.87	11.78	77.83	2.09	5.30	14.25
Narsinghpur	957399	179627	74.61	28.42	87.69	22.14	51.36	5.45	7.45	22.94
Dindori	579312	126318	37.26	5.84	47.01	3.71	85.49	0.99	0.79	8.10
Sagar Division										
Chhatarpur	1474633	263817	46.58	15.29	36.10	16.85	54.53	1.94	6.47	22.60
Damoh	1081909	222743	64.73	13.88	54.19	13.86	53.66	1.32	6.19	18.27
Panna	854235	173228	34.59	11.06	48.71	8.78	60.48	0.89	4.18	15.53
Sagar	2021783	370377	69.16	21.29	54.67	22.17	50.26	2.71	10.63	27.95
Tikampur	1203160	213744	49.27	10.98	33.83	18.95	50.27	0.76	5.45	25.20

(Contd...)

1	2	3	4	5	6	7	8	9	10	11
Ujjain Division										
Dewas	1306617	222318	89.10	28.27	67.16	30.28	69.54	4.30	14.51	34.28
Mandsaur	1183369	215337	86.78	18.82	59.67	18.35	49.85	3.45	13.63	44.35
Neemuch	725457	135865	90.43	21.15	64.32	22.84	50.56	4.22	17.28	47.14
Ratlam	1214536	215477	81.38	29.40	80.87	28.50	42.07	3.52	21.13	43.93
Shajapur	1290230	219259	90.32	18.38	73.07	23.05	56.05	3.48	7.54	45.21
Ujjain	1709885	293415	90.15	37.16	82.31	38.36	62.66	4.94	27.39	46.85

Table 4.2: Per cent distribution of SC, ST and others women by Background characteristics in divisions of Madhya Pradesh -DLHS-RCH-II

Background Characteristics	BHOPAL				UJJAIN				JABALPUR			
	SC	*ST*	*OBC*	*Others*	*SC*	*ST*	*OBC*	*Others*	*SC*	*ST*	*OBC*	*Others*
1	*2*	*3*	*4*	*5*	*6*	*7*	*8*	*9*	*10*	*11*	*12*	*13*
Age												
15-19	4.4	4.2	3	2.3	4.7	6.3	4.1	3.5	3.7	6.6	3	1.3
20-24	21.8	22.4	20	15.9	22.5	24.4	22.8	18.8	20.1	21.7	17.5	9.7
25-29	19.7	23.4	22.9	24.6	22.7	19.5	21.8	19.6	22.5	22.1	22	22.5
30-34	20.6	21.1	22	20	19.5	20.9	19.7	21	23.2	19.7	22.7	24.1
35-39	18.6	15.3	17.7	20.3	15.1	17.7	17.1	19.4	17.5	16.8	18.8	22.4
40-44	14.8	13.6	14.4	16.9	15.5	11.2	14.5	17.6	13.1	13.1	16	20
Education												
Illiterate	70.8	85.5	56.8	37.2	79.8	84.8	65.9	46.1	55.5	77.4	46.7	18.5
Literate	29.2	14.5	43.2	62.8	20.2	15.2	34.1	53.9	44.3	22.6	53.3	81.4
Husband-Education												
Illiterate	40.2	59.8	28	17	41	58.7	24.8	17.3	28.8	44.4	20.3	6.5
Literate	59.6	38.9	71.7	82.9	58.9	41.1	75	82.7	71.2	54.8	79.3	93.3

(Contd...)

Table 4.2 (Contd...)

1	*2*	*3*	*4*	*5*	*6*	*7*	*8*	*9*	*10*	*11*	*12*	*13*
Place of residence												
Rural	73	88.7	69	43.3	77.6	84.4	72.5	57.9	71.5	90.3	68.6	30.6
Urban	27	11.3	31	56.7	22.4	15.6	27.5	42.1	28.5	9.7	31.4	69.4
SLI												
Low	62.6	81.9	43.4	24.4	62.8	76.7	38.6	27.9	65.8	87.8	52.4	17.8
Medium	25.2	14.2	34.7	30.1	26.3	18.4	38.1	30.8	22.6	9.6	29.5	21.6
High	12.2	4.9	21.9	45.5	10.9	4.9	23.3	41.3	11.6	2.6	18.1	60.6
Child survival Ratio												
Less than 1	41.6	42.9	30	21.9	36.1	35.8	25	20.6	35.5	39.2	30.5	18
equal to 1	58.4	57.1	70	78.1	63.9	64.2	75	79.4	64.5	60.8	69.5	82

(Contd...)

Background Characteristics	SAGAR				CHAMBAL				Madhya Pradesh			
	SC	*ST*	*OBC*	*Others*	*SC*	*ST*	*OBC*	*Others*	*SC*	*ST*	*OBC*	*Others*
1	*14*	*15*	*16*	*17*	*18*	*19*	*20*	*21*	*22*	*23*	*24*	*25*
Age												
15-19	4	2.6	3.1	1.4	2.7	4.8	3.7	2.3	10.4	12.2	8.7	6.2
20-24	21.1	27	23	16.1	19.8	17.6	18.4	14.9	23.1	23.5	22.8	18.9
25-29	19.9	24.5	24.5	23.1	21.9	28	22.7	23.8	20.1	21.4	21.1	21.7
30-34	23.4	17.5	19.8	24.2	24.5	24.8	23.4	23.9	19.6	17.8	19.1	20.1
35-39	21.2	16.8	15.9	20.5	17.9	12	17.7	20.1	15.7	14.1	15.8	18.1
40-44	10.3	11.7	13.7	14.6	13.1	12.8	14.2	15.1	11.1	11	12.5	15
Education												
Illiterate	74.8	87.3	67.1	33.5	82.9	91.3	76.3	35.1	70.2	82.5	58.1	33.7
Literate	25.2	12.7	32.9	66.5	16.8	8.7	23.7	64.9	29.8	17.5	58.2	33.8
Husband-Education												
Illiterate	38.6	57.7	32.9	13.2	30.1	59.5	31.7	9.4	35.8	56.3	25.4	13.3
Literate	61.1	42.3	67	86.8	69.5	39.7	68	90.6	63.9	43.2	74.2	86.6

(Contd...)

1	14	15	16	17	18	19	20	21	22	23	24	25
Place of residence												
Rural	69.5	85.5	73.4	61.3	74.5	84.8	75.3	56.1	72.2	89.9	69.9	49.2
Urban	30.5	14.5	26.6	38.7	25.5	15.2	24.7	43.9	27.8	10.1	30.1	50.8
SLI												
Low	73.5	87.6	63.5	36	66.9	84	60	27.4	64.1	85.9	49.4	25.4
Medium	19.8	8.9	25.5	27.6	22.4	12	25.9	31.9	23.4	10.7	30.9	27.7
High	6.7	3.5	11	36.4	10.8	4	14	40.7	12.5	3.4	19.8	47
Child survival Ratio												
Less than 1	46.6	49.5	36.1	24.1	42.6	54.8	40.5	24.9	33.9	36.2	27.2	19.4
equal to 1	53.4	50.5	63.9	75.9	57.4	45.2	59.5	75.1	66.1	63.8	72.8	80.6

Among 6717 currently married women age 15-44 in the Bhopal division, majority of women are from rural areas (73 per cent) and only 29.2 per cent women are found to be literate. Twenty-five per cent women belong to the highest standard of living (SLI). Thirty per cent of women are from Other Backward Castes, and 22 per cent belong to other caste category while 43 per cent women belong to Scheduled Tribes.

In Ujjain division 5532 currently married women age 15-44 were covered by the DLHS-2. Majority of women in this division are from rural areas (77.6 per cent) compared to their urban counterparts. Literate women account for only 35.6 per cent of the total women. Twenty-five per cent women belong to the highest standard of living (SLI). Thirty six per cent women are from the Scheduled Tribes and 25 per cent belong to Other Backward Castes, while 20.6 per cent women belong to other caste category.

The Sagar division accounts for 3863 currently married women age 15-44 according to the DLHS-2 coverage. 35.7 per cent women are literate and Per cent literate husband found to be more to women literate. Around three fourths of the women are from rural areas (71.2 per cent) compared to the urban areas. Only fourteen per cent women come from the highest standard of living (SLI). 24.1 per cent women belong to other caste category while Other Backward Castes women accounted for 36.1 per cent and another 50 per cent women belong to Scheduled Tribes.

Among 2485 currently married women age 15-44 in the Chambal division, about two fifths of the women are literate and three fourths of them hail from rural areas (71.2 per cent) compared to urban areas. Twenty one per cent women are from the highest standard of living (SLI). One fourth of the total women belong to other caste category while Other Backward Castes women accounted for 40.5 per cent and more than half of the women (54.8 per cent) belong to the Scheduled Tribes.

Out of 6680 currently married women age 15-44 surveyed under DLHS-2 in the Jabalpur division, about half of the total women population are literates while majority of them are from rural backgrounds (69.8 per cent). Only nineteen per cent women belong to the highest standard of living (SLI). Eighteen per cent women belong to other caste category while Other Backward Castes women accounted for 30.5 per cent and another 39.2 per cent women belong to the Scheduled Tribes category.

2. Per cent distribution of women by caste categories and housing characteristics.

Table 4.3 presents variations by caste categories and housing characteristics among women in Madhya Pradesh. The household and environmental factors reveal that more than one fourth of the total population and 38.6 per cent of ST population are not having electricity facilities at household level. About three fifths (57 per cent) of the ST population and 47 per cent of the remaining population are using well and hand pump as source of drinking water. Further, the table shows that 93 per cent of the ST population is not having toilet facilities either. Majority of SC and ST population of Madhya Pradesh are living in kaccha house. 94 per cent of ST population and 83 per cent of SC population are using wood as source of fuel used for cooking, while about half of the women belonging to other caste category use LPG as source of fuel for cooking.

Variations by caste categories and housing characteristics and environmental factors among women in Bhopal show that nearly 19 per cent of ST population and 16 per cent of SC population are not having electricity facilities at household level. Among the women belonging to Scheduled tribes category, 21 per cent of them are using well and another 61 per cent are using hand pump as the major source of drinking water. 90 per cent of the ST population is not having toilet facilities. Majority of SC and ST population of Bhopal division live in kaccha houses. 93 per cent of ST population and 80 per cent of SC population are using wood as source of fuel used for cooking, while LPG as source of fuel for cooking is used by 42 per cent of women belonging to other caste category.

Table 4.3: Per cent distribution of SC, ST and other women by housing characteristics in divisions of Madhya Pradesh-DLHS-RCH-II

Housing characteristics	BHOPAL				UJJAIN				JABALPUR			
	SC	*ST*	*OBC*	*Others*	*SC*	*ST*	*OBC*	*Others*	*SC*	*ST*	*OBC*	*Others*
1	2	3	4	5	6	7	8	9	10	11	12	13
Electricity												
Having	84.4	81	88.3	93.4	89.9	75.7	93.3	94.9	79.1	54.1	77.4	92
Not Having	15.6	19	11.7	6.6	10.1	24.3	6.7	5.1	20.9	45.9	22.6	8
Sources of Drinking Water												
Tap	28.6	16.4	32.3	50.1	20.1	17	29	41.3	32.7	11.1	40	69.3
Hand pump	50.6	60.8	45.8	36.4	56.4	57.8	45.5	43.2	47.3	53.5	37.1	22.5
Well	18.8	20.8	20.2	12	22.2	24	24.2	14.3	19.2	30.6	22.1	7.7
Others	2.1	2	1.7	1.6	1.4	1.2	1.3	1.2	0.8	4.8	0.8	0.5
Type of Toilet Facility												
Having toilet	20.6	9.4	34.9	59.2	14.9	7.7	26.4	47.8	19.8	5.4	30	74
Public & share	1.6	9	1.3	1.2	2.4	1.5	2.7	2.8	0.8	0.4	0.7	0.9
No toilet	77.8	89.7	63.8	39.6	82.7	90.6	70.9	49.3	79.5	94.2	69.3	25.1

(Contd...)

Table 4.3 (Contd...)

1	*2*	*3*	*4*	*5*	*6*	*7*	*8*	*9*	*10*	*11*	*12*	*13*
Type of House												
Kaccha	65.2	78.8	43.8	25.2	62.4	74.1	38.1	30.3	69.4	80.2	62	24.3
Semi-pucca	19.4	15.5	30.8	27.9	19.8	13.1	27.5	21.4	17.5	16.5	21.2	21.5
pucca	15.5	5.7	25.4	46.9	17.8	12.8	34.4	48.3	13.1	3.3	16.7	54.1
Type of Fuel for Cooking												
LPG-Electricity	13.9	4.2	19.5	44.2	11.9	6.3	16.4	37.8	12.7	2.8	16.5	60.8
Kerosene	4.1	1.9	2.6	5.2	1.4	1.7	1.8	2.2	2.2	1.3	2.7	3.1
Wood	80	93.3	76	49.6	86.1	91.8	81	59.4	83.5	95.6	78.6	34
Others	2	0.6	2	1	0.6	0.2	0.8	0.6	1.6	0.3	2.2	2.1

(Contd...)

Housing characteristics	SAGAR				CHAMBAL				Madhya Pradesh			
	SC	*ST*	*OBC*	*Others*	*SC*	*ST*	*OBC*	*Others*	*SC*	*ST*	*OBC*	*Others*
1	*14*	*15*	*16*	*17*	*18*	*19*	*20*	*21*	*22*	*23*	*24*	*25*
Electricity												
Having	66.6	47.6	69.3	86.7	68.1	76.2	63.3	73.9	75.7	61.4	79.5	89.7
Not Having	33.4	52.4	30.7	13.3	31.9	23.8	36.7	26.1	24.3	38.6	20.5	10.3
Sources of Drinking Water												
Tap	20.5	10.8	17.9	27.1	20	10.3	17.3	39.2	26.6	11.7	29.8	46.9
Hand pump	40.3	33.7	33.6	36.2	63.5	81	56.5	45.6	47.7	56.9	41.7	33.2
Well	34.1	45.4	46.3	33.8	16.2	7.9	25.9	14.9	23.6	27.2	27.1	17.6
Others	5.1	10.2	2.1	2.9	0.2	0.8	0.3	0.3	2.1	4.2	1.5	2.2
Type of Toilet Facility												
Having toilet	9.1	4.1	15.9	40.6	12.1	9.5	16.8	45	18.3	6	26.7	54.9
Public & share	1.3	0	0.6	0.7	0.4	0.8	0.9	1.6	2.1	1.1	1.6	1.9
No toilet	89.6	95.9	83.5	58.7	87.5	89.7	82.3	53.4	79.6	92.9	71.7	43.2

(Contd...)

1	*14*	*15*	*16*	*17*	*18*	*19*	*20*	*21*	*22*	*23*	*24*	*25*
Type of House												
Kaccha	73.2	82.2	63.2	39.8	50	85.7	37.5	10.4	63	78.7	49.1	28.4
Semi-pucca	11.7	10.5	18.9	20.5	28.5	6.3	30.5	18.2	18.8	15.7	25.6	20.8
pucca	15.2	7.3	17.9	39.8	21.5	7.9	32	71.4	18.2	5.6	25.3	50.8
Type of Fuel for Cooking												
LPG-Electricity	7.1	2.2	9.7	34.6	7.4	1.6	8.7	37.5	13.9	3.7	17.6	45.9
Kerosene	1.2	0.6	1.3	1.6	0.8	4.8	1.4	1.7	2.2	1.7	2.2	3.2
Wood	91.6	97.1	88.6	63.2	91.8	93.7	89.9	60.7	82.6	94	78.8	49.8
Others	0.1	0	0.4	0.5	0	0	0	0.1	1.3	0.6	1.4	1.1

Table 4.4: List of Variables Considered for Analysis in Measuring Influence of Environment factor in Child Survival in Divisions of Madhya Pradesh

Indicators	*Descriptions*	*Score*
Indirect Household factors		
Respondent's Literacy	Illiterate	0
	Literate	1
Husband's Literacy	Illiterate	0
	Literate	1
Standard of living index	Low	0
	Medium	1
	High	2
Household Factors Index		
Score <1poor household environment		
Score >1poor household environment		
Direct Environment factors		
Electricity	No	0
	Yes	1
Sources of Drinking Water	Others	0
	Well	1
	Hand pump	2
	Tap	3
Type of Fuel for Cooking	Wood	1
	Kerosene	2
	LPG	3
	Others	4
Type of house	Kaccha	0
	Semi-kaccha	1
	Pucca	2
Toilet Facility	Not having	0
	Public & Share	1
	Having	2
Environmental Index		
Score <5poor household environment		
Score >5poor household environment		

In Ujjain, per cent of women by household and environmental factors reveal that nearly one-fourth of the ST population and 10 per cent of SC population are not having electricity facilities at household level, while 24 per cent and 58 per cent of ST population are using well and hand pump as source of drinking water, respectively. More than 90 per cent of the ST populations are not having toilet facilities and majority of SC and ST population of Ujjain division reside in kaccha houses. Ninety-two per cent of ST population and 86 per cent of SC population utilize wood as source of fuel for cooking purposes, while 38 per cent of women from other caste category are using LPG as source of fuel.

The per cent distribution of women by household and environmental factors in Chambal depict that nearly one fourth of the ST population and 32 per cent of SC population are not having electricity facilities at in their households. Well and hand pump as source of drinking water is used by eight and 81per cent of ST population, respectively. Ninety per cent of ST and 88 per cent of SC population are not having toilet facilities in the Chambal region. Majority of SC and ST population of the area inhabit kaccha houses. Only 38 per cent of women belonging to other caste category are using LPG as source of fuel used for cooking whereas, 94 per cent of ST population and 92 per cent of SC population are using wood as major source of fuel for cooking.

The environmental factors and household differentials among women belonging to the Jabalpur division show that nearly half of the ST population and one fifth of the SC population are not having electricity facilities in households. Majority of the ST population are using well and hand pump as source of drinking water (31 and 54 per cent respectively). Ninety-four per cent of ST population and four fifths of the SC population are not having toilet facilities in their households. Majority of SC and ST population of Jabalpur division reside in kaccha houses. About three fifths of women from other caste category use LPG as source of fuel used for cooking while, 96 per cent of ST population and 84 per cent of SC population are using wood as major source of fuel for cooking purposes.

In Sagar division, variations among women by their household and environmental characteristics present that more than half of the ST population and one third of the SC population are not having electricity facilities at the household level. 46.3 per cent of OBC population and 40 per cent of SC are using well and hand pump as source of drinking water. 96 per cent of ST population and 90 per cent of SC are devoid of toilet facilities in their households. Majority of SC and ST population of Sagar division are living in kaccha houses. 97 per cent of ST population and 92 per cent of SC population are using wood as source of fuel used for cooking whereas 35 per cent of women from other caste category use LPG as source of fuel.

3. Odds ratios from regression analyses assessing likelihood of influence of environment factors on child survival by selected background characteristics of women.

Table 4.5 presents the multivariate results for child survival influenced by environmental and household factors in Madhya Pradesh by caste variations among the women population. It is observed that in case of both environmental and household factors, the odds for child survival are highest among women from other caste category, followed by women belonging to other backward castes and scheduled castes women. The likelihood for child survival is lowest (less than one) among tribal women. Moreover, it is also revealed that the odds ratios for child survival are higher with respect to household factors as compared to the environmental factors, among all the four caste categories of women.

In the Bhopal region, the multivariate results for child survival influenced by environmental and household factors by caste variations among the women population reveal that considering both environmental and household factors, the odds for child survival are highest among women from other caste category, followed by women belonging to other backward castes and scheduled castes women. The likelihood for child survival is lowest (less than one) among the tribal women. Further, it is also observed that the odds ratios for child survival are higher with respect to household factors as compared to the environmental factors, by all four caste categories.

Table 4.5: Legit Regression Analysis of Households and Environmental Variables Influencing Child survival in divisions of Madhya Pradesh

Independent variable		Exp(B)			
Madhya Pradesh					
	Household (HHF) and Environmental (ENF) Factors	*SC*	*ST*	*OBC*	*Others*
ENF	Less than 5	1	1	1	1
	Greater than 5	1.047	0.487	1.282	2.664
HHF	Less than 1	1	1	1	1
	Greater than1	1.749	0.853	2.61	5.02
Bhopal					
ENF	Less than 5	1	1	1	1
	Greater than 5	1.105	0.527	1.245	2.773
HHF	Less than 1	1	1	1	1
	Greater than1	1.528	0.696	2.654	3.874
UJJAIN					
ENF	Less than 5	1	1	1	1
	Greater than 5	0.829	0.777	1.169	1.974
HHF	Less than 1	1	1	1	1
	Greater than1	1.231	0.69	2.478	3.434
JABLAPUR					
ENF	Less than 5	1	1	1	1
	Greater than 5	1.075	0.348	1.428	7.836
HHF	Less than 1	1	1	1	1
	Greater than1	2.093	0.979	2.818	4.587
SAGAR					
ENF	Less than 5	1	1	1	1
	Greater than 5	1.012	0.645	1.094	2.414
HHF	Less than 1	1	1	1	1
	Greater than1	1.479	0.669	1.956	5.099
CHAMBAL					
ENF	Less than 5	1	1	1	1
	Greater than 5	1.185	1.14	1.143	2.426
HHF	Less than 1	1	1	1	1
	Greater than1	1.101	0.55	1.492	5.393

The multivariate results for child survival among women by caste variations influenced by environmental and household factors in the Ujjain division show that with respect to both environmental and household factors, the odds for child survival are highest (ranging between 1.1 times to 3.4 times) among women from other caste category followed by women belonging to other backward castes and scheduled castes women. However, it is revealed that the likelihood of child survival influenced by environmental factors is about 20 per cent lesser among the SC women. The likelihood for child survival is lowest (less than one) among tribal women. Besides, it is also observed that the odds ratios for child survival are higher with respect to household factors as compared to the environmental factors, irrespective of caste affiliations of the women in the Ujjain region.

In the Chambal division, regression results for child survival by environmental and household factors by caste variations among the women reveal that in case of both environmental and household factors, the odds for child survival are highest among women from other caste category, followed by women belonging to other backward castes and scheduled castes women. The likelihood for child survival is lowest (less than one) among tribal women. Moreover, it is also observed that the odds ratios for child survival are higher with respect to household factors as compared to the environmental factors, among all caste categories.

The regression results for child survival in the Jabalpur area influenced by its environmental and household factors by women's caste differentials present that with regard to both environmental and household factors, the odds for child survival are highest among women from other caste category, followed by women belonging to other backward castes and scheduled castes women. The likelihood for child survival is lowest (less than one) among tribal women. Moreover, it is also revealed that the odds ratios for child survival are higher with respect to household factors as compared to the environmental factors, among all the four caste categories of women.

In the Sagar division of Madhya Pradesh, the multivariate outcomes for child survival by women's caste affiliations and the region's environmental and household factors depict that regarding both environmental and household factors, the odds ratios values for child survival are highest among women from other caste category, followed by women belonging to other backward castes and scheduled castes women. The likelihood for child survival is lowest (less than one) among tribal women, however, in case of environmental factors, the odds ratio for child survival is 1.14 times higher among those women having more than five positive environment factors in their households. Moreover, it is also revealed irrespective of women's caste associations, the odds ratios for child survival are higher with respect to household factors as compared to the environmental factors.

SUMMARY AND CONCLUSIONS

In conclusion, the following points emerge from this study on influence of environmental factors on child survival among ever married women age 15-44 in Madhya Pradesh and its divisions:

- Per cent literate husband found to be more to women literate.
- Majority of women are from rural areas compared to urban areas.
- More than thirty –five per cent women belong to ST showed that survival ratio less than one in Madhya Pradesh.
- 93 per cent of ST populations are not having toilet facilities in Madhya Pradesh
- 94 per cent of ST population and 83 per cent of SC population are using wood as source of fuel used for cooking in Madhya Pradesh and For ST, OBC & Others; both factors had significantly greater odds of being influence of environmental factors on child survival in Madhya Pradesh.
- In multivariate analyses for Ujjain division, for SC population, both factors are not playing significantly role

of being influence of environmental factors on child survival. And for Sagar division, For SC, ST & OBC, Environmental factors had significantly low odds than household factors being influence of environmental factors on child survival.

REFERENCES

Gubhaju B., Streadfield K., and Majumder, A.K. (1991): "Socio-economic, Demographic and Environmental Determents of Infant Mortality in Nepal", Journal of Biosocial Science. Oct; 23(4): 425-435.

Hoque, BA., Chakraborty J., Chowdhury JT. Chowdhury U.K., Ali. M., Arifeen. S., and Sack R.B. (1999): "Effects of Environmental Factors on Child Survival in Bangladesh: A Case Control Study" *Public Health*. Mar; 113(2): 57-64.

Jatrana, S. (2001): "Household Environmental Factors and Their Effects on Infant Mortality in Mewatregion of Haryana State", *Demography India,* Jan-Jun, 30(1): 31-47.

Majumder, A.K., Islam, S.M. (1993): Socio-economic and Environmental Determinants of Child Survival in Bangladesh. *Journal of Biosocial Science*. Jul; 25(3): 311-318.

Mishra, Vinod, Robert D. Retherford and Kirk Smith (1997) "Effects of Cooking Smoke on Prevalence of Tuberculosis in India", East-West Centre Working Paper, Population Series No. 92, October 1997.

5

Socio-Economic Inequalities in Health Care and Nutritional Status Across the Newly Formed States of India

Uttarakhand, Jharkhand and Chhattisgarh

Sandhya Mahapatro
M. Siva Kumar

ABSTRACT

Although the primary health care centres (PHC) have been set up as a part of government's 'Health for All' programme, still there exist huge inequalities in health care and nutritional status in the society, particularly among the poor sections of the population. This paper, therefore, attempts to examine the inequalities in health care and nutritional status between the caste groups in the three newly formed states of India; Uttarakhand, Jharkhand and Chhattisgarh. This paper examines how far the inequalities in health care and nutritional status are as a result of social stratification or whether it could be due to differential in economic condition of an individual belonging to different caste groups.

The data for the study are drawn from the National Family Health Survey-3 (NFHS-3). The following indicators on health and nutritional status will be examined: ante natal care (ANC), institutional delivery, child immunization, body mass index (BMI), and anaemia level. Bivariate analysis will be carried out to examine the extent of inequalities between caste and income groups. Logistic regression analysis will be used to ascertain the individual effect of socio-economic factors in health and nutritional status after controlling for other factors.

BACKGROUND

There has been a serious concern on the various forms of inequality prevailing in the Indian society. The inequality that exits among regions, class, caste and gender hinders the overall development of health society. It is feared that such inequality might intensify in the liberalisation era. Among others, inequality that exists in education and health are recognised to have major influence in human development. As stated by Dreze and Sen (1995) health and education can promote the freedom and ability of individuals to make use of available opportunities. Several programmes in India are trying to narrow down various dimensions of inequality.

India is a signatory to UN's "Health for All" and it is committed to address the wide disparities in various dimensions of health such as incidence of diseases, disability, death, care seeking behaviour, diagnosis and treatment. Individual's age, economic status, , ethnicity, caste, gender etc. could lead such inequality in health. Among all these domains caste and economic status of the individual plays a significant role. Caste occupies a prime role especially in Indian society as it by and large governs the status of the household (Yadav, 2002). Social stratification system determines the living condition, privileges, obligations and other cultural practices surrounding the life of a person which in turn affects their perception regarding health, knowledge of health care and accessibility of health care practices. Caste is also likely to influence the health behaviour of individuals. Caste differences may lead to disparities in accessibility, utilization and quality of health care services.

Caste is an important factor in the social system, particularly in rural communities that exerts and influences the utilization of MCH services. Earlier studies showed a strong association of the caste and utilisation of maternal care services (Singh, 2005 and Kavitha and Audinarayana, 1997). Tiwary and Prasad (2002) observed that the main impediments for not receiving proper antenatal care are socio-economic and demographic characteristics of the women like age, place of residence, religion and caste. Roy *et al.*, (2004) highlight that differentials in health care indicators between SC, ST, OBC and women in other category exists even after controlling for socio economic factors in some states of India.

Evidence from various studies suggests that not only caste results in poorer health status and negative health outcomes but economic status of the household which also greatly influences the utilisation of health care services. Based on the Demographic Health Survey (DHS) data for more than 50 countries, it was found that the poorest quintiles far worse than better off groups on a range of health outcomes, including childhood mortality and nutritional status (Carr, 2004). On an average a child from the poorest health quintile is twice as likely as a child in richest quintile die before age 5. Similarly the study showed that the people in the poorest quintile are less likely than those in better off quintile to use basic health services such as immunization, maternity care and family planning. In Indian context the disparities in health outcome and health care utilization is even larger among the rich and poor. The estimated under five mortality of poorest quintile is 141 per 1000 live births, as compared to 46 per 1000 live birth for the richest. Ahemed (2004) using DHS data of Bangladesh showed that there is differential in contraceptive use, fertility level, unmeet need, fertility preference and maternal health care utilization by socio-economic status.

The Indian society stratified in such a way that there is glaring inequalities among different social groups. Among the social groups those belonging to traditionally oppressed sections of the society called Scheduled Caste and Scheduled Tribe (SC/ST), live in relative isolation and are often permitted easy access to common facilities in spite of legal provisions prohibiting such discrimination. Moreover health worker may also be reluctant to visit localities or hamlets or SC/ST (Sivakami, 2003). Thus the poorer and the socially weaker sections of the society are at disadvantage condition in utilization of health care services and nutritional status. Although a large number of primary health centres and sub centres has been created in order to reach out the marginalised group and bridge the gap between the social groups and the rich and before as a part of government's 'Health for All' programme, most of the states in India still are far away from this goal. This paper attempts to examine the extent of inequalities of health and nutrition in the newly formed states of Uttarakhand, Jharkhand and Chhattisgarh with a special focus to social and economic groups. Further, it also assess the net effect of these groups on health and nutrition after controlling for other socio economic and other demographic characteristics of the individual.

OBJECTIVE

1. To examine the extent of differential in health and nutritional indicators by social groups.
2. To examine the extent of economic differentiation in health and nutritional indicators.

DATA SOURCE

This study uses the data from National Family Health Survey-3, a large scale sample survey that was carried out by International Institute for Population Sciences (IIPS) under the aegis of the Government of India; The NFHS-3 covered a sample of over 109,041 sample households, 124,385 women age 15-49. It provides estimates for the country as a whole and all the 29 states. The survey was conducted with the primary objective of providing reliable and comparable estimates of fertility, infant mortality, contraceptive use , reproductive health, family size etc. for different states of India.

Apart from this, it also gives data on basic socio economic characteristics of household and women. The survey also provides information on social groups namely, Scheduled castes (SC), Scheduled tribes (ST), Other backward classes (OBC) and Others.

METHODOLOGY

The following indicators of the health and nutrition are examined in the present paper.

Full immunization: Children who received one dose each of the BCG and measles Vaccines and three doses each of the DPT and polio vaccines are considered as fully immunized.

Under weight: Children whose weight-for-age is below minus two SD from the median reference of population.

Anemia: Children whose hemoglobin level is less than 11.0g/dl.

Full ANC: Full ANC is that the minimum of three antenatal visits, two or more TT Injection received and receipt of more than hundred IFA tablets/syrup.

Safe Delivery: Safe delivery is considered as the institutional delivery performed in health institutions.

Anaemia level: women whose haemoglobin level is less than 11.0g/dl.

Bivariate analysis is used to carry out the extent of differential in health and nutritional indicators among the individuals belonging to different caste and income groups. Besides *logistic regression* analysis is used to assess the influence of certain variables on the probability of occurrence of an event. 3 sets of separate logistic regression have been carried out for each of the health and nutritional indicator for women and child.

DISCUSSION

Profile of the Study Population

Uttarakhand, Jharkhand and Chhattisgarh have distinct geographical and topographical characteristics. Chhattisgarh and Jharkhand are on a plateau, while Uttarakhand is on the lap of the middle and lower Himalayas. All three are land-locked states. For administrative purposes, Jharkhand is divided into four division and 22 districts, Uttarakhand and Chhattisgarh in to 13 and 16 districts respectively.

Table 5.1: Socio-Economic and Demographic Characteristics of the States

Variable	*Year & Source*	*Uttarakhand*	*Jharkhand*	*Chhattisgarh*
Demographic variable				
Total population(million)	Census 2001	8.49	26.94	20.83
CBR	SRS(20006)	20.5	26.2	27.4
CDR	SRS(2006)	7.2	8	7.7
TFR	SRS(20004)	3.6	3.5	3.4
IMR	SRS(20006)	42	49	60
Sex ratio	Census 2001	962	941	989
Decadal growth rate	Census 2001	20.4	23.4	18.3
MMR	SRS(2001-03)	517	371	379
Social variable				
Literacy	Census 2001			
Male		83.3	67.3	77.4
Female		59.6	38.9	51.9
Total		71.6	53.6	64.7
Life expectancy	SRS(20004)			
Male			61.8	57.5
Female			69.9	57.2
% of people live BPL				
Economic Variables				
GSDP(in crore)	(2004-05)	11057	26788	

Uttarakhand is a state with 8.49 million people accounts for one per cent of total population of the country. The state being a hilly one, is the most sparsely populated state in the country. 72 per cent of total population of state is literate which is higher than national average. Chhattisgarh is a state which fulfils the long cherished demand for tribal people. It is a state of 20.8 million people accounts for 2.5 per cent of total population of the country. The decadal growth rate is lower than national average. The state of Jharkhand with a population of 26.9 million population accounts for 3 per cent of total population of the country. Jharkhand is one of the mineral rich regions in the country.

To understand the socio-economic inequality the distribution of women by caste and wealth Index is shown in the

Table 5.2. For the purpose of study OBC and others are combined into one category considered as General. Caste wise distribution of women in all the three States shows that in Uttarakhand less than five per cent women belong to ST category whereas two-fifths of population belongs to SC category and more than 70 per cent women are general. Compared to Uttarakhand in Chhattisgarh and Jharkhand more than 50 per cent of population belong to general category, 30 per cent of women belong to ST category and it is less than 20 per cent for SC.

Table 5.2: Distribution of women by caste and wealth in three States

	Uttarakhand	*Jharkhand*	*Chhattisgarh*
Caste			
SC	23.4	12.0	15.4
ST	4.1	30.3	30.5
General	72.4	57.7	54.11
Wealth Index			
Poorest	8.0	57.2	44.2
Poorer	16.8	16.2	26.9
Middle	23.1	10.8	14.6
Richer	24.2	9.5	7.3
Richest	27.9	6.3	7

To know the economic inequality in these three States, the wealth index is used as appropriate measure. The distribution of women by wealth index shows that proportion of women falling in poorest quintile is 8 per cent where as it is 28 per cent in richest quintile. Compared to Uttarakhand, in Chhattisgarh 44 per cent people falling under poorest quintile and 57 per cent in Jharkhand whereas it is about 7 per cent for richest quintile. This shows that economic inequality is higher in Jharkhand, followed by Chhattisgarh and though inequality exist but it is low in Uttarakhand.

Social Inequality in Uttarakhand, Jharkhand and Chhattisgarh

The social inequality by caste in all the three States by background characteristics women shown in Table 5.3.

The background characteristics include age of women, education of women, wealth Index, religion and place of residence. It may be seen that 78.4 per cent SC women lives in rural area whereas it is more than 80 per cent for Chhattisgarh and Jharkhand. Similarly about 90 per cent ST women in Uttarakhand lives in rural area and it is 95 per cent for Jharkhand and Chhattisgarh. The economic differential among the caste groups is remarkable in three States. In case of Uttarakhand 11 per cent of SC are classified in the poorest quintile as compared to 7 per cent among ST and 8 per cent among general. In case of Jharkhand and Chhattisgarh the proportion of poor is relatively higher for ST and SC compared to others. In Jharkhand 75 per cent of ST fall under poorest quintile, for SC it is 69 per cent followed by general which is 45 per cent. This pattern is similar for Chhattisgarh. The religion differential among the caste group is sharp which shows that proportion of Hindu is higher for all the caste as compared to Muslims and others. This is true for all the states. The educational differentiation by caste shows that the proportion of women who are illiterate is higher among ST's followed by SC's followed by General. In Uttarakhand it is 73 per cent for ST, 55 per cent for SC and 35 per cent for others. This pattern is same for all the three states.

Differential in Health and Nutritional Status by Caste groups

Table 5.4 presents the extent of inequality in all the 7 MCH indicators between the caste groups. From the table it is found that SC and ST are poorly performed in all the health and nutritional indicators as a whole in comparison to generals.

Looking into the full immunisation coverage, say for Uttarakhand it is 42 per cent among ST followed by SC that is 54 per cent followed by General that is 63 per cent. This pattern is same for Chhattisgarh. Where as in Jharkhand it is found that full immunisation coverage is lowest among SC's that is 25 per cent, 31 per cent for ST's and 39 per cent for General. If we compare full immunization coverage between the 3 states, it is found that the coverage is lower in Jharkhand as compared to Uttarakhand and Chhattisgarh. Out of various components of immunization, it is found that the coverage of measles is lower as compared to other vaccination in all the three States.

Table 5.3: **Distribution of women in different social groups by background chrematistics**

Background Variable	Uttranchal				Chhattisgarh				Jharkhand			
	SC	ST	GENERAL	Total	SC	ST	GENERAL	Total	SC	ST	GENERAL	Total
1	2	3	4	5	6	7	8	9	10	11	12	13
Residence				1234								
Urban	21.63	10.81	24.79	290	19.61	4.88	25.76	325	16.88	4.19	23.39	273
Rural	78.37	89.19	75.21	944	80.39	95.12	74.24	1413	83.12	95.81	76.61	1380
Wealth index				1234				1738				1654
Poorest	11.33	6.08	7.08	99	68.51	75.53	45.2	994	45.69	68.52	30.17	732
Poorer	25.21	42.57	12.56	207	14.49	11.57	19	282	29.59	18.64	30.92	446
Middle	28.67	16.22	21.68	285	6.32	5.91	14.25	187	15.63	9.24	17.14	240
Richer	16.22	27.48	26.6	299	7.55	5.43	12.1	166	6.95	2.79	9.88	120
Richest	18.57	7.66	32.08	344	3.13	1.57	9.45	109	2.14	0.81	11.89	116
Religion				1234				1732				1653
Hindu	95.31	82.88	80.3	1035	95.68	48.6	69.52	1149	98.47	99.05	94.3	1594
Muslim	3.3	13.06	13.14	134	2.04	0.91	29.7	305	0	0	5.25	46
Others	1.39	4.05	6.56	65	2.28	50.49	0.78	278	1.53	0.95	0.46	13

(Contd…)

1	2	3	4	5	6	7	8	9	10	11	12	13
Education of women												
No education	55.31	72.97	35.29	513	74.64	74.07	61.48	1162	55.49	69.29	44.62	890
Primary	13.2	15.31	12.45	157	12.35	8.23	11.94	189	20.11	12.79	22.24	315
Secondary	28.15	9.91	37.18	419	11.68	16.12	23.37	343	22.34	17.05	26.92	384
Higher	3.34	1.8	15.08	145	1.33	1.59	3.21	43	2.06	0.87	6.22	65
Age of women								1737				1653
15-24	31.65	53.83	28.3	372	51.59	40.93	49.24	817	42.32	40.31	45.23	716
25-34	59.52	44.37	63.74	765	37.39	48.61	43.54	770	45.11	50.62	49.97	817
35-49	8.83	1.8	7.96	97	11.02	10.45	7.23	150	12.57	9.06	4.8	120

Table 5.4: Health and nutrition status by Caste/Tribes

Health & nutrition indicators	*Uttarakhand*				*Jharkhand*				*Chattisgarh*			
	SC	*ST*	*Non SC/ST*	*N*	*SC*	*ST*	*Non SC/ST*	*N*	*SC*	*ST*	*Non SC/ST*	*N*
Child indicator												
Full immunization	54.1	41.9	63.0	219	25.07	31.5	39.1	303	47.8	42.2	52.9	284
Received BCG	78.3	71.0	85.9		63.85	75.2	73.5		79.5	81.2	87.9	
Received DPT	57.8	71.0	70.1		32.65	39.3	44.1		62.1	62.3	63.8	
Received polio	72.7	71.0	83.4		63.85	80.5	81.5		82.6	82.5	87.3	
Received measles	65.1	56.5	74.5		44.61	42.5	52.6		62.1	55.6	66.4	
Nutritional status				1030				1387				1442
Stunting	54.9	47.9	41.4		53.48	55.2	46.5		57.7	52.6	53.3	
Wasting	21.3	21.4	18.0		29.59	40.2	29.3		14.8	27.1	17.7	
Underweight	44.9	50.3	35.3		56.79	65.5	53.0		46.4	53.3	44.8	
Anemia level	73.5	72.3	57.5		76.44	80.5	64.6	1300	69.0	78.1	69.4	1295
Women indicator												
Safe delivery	24.4	7.9	36.9	1227	15.24	7.9	24.7	1726	11.3	3.9	21.1	1653
Full ANC	19.3	9.2	30.1	869	13.51	12.2	26.4	1196	20.3	15.1	27.5	1197
3 & more visits	38.8	22.9	50.7	833	27.79	25.9	43.0	1193	48.0	48.1	59.6	1195
TT injection	63.2	65.1	71.0	867	63.88	54.2	75.7	1193	76.3	68.2	78.4	1192
IFA tablets	36.2	24.3	46.6	527	21.49	29.5	31.0	579	21.9	24.7	32.2	876
Anemia level	60.0	71.4	53.1	2839	72.58	85.0	62.4	2779	51.9	74.0	50.3	3776
Undernutrition	37.9	48.9	26.6	2735	39.3	47.01	42.01	2624	38.4	50.4	40.9	3582

Coming to nutritional status it is found that proportion of underweight children is higher among STs followed by SCs followed by General. In Jharkhand it is 66 per cent for ST, 57 per cent for SC followed by General. This pattern is same for other two states. Looking into the nutritional status of women it is higher for ST that is 48 per cent, 37 per cent for SC and 26 per cent for General. But in Jharkhand it is higher for ST that is 46 per cent followed by others that is 42 per cent followed by SCs. This pattern is same for Chhattisgarh.

Similar is the case with anaemia level both for children and women. It is observed from the table that anaemia level is higher in all the 3 states among all the castes particularly among STs. In Jharkhand more than 80 per cent children and women among STs become anaemic. In Uttarakhand only proportion of anaemic children higher among SCs followed by ST and General.

Looking into other two programmes related indicators the situation is same and it is much sharper. If we observe the safe delivery case in Uttarakhand it is 8 per cent STs followed by SCs that is 24.4 per cent followed by General that is 37 per cent. This pattern is same for other two states. In Chhattisgarh the differential is much higher. Only 4 per cent of STs go to health institution.

If we look the results it is found that in all states, the proportion of women going to health institutions for delivery is lower among all the castes. And it is much lower for Chhattisgarh compared to other two states. In Uttarakhand even though economic inequality is low among the caste groups, still there exists social inequality in utilisation of these services.

In case of antenatal care, it is observed that the coverage of complete ANC is lowest for STs followed by SCs and General. In Uttarakhand the coverage of Full ANC is 9 per cent for ST, 19 per cent for SC and 30 per cent for General. Like safe delivery, FANC coverage is lower in all the 3 states. The possible reasons for not utilising these services are lack of awareness among women, lack of accessibility of these services both physical and economical.

Economic Differential in Health and Nutritional Status Between the 3 States

Table 5.5 presents economic inequalities in these three States with respect to all 7 indicators selected for the analysis. Wealth Index is used to examine the extent of inequality prevailing in different income groups with respect to such indicators. The differential in full immunization coverage varies directly with wealth quintile in Chhattisgarh. In Jharkhand it is lowest for poorest followed by middle, poorest and so on. Where as in Uttarakhand it is lowest for poorer followed by poorest, middle, rich and richest.

Looking into the safe delivery case in Uttarakhand it is 8 per cent for poorer followed by poorest that is 12 per cent, 16 per cent for middle, 30 per cent for rich and 70 per cent for richest. Similarly in Chhattisgarh it is 4 per cent for poorest, 5 per cent for poorer, 17 per cent for middle, 37 per cent for richer and 88 per cent for richest. This shows that not only inequality exists among the income groups but also the extent of inequality is sharp. This situation is same with coverage of FANC.

Looking in to the table it is found that, though inequality exists among the income groups with respect to such indicators, the extent of inequality is higher in safe delivery and coverage of FANC in all the States.

There are certain other correlates of health and nutrition indicators except caste/tribe or income. If higher percentage of SC/ST or low income group people do not go for FANC or if they are anaemic may not be due to their caste per se or belong to low income. It can be due to certain other factors. Thus besides caste and Wealth Index a set of independent variables are taken for examining the differentials in health and nutritional status between the individuals belonging to different socio economic group. These are type of residence, women's education, religion of the women, age of the mother, sex of the child, birth order, work status of women, exposure to mass media etc. For this logistic regression carried out to capture the significance of other variables.

Table 5.5: Health and nutrition satus by wealth index

Health & nutrtion indicators	*Uttrakhand*						*Jharkhand*						*Chhattisgarh*					
	Q1	*Q2*	*Q3*	*Q4*	*Q5*	*N*	*Q1*	*Q2*	*Q3*	*Q4*	*Q5*	*N*	*Q1*	*Q2*	*Q3*	*Q4*	*Q5*	*N*
Child indicator																		
Full immunization	39.1	32.4	60.4	63.3	80	219	24.5	41.5	28	62	76.3	304	37.0	48	53	68	94.4	285
Receive BCG	55.9	73.0	82.9	86.6	95.7		63.5	82.6	77	90	100		76.8	89.1	84.2	100	100	
Receive DPT	39.1	45.1	70.5	69.2	84.5		29.7	50.2	40	67	79.2		52.2	65.4	60.6	86	100.0	
Receive polio	61.5	57.5	80.6	88.4	92.9		73.7	91.3	80	87	88.1		78.6	87.7	90.6	83	100.0	
Receive Measles	55.9	40.0	73.0	80.9	87.1		39	60.6	36	70	85.2		49.3	67.3	63.5	90	94.4	
Nutritional status						1030						1390						1445
Stunting	62.5	63.6	53.1	46.4	22		55	53	43	47	13.5		58.1	59.1	49.9	50	20.4	
Wasting	25.9	25.4	23.5	16.4	11.9		36	32.4	32	24	17.3		24.6	15.9	20.6	11	15.8	
Underweight	57.4	54.1	44.2	39.8	18.2		63.5	61.2	49	49	17.1		55.6	51.2	40.3	31	17.8	
Anemia level	77.7	69.4	67.3	58	51.6	887	76.9	68.7	59	64	47.3	1303	76.1	74.9	67.8	66	52.7	1297
Women indicator																		
Safe delivery	11.6	8.1	16	30.2	69.8	1227	5.39	15	28.6	42.3	91.9	1729	3.7	4.91	17.1	37	88.0	1665
Full ANC	9.3	7.3	15.5	24.5	52.9	870	9.7	19.8	33.1	36.9	65.3	1200	14.2	19.6	23.6	44	58.2	1198
3 & more visits	13.1	20	34.7	45.1	80.5	833	18.8	40.2	58.3	62.9	89.2	1196	41.8	50.5	63.3	84	92.2	1196
TT injection	37.0	43	64.8	71.6	92.5	868	56.1	79.1	81.3	82.9	95.3	1196	65.6	75.1	85.4	91	90.5	1193
IFA tablets	33.6	25	25.1	39.2	60.3	527	19.2	27.3	37.9	34.3	62.2	579	22.7	22.4	26.1	40	63.6	876
Anemia level	61.6	56	60	59.2	48.2	2842	76.6	71.4	64	60	55	2786	65.4	56.5	55.3	48	43.9	3768
Under nutrition	39.9	43	37	31	18.3	2738	50	47.8	47.7	35.1	17.5	2630	52.7	46.9	41.1	32	16.4	3585

RESULTS OF LOGISTIC REGRESSION

FANC: Differential between SC women and General regarding full ANC disappear in all the 3 states. Where as in Jharakhand and Chhattisagarh 'ST' women are less likely to get FANC. It can be that programme should be taken specific care to focus on tribes. Except caste, in Jharkhand it is found that women belong to richest quintile are more likely to FANC. Thus, in Jharkhand it is income which matters in utilisation of ANC.

Safe delivery: Differential between SC/ST women and women in General category disappear in all the three States. Thus here caste does not play any role. Economic factor play an important role here. In Uttarakhand women belong to richer quintile 3 time more likely to go to health institutions, in Jharkhand it is 2 times and in Chhattisgarh 4 times.

Anaemia: It is found that ST women are 2 times more likely to get anaemic in all the 3 states. SC women in Uttarakhand and Chhattisgarh more than 1 time likely to be anaemic than general.

Under nutrition: Differential between SC/ST and General persist regarding BMI in Uttarakhand. The Odds of having low BMI is 2.07 for ST and 1.47 for ST where as in Jharkhand and Chhattisgarh SC women are less likely to be underweight compared to General. In Chhattisgarh it found that women belong to richest quintile have low BMI. This is the case with Jharkhand also.

Full Immunisation: Differential between SC/ST and General disappear regarding immunisation. This is also happen in different income groups also.

Malnutrition: Differential between SC/ST and General disappear regarding malnutrition. This states that Cast does not have any effect on Malnutrition. In Chhattisgarh it is income which plays a significant role for this. This is the case with Uttarakhand and Jharkhand.

Anameia: Differential between SC and General persist in Uttarakhand and Jharkhand regarding Anaemia. The odds of having anaemia for SC is 1.8 in Uttarakhand, 1.6 in Jharkhand but in Chhattisgarh caste does not have any effect on Anaemia.

Table 5.6: Results of Logistic regression for women

	Uttarkhand				*Jharkhand*				*Chhattisgarh*			
	Full ANC	*Safe delivery*	*Anaemia*	*under-nutrition*	*Full ANC*	*Safe delivery*	*Anaemia*	*under-nutrition*	*Full ANC*	*Safe delivery*	*Anaemia*	*under-nutrition*
1	2	3	4	5	6	7	8	9	10	11	12	13
Caste												
General[R]												
SC	1.01	1.12	1.29*	1.47*	0.72	0.72	1.36**	0.8*	0.82	1.04	1.01	0.74***
ST	0.44	0.38	2.01*	2.07*	0.38*	0.88	2.62***	0.92	0.66*	0.61	2.48***	1.03
Wealth Index												
Q1[R]												
Q2	0.87	1.63	0.78	0.78	1.61*	1.73*	0.89	0.91	1.17	0.92	0.85*	0.80***
Q3	1.20	1.92	0.98	0.98	3.09***	2.14**	0.69**	0.95	1.42	2.49**	0.85	0.70***
Q4	1.69	3.53**	0.96	0.96	3.48***	2.61***	0.62***	0.56***	2.45**	4.96***	0.65***	0.49***
Q5	2.42	7.85***	0.71	0.71	4.52***	16.07***	0.55***	0.25***	1.72	22.59***	0.55***	0.23***
Place of residence												
Urban[R]												
Rural	0.61**	0.59**	1.18	1.45***	1.05	0.44**	1.01	0.94	0.61**	0.25***	0.81**	1.13

(Contd...)

1	2	3	4	5	6	7	8	9	10	11	12	13
Religion												
Hindu^R												
Muslim	1.62	0.77	1.74***	1.31	1.07	0.83	0.89	1.13	0.70	3.02**	0.96	0.95
Others	1.21	4.86***	1.12	1.08	1.49	0.35**	1.10	0.98	0.98	0.73	0.73	1.52*
Education												
No^R												
Primary	1.84*	1.17	0.96	0.95	1.53	0.80	1.01	0.74**	1.13	0.98	0.87	0.96
Secondary	3.10***	1.93***	0.95	0.97	1.38	2.90***	0.92	0.73***	1.33	1.70	0.80**	0.90
Higher	7.83***	10.54***	0.74**	0.67**	3.47***	15.63***	0.81	0.87	3.07**	4.42***	0.76	0.76
Age of women												
15-24^R												
25-34			1.00	0.57***			1.04	0.69***			0.85*	0.74***
35+			0.77***	0.51***			1.17	0.53***			0.91	0.45***
Birth order												
1^R												
2	0.69*	0.52***			0.79	0.51***			0.81	0.44***		
3	0.47**	0.41***			0.69	0.32***			0.69	0.23***		
4+	0.61	0.41***			0.69	0.30***			0.61**	0.20***		
Full ANC												
No^R												
Yes		2.23***				2.13***				1.36		

Table 5.7: Results of Logistic regression for children

	Uttarakhand			*Jharkhand*			*Chhattisgarh*		
	Full Immunisation	*Malnutrition*	*Anaemia*	*Full Immunisation*	*Malnutrition*	*Anaemia*	*Full Immunisation*	*Malnutrition*	*Anaemia*
1	*2*	*3*	*4*	*5*	*6*	*7*	*8*	*9*	*10*
Caste									
General[R]									
SC	0.97	1.18	1.79***	1.00	0.96	1.59**	0.44	0.89	0.97
ST	1.18	1.11	1.78	1.01	1.14	1.56**	0.71	1.09	1.29
Wealth Index									
Q1[R]									
Q2	0.63	0.91	0.63	1.12	1.03	0.76	2.44**	0.93	0.99
Q3	1.27	0.69	0.61	0.88	0.74	0.59**	0.69	0.67**	0.75
Q4	1.45	0.64	0.43**	1.29	0.75	0.68	4.23***	0.56**	0.71
Q5	2.47	0.33***	0.38***	6.68*	0.22***	0.40***	2.12	0.43**	0.31***
Place of residence									
Urban[R]									
Rural	0.71	1.67**	1.09	0.68	1.09	1.08	1.44	1.10	0.58***

(Contd...)

1	2	3	4	5	6	7	8	9	10
Religoin									
Hindu[R]									
Muslim	0.53	1.78**	1.84**	1.24	0.86	1.19	0.61	0.77	1.73
Others	4.72	0.99	1.07	0.49	1.38	1.25	0.90	0.64	0.20**
Education									
No[R]									
Primary	0.63	0.76	0.75	1.42	0.79	0.62**	0.45*	1.04	0.85
Secondary	2.24*	0.62***	0.86	2.55**	0.66**	0.80	2.35***	0.61***	0.72*
Higher	0.86	0.39*	0.69	1.24	0.30**	0.71	3.81	0.29***	0.56
Age of child									
< 1yr[R]									
<25 month		1.43	1.75**		2.42***	0.92		1.31	0.81
25+		2.23***	0.59**		2.31***	0.34***		1.30*	0.25***
Birth order									
1[R]									
2	0.82			0.83			0.87		
3	0.83			1.37			0.58		
4+	0.37*			0.82			0.52***		
Anemia of women									
no[R]									
yes			2.08***			2.49***			1.58***

*<=0.10, **<=0.05, ***<=0.01

R= Reference Category.

CONCLUSION

The study is a preliminary attempt to show the socio-economic inequality in health and nutritional indicators. It uses the caste and wealth quintiles as the basis of analysis followed by logistic regression. The study focus on three states which are the newly formed state of India and lagging behind in various socio, economic and demographic indicators. It found that there is greater inequality in these health and nutritional indicators by distribution of wealth and by different social groups. Instead of Caste and wealth certain other factors also contributing to this such as educational level of women, age of the women, Religion, Birth Order etc. In all the Indicators STs are lagging behind followed by SCs and General. The level of immunization, ANC and safe deliveries, the three main components of RCH services and also other nutritional indicators varies directly with the wealth index in both the states of Jharkhand and Chhattisgarh whereas in Uttarakhand it is the poorer quintile who are lagging behind in all three RCH indicators. The result of logistic regression shows that caste is not a significant predictor except for anemia of women. Where as Wealth index has a significant predictor in many indicators. Though inequality persist in all indicators both by caste and distribution of wealth, the extent of inequality is relatively higher for ANC and safe delivery as compared to other indicators for all the three states.. The implication is that more programmatic stress should be given to improve ANC and safe delivery for poorer section and also for the backward sections of the society.

LIMITATION

1. The wealth index is not exact quintile distribution.
2. The rigorous statistical exercise could not be carried out owing to time constraint.

SOME IMPLICATIONS

Some of the implications of our analyses can be stated as follows:

1. There is a greater disparity in the health and nutritional indicators by Caste and the economic status of the women.

So there is a greater need to focus on the weaker and disadvantaged section of the society in the health care matter.

2. The more programmatic stress should be given to improve ANC and safe delivery for poorer section of the society.

3. Besides more research is required to find out the reasons of not utilizing public health services.

REFERENCES

Ahmed, S. (2004). "Does Family Planning Programme Reduce Inequality In Contraceptive Use, Fertility and Other Health Care Utilization? Evidence from Bangladesh", Paper presented in *Population Association of America* (PAA), USA.

Bishoyi, D (2005): "Economic inequality in Utilisation of Reproductive and Child Health Services: A Comparative Study of Orissa and Bihar", Seminar Paper Presented in IIPS.

Carr, D. (2004). "Improving the Health of the World's Poorest People", *Health Bulletin 1*, Population Reference Bureau, Washington, DC.

International Institute for Population Science and ORC Macro (2007): National Family Health Survey (2005-06): India, IIPS, Mumbai.

Negi, N.S (2007): "Utilization of Maternal and Child Health Services Among Tribles in Chhattisgarh, M.Phil Dissertation Presented in IIPS.

Pandey,et.al(2004): "Maternal Health Care Services: Observation from Chhattisgarh, Jharkhand and Uttaranchal", *Economic and Political Weekly*.

Roy, et.al (2004): "Social Inequalities in Health and Nutrition in Selected States", *Economic and Political Weekly*.

Sivakami, M and Kulkarni, P.M (2003): "Are Socially and Economically Weaker Sections Deprived of Maternal Health Care in Tamilnadu in India", *Journal of Health and Population in Developing Countries*.

Tiwary, M. and Prasad, R. (2002). *Status of Maternal Health Care in Jharkhand: A District Level Analysis*.

6

An Investigation into Causes and Consequences of Disability in India
A Case of Working Age Population

Sangram Kishor Patel

ABSTRACT

This study makes an attempt to unearth the fact that certain types of disability can be avoided with preventive measures by analysing the causes of disability among working age population (15-59) in India. The chapter also highlights the economic consequences of disability in terms of likelihood of loosing work or has to change job due to disability and economic status of disabled working population.

The National Sample Survey Organisation (58th round, 2002), survey of disabled persons unfolds that more than 53 per cent of them have limited ability to physical movement (Locomotor), while as many as 15 per cent have mental disability. At the same time, around 11 per cent have multiple type of disability. Those having visual and hearing difficulties are around 8 per cent each and the rest have speech related challenge. Polio and injury other than burns are found to be the most vital causes of physical immobility while serious illness during childhood, head injury in childhood, heredity and pregnancy and birth related causes are significantly associated with mental disability, a large proportion (77 per cent) of such cases are either due to other or unknown causes. Twenty-five per cent of visual disability is due to eye diseases and 15 per cent is due to cataract disease. The other subsidiary causes of visual disability are glaucoma, corneal opacity, small fox, burns, injury and surgical intervention. The main reason, which caused hearing problems, is other illness and ear discharge constituting with 31 and 20 per cent respectively. Where as in case of speech disability, 26 per cent is due to other illness, followed by paralysis, voice disorder and mental illness/retardation making 18, 9 and 9 per cent respectively of the totality. Bivariate analysis also reveals that burns/injuries related disabilities are caused mostly due to transport accident, home accidents and working in manual activities. Around 62 per cent of disabled persons have either changed or loosed their works due to onset of disability. The proportion of persons who have changed or loosed their works due to onset of disabilities related to visual, mental and locomotor disability are 71, 83 and 66 per cent respectively. As compared to hearing/speech related challenged persons it is 10, 11, 27 and 10 times more likely that disabled persons having locomotor, visual, mental and multiple disabilities of either loosing or changing work due to the onset of these disabilities Among working disabled population, around 54 per cent are continuing their works as before or either changed to a new work, after the onset of disability.

The present study brings to light main causes of all forms of disabilities which will enable policy makers to implement preventive and precautionary steps to control incidence of disability. It is also evident that to save disabled persons from economic dilution we need to have a national network of vocational training centers for imparting knowledge and skill which will help them to remain economically active. It is in this sense that the paper has certain policy relevance.

Key words: Disability, causes, consequences, working age population and India.

INTRODUCTION

As disability is a complex phenomena, and accurately measuring its prevalence in a national-level survey present many challenges and the way these definition are operationalised through questions, wording and placement influence the levels of disability estimated and characteristics of the disabled population (Kramarow and Pamela, 2004). Given these complexities, the lack of agreement about optimal measures of disability is not surprising (Altman, 2001). Then also the standard definition given by, WHO (1980) define disability as any restriction or lack (resulting from an impairment) of ability to perform an activity in the manner or within the range considered normal for a human being.

The disabled population is increasing every year by some 15 million as a result of war, accident, malnutrition and diseases (Harper and Momm, 1989). Each year 35 million children die and another 35 million become disabled (World Bank, 1993). For every disabled person in the world, it is estimated that at least four members of the immediate family will be directly affected through having to adapt to and meet the needs of their relative (Krishna, et al., 2001). According to Census of India 2001 around two per cent of the total populations in our country are disabled persons. NSSO (58th round- 2002) estimated that around 19 million people are disabled in India. Of this, 11 per cent of disabled persons suffer from more than one type of disability. Among the different types of disabilities, the prevalence of locomotors disability is the highest in the country. Further, NSSO has estimated that 69 persons per Lakh population were either born disabled or become disabled for some reasons. About 13 per cent of the physically disabled were observed to be severely disabled, as they could not take self-care even with aid/appliance.

From the replies received from international agencies, governmental and non-governmental sources, the causes of disability mentioned most often are the following: heredity, birth defects, lack of care during pregnancy and child birth because of lack of coverage of ignorance, insalubrious housing, natural disasters, illiteracy and the resulting lack of information available on health services, poor sanitation and hygiene, congenital diseases, malnutrition, traffic accidents, work-related accidents and illness, sports accidents, the so-called diseases of 'civilisation' (cardiovascular disease, mental and nervous disorders, the use of certain chemicals, change of diet and life style etc.), marriage between close relatives, accidents in home, respiratory diseases, metabolic diseases (diabetes, kidney failure etc.), drugs, alcohol, smoking, high blood pressure, old age, chugs disease, poliomyelitis, measles etc. Non-governmental sources also place particular emphasis on factors related to the environment, air and water pollution, scientific experiments conducted without the informed consents of the victims, terrorist violence, wars, intentional physical mutilations carried out by the authorities and other attacks on the physical and mental integrity of persons, as well as violations of human rights and humanitarian law in general (Stace, 1986; Krishna, *et al.*, 2001).

The morbidity experience of men and women; different working age groups population varies substantially over the life course. Men are more likely then women to encounter a series chronic illness that increases risk of mortality, such as coronary heart disease, atherosclerosis, emphysema (Verbrugge, 1985). Conversely, women are more likely than men to encounter chronic diseases that are physically limiting, but not life threatening (Verbrugge, 1985). For example, arthritis is the leading cause of locomotor disability and women are twice as likely as men to be limited by arthritis (Mutt, *et al.*, 1996).

Like other members of the society, the disabled individuals also have hopes, aspiration, rights and privileges. This basic and simple proposition, how ever is not widely acknowledged. It may be gauged from the fact that given the vast magnitude of the problem affected by the ravages of disability, even the industrialized countries, which claim to achieved medical, scientific and technological advancement as also economic prosperity – have not been able to integrate these disabled citizens in to active social and economic life. As long as the problem of appalling poverty, illiteracy and unemployment is rampant, the persons with disabilities are bound to suffer more than most. In Third World countries such as India, their prospects of securing employment in the open labour market are, so to say the least or non-existent. So much so that even in developed countries, their rate of unemployment is often double than that of none disabled workers.

Cynics could assume this to be merely a question of lack of opportunity for the disabled and a problem, which deserves to be tackled with the over all improvement in the economic sphere. In deed, such a parochial and discriminatory approach undermines not only their basic human rights but also the economic benefits occurring to themselves, their families and the state itself if they were to be productively engaged in to the fabric of society. It presents, in fact a sordid picture in human terms with the persons with disabilities gripped by the feelings inadequacy, dependency and insecurity; normally relegated to the margin of society to turning to charity or begging as a means of sustenance.

In America (1998), 17.2 millions working age-men and women had a work disability of which nearly one third or 5.2 millions were active in labour forces. More over, because older adults are more likely to encounter a disabling health condition than younger adults (Crimmins, *et al.*, 1999; La Plante 1993), the impact of disability is particularly salient for older workers.

The male model of impact of disability suggests that labour supply is severely curtailed at onset of a disability health condition as evidenced by both high rate of labour force exit and by low rate of labour force re-entry (Hayward, *et al.*, 1989). There are few studies that have compared women and men show that prevalence rate of work disability does not differ by gender (Daly and Bound 1996; Loprest *et al.*, 1995). None the less, it is widely recognized that women and men experience different types of health problems and have substantially varying labour market experiences (Daly and Bound, 1996).

Different employers might differ different levels of or types of accommodation for disabilities. In general, work related disability out comes improve when companies/government have policies in place such as worker safety, safety training and proactive return-to-work programs (Habeck, *et al.*, 1998). Analyzing retrospective disability data from the health and retirement study, Daly and Bound (1996) found that 29.2 per cent of men and 36.9 per cent of women mentioned specific ways in which their employer had accommodated them. The most common types of accommodation for those who remained with their employer were: alteration in job dilution, assistance with the job, a change in schedule or a shorter work day, and more breaks. Although, workers who changed employers after the onset of disability were likely to experiences a change in job demands, these women significantly less likely than women who remained with their original employers to receive employer accommodations.

Again, measuring functional limitations and reducing work disability among the working population is an important issue on the scientific and policy agenda in many countries (Kapteyan, 2004). Waidmann (2002) models work limitations and finds that disability is significantly associate with work limitations. Favreault and Wolf (2002) estimates model of self reported health status similar to Waidmann's, but for an older population and finds that age, educational attainment, wealth and impending mortality all significantly predict entries into poor health (disabled stage).

NEED FOR THE STUDY

So far research on disability is very limited and focused only to old age population in developed world as well as developing countries. However, after International Year of Disabled (IYD) – 1981, some focused has given to disability studies and research. Worldwide very few studies are available which can sight some light simultaneously on disabilities, their causes and economic consequences among working age population. In India, the research on working age disabled is scarce and never explored. Further, there is no literature available which can demonstrate the causes of disability and their consequences on works due to disability among working age population in India. A nation like India, where the working age population is around 57 per cent of total population and more than 2 per cent of the working age population is disabled. One of the major concerned is that, on set different types of disabilities among working age population directly affecting the nation's productivity and economy. NSS-58th round data on disabled persons provides information about basic socio-economic and demographic characteristics of disabled persons and household members. So the problems need exploration. This study is an attempt in this direction that certainly raises some researchable issues and further understanding the causes and consequences of disability among working age population in India is an important step for the policy and program points of view, also for the future research.

OBJECTIVES

The specific objectives of the study are as follows:

1. to assess the causes of different types of disability among working age population (15-59) years according to different back ground characteristics in India;
2. to study the factors associated with, change or loss of works due to onset of disabilities among working age population in India.

MATERIALS AND METHODS

The present study is based on the National Sample Survey – 2002 (58th round - Disabled Persons of India) data source. For the purpose of this present study only selected working age (15-59) years' disabled population data have used here. Here the number of cases is 42,202 extracted from the disabled file. The survey has covered 35 States/UTs. The NSS has collected data on its fifty-eighth round from 1st July 2002 to 31st December 2002. The fifty-eighth round of NSS is earmarked for collection of data on disability, housing condition, village facilities and slum particulars besides that on household consumer expenditure and employment-unemployment.

The National Sample Survey made its first attempt to collect information on the number of physically disabled persons during 15th round (July 1959 - June 1960). Thereafter, data on disabled persons were collected in the 16th (July 1960 - June 1961), 24th (July 1969 - June 1970), 28th (October 1973 - June 1974), 36th (July - December, 1981) and 47th (July - December, 1991) rounds. The surveys undertaken during 15th, 16th, 24th and 28th rounds were intended mainly to get a count of the disabled persons of various kinds. In the surveys undertaken during the 36th and 47th rounds, detailed inquiry was made on each type of disability along with the socio-economic characteristics of the disabled. The fifty-eighth round of NSS will cover disability (both physical and mental), housing conditions, village facilities and slum particulars. In addition, the annual consumer expenditure enquiry covering some key characteristics of employment-unemployment will also be carried out on a sample of four households in each sample FSU.

A stratified multi-stage design has been followed for the conduct of survey of NSS 58th round. The first-stage units are census villages (panchayat wards for Kerala) in the rural sector and the NSSO Urban Frame Survey (UFS) blocks in the urban sector. The ultimate stage units are households in both the sectors. For the disability data collection in each selected village/ block/segment, three second stage strata (SSS) were formed on the basis of disability type. SSS1 are households having at least one person with mental disability, SSS2 are households having at least one person with speech/hearing/visual disability out of remaining households and SSS3 are households having at least one person with locomotor disability out of remaining households. The sample households were selected by SRSWOR from each SSS. For a household having a person with more than one disability (i.e multiple disability), SSS was assigned by priority criterion e.g. a household having a person with mental disability as well as locomotor disability was classified under SSS1 and a household having one person with speech disability and another person with locomotor disability was classified under SSS2.

Disability concepts, definitions are varying from country to country, from decades to decades. How ever for the present study the definitions are from NSS defined, which are described as follows:

Disability: A person with restrictions or lack of abilities to perform an activity in the manner or within the range considered normal for a human being is treated as having disability. It excludes illness/injury of recent origin (morbidity) resulting into temporary loss of ability to see, hear, speak or move.

Mental disability: Persons who have difficulty in understanding routine instructions, who do not carry out their activities like others of similar age or exhibit behaviours like talking to self, laughing/crying, staring, violence, fear and suspicion without reason would be considered as mentally disabled for the purpose of the survey. The "activities like others of similar age" will include activities of communication (speech), self-care (cleaning of teeth, wearing clothes, taking bath, taking food, personal hygiene, etc.), home living (doing some household chores) and social skills.

Visual disability: By visual disability, it is meant, loss or lack of ability to execute tasks requiring adequate visual acuity. For the survey, visually disabled will include: (a) those who do not have any light perception - both eyes taken together; and (b) those who have light perception but cannot correctly count fingers of hand (with spectacles/contact lenses if he/she uses spectacles/contact lenses) from a distance of 3 metres (or 10 feet) in good day light with both eyes open. Night blindness is not to be considered as visual disability.

Hearing disability: This refers to persons' inability to hear properly. Hearing disability is to be judged taking into consideration the disability of the better ear. In other words, if one ear of a person is normal and the other ear has total hearing loss, then the person is to be judged as normal in hearing for the purpose of the survey. Hearing disability will be judged without taking into consideration the use of hearing aids (i.e., the position for the person when hearing aid is not used). Persons with hearing disability may have different degrees of disability, such as profound, severe or moderate. A person will be treated as having 'profound' hearing disability if he/she cannot hear at all or can only hear loud sounds, such as, thunder or understands only gestures. A person will be treated as having 'severe' hearing disability if he/she can hear only shouted words or can hear only if the speaker is sitting in the front. A person will be treated as having 'moderate' hearing disability if his/her disability is neither profound nor severe. Such a person will usually ask to repeat the words spoken by the speaker or will like to see the face of the speaker while he/she speaks or will feel difficulty in conducting conversations.

Speech disability: This refers to persons' inability to speak properly. Speech of a person is judged to be disordered if the person's speech is not understood by the listener. Persons with speech disability will include those who cannot speak, speak only with limited words or those with loss of voice. It also includes those whose speech is not understood due to defects in speech, such as stammering, nasal voice, hoarse voice and discordant voice and articulation de-fects, etc.

Locomotor disability: A person with: (a) loss or lack of normal ability to execute distinctive activities associated with the movement of himself/herself and objects from place to place; and (b) physical deformities, other than those involving the hand or leg or both, regardless of whether the same caused loss or lack of normal movement of body – will be considered as disabled with locomotor disability. Thus, persons having locomotor disability will include those with: (a) loss or absence or inactivity of whole or part of hand or leg or both due to amputation, paralysis, deformity or dysfunction of joints which affects his/her "normal ability to move self or objects"; and (b) those with physical deformities in the body (other than limbs), such as, hunch back, deformed spine, etc. Dwarfs and persons with stiff neck of permanent nature who generally do not have difficulty in the normal movement of body and limbs will also be treated as disabled.

The various background characteristics considered in the analysis are: (1) Place of residence (Rural, Urban); (2) Sex (Male, Female); (3) Working age group (15-29, 30-44, 45-59); (4) Caste (Scheduled caste/tribes - SC/ST, Other Backwards Classes – OBCs, Other castes); (5) Education attainment (Illiterate, Literate up to Middle School, Secondary and above); (6) Average

Monthly Consumer Expenditure of Household (<3000, 3000-6000, 6000+) (This is classified according to WHO's definition of poverty as below 2$ per day, then 2$ to 4$ and 4$+ etc. as proxy economic status.); (7) Living arrangements (Alone, with spouse/ other members, without spouse/with parents/children/ relatives); (9) Disability type (Hearing, Speech, Visual, Mental, locomotor and Multiple); (10) Extent of disability (Mild/Others: can take self-care without aid/appliance and aid/appliance not tried/not available; moderate: can take self-care with only aid/ appliance; severe: cannot take self care even with aid/appliance; (11) Region (Northern: Jammu and Kashmir, Himachal Pradesh, Punjab, Chandigarh, Haryana, Delhi and Rajasthan; Central: Uttar Pradesh, Uttarakhand, Madhya Pradesh and Chhattisgarh; Eastern: Bihar, Jharkhand, Orissa and West Bengal; Northeastern: Arunachal Pradesh, Assam, Manipur, Meghalaya, Mizoram, Nagaland, Sikkim and Tripura; West: Goa, Daman and Diu, Dadra and Nagar Haveli, Gujarat and Maharashtra; South: Andhra Pradesh, Karnataka, Tamil Nadu, Kerala, Pondichery, Andaman and Nicobar Islands, and Lakshadweep).

Calculation of proportions, and chi-square χ^2 tests were used to assess the significance of univariate and bivariate relationships and multiple logistic regression analysis were employed to assess the significance of independent factors on the dependent variable.

FINDINGS

Prevalence of Causes of Disability

Table 6.1 depicts the percentage distribution of different types of disabilities among working age population in India. It shows that among the different types of disabilities, locomotor is highly (53 per cent) prevalent followed by mental and multiple disability with 15 and 11 per cent respectively.

Table 6.1: Percentage distribution of different types of disability among working age population, India, 2002

Types of Disability	*Percentage*
Mental	15.3 (6463)
Visual	8.0 (3397)
Hearing	8.3 (3482)
Speech	4.9 (2063)
Locomotor	52.7 (22249)
Multiple	10.8 (4548)
Total	**100.0 (42202)**

Results from Table 6.2, 6.3, 6.4, 6.5 and 6.6 illustrate about causes of different types of disabilities among working age populations; which are distributed according to different background characteristics such as place of residence, caste, age group, educational attainment of disabled person and average monthly consumer expenditure of households etc.

Results from these tables explain that there is a considerable amount of disabled persons' causes are either not known or are from other kinds of causes which have not mentioned here. Results from Table 6.2 show that there is significant association between different causes of mental disability and background characteristics of disabled persons. Among the different causes of mental disability, around 77 per cent of causes are either not known or due to other reasons. From the rest of the given causes, serious illness during childhood, head injury in childhood, heredity and pregnancy and birth related causes are the major ones, which caused mental problems between working age population in India. However persons belong to rural resident, male, other backward castes, illiterate and lower standard of living background characteristics are having more mental problems than their other counter parts. One of the interesting finding is that persons from middle working age group (30-44) years have correspondingly 15 and 3 per cent significantly higher mental problems than (45-59) and (15-29) years. Pregnancy and birth-related cause is highest (around 74 per cent) among rural resident disabled; while urban has only 26 per cent. But in case of pregnancy and birth related cause, female are more (79 per cent) affected than male (21 per cent). At the same time, heredity cause of mental disability showing a different picture. Results from the table indicate that literate up to middle, illiterate, and secondary and above categories mental disabled person are 54, 37 and 10 per cent respectively of having heredity cause.

Results from Table 6.3 depict that there is a significant association between different causes of visual disability and different background characteristics among working age population in India. Number of cases is very less in sore eyes during the first month of life and visual disability due to burns causes in India. However sufficient cases are available for making interpretation for others causes of visual disabilities. Among the different causes of visual disability among working age population, other eye diseases (25 per cent) is the main cause follows with cataract (15 per cent), injury other than burns (9 per cent) and small-pox (7 per cent) respectively. Among other major causes of visual disability between working age population are other reasons, glaucoma, corneal opacity, old age and medical/ surgical intervention etc. Burns/injury that caused visual disability are mainly due to home accidents (32 per cent), agricultural field accidents (22 per cent) and others places (20 per cent) respectively. As per mental disability, visual disability causes are also significantly high among persons from rural resident, illiterate, lower household standard of living and older working age group (45-59) years. In totality there is not much differences between male and female of having visual disability. But sore eyes after one month, injury other than burns, small pox, corneal opacity causes of visual disability are significantly higher among male; while cataract, glaucoma and old age causes of visual disability are more among female. Small pox cause of visual disability is highest (80 per cent) in illiterates as against literate up to middle (14 per cent) and secondary and above (6 per cent) respectively.

Table 6.2: Causes of mental disability among working age population according to different background characteristics in India, 2002

Background Charecteristics	*Causes*						
	Pregnancy and Birth related	*Serious illness during childhood*	*Head injury in childhood*	*Heredity*	*Other reasons*	*Not known*	*Total*
1	*2*	*3*	*4*	*5*	*6*	*7*	*8*
Place of residence							
Rural	73.6	52.9	54.3	66.2	65.6	74.3	66.8
Urban	26.4	47.1	45.7	33.8	34.4	25.7	33.2
Sex							
Male	20.9	63.1	67.1	59.2	65.8	63.4	63.0
Female	79.1	36.9	32.9	40.8	34.2	36.6	37.0
Age Group							
15-29	39.2	65.6	64.7	30.0	34.4	26.6	36.4
30-44	37.8	28.2	30.1	36.2	40.8	43.0	39.4
45-59	23.0	6.2	5.2	33.8	24.8	30.4	24.2

(Contd...)

1	2	3	4	5	6	7	8
Caste							
ST/SC	29.7	25.1	25.0	23.0	27.9	29.9	28.0
OBCs	29.1	35.6	33.1	42.3	35.5	37.7	36.1
Others	41.2	39.3	41.9	34.6	36.7	32.5	35.8
Educational Level							
Illiterate	57.4	68.3	51.4	36.4	39.2	49.3	47.6
Lit. up to Middle	37.8	29.5	43.4	53.5	44.8	39.9	41.0
Secondary & above	4.7	2.2	5.2	10.1	16.0	10.8	11.4
Hhd. Avg. MCE							
<3000	53.4	46.4	44.5	62.3	60.1	64.9	59.3
3000-6000	39.9	44.4	43.4	32.3	34.5	30.9	35.0
6000+	6.8	9.3	12.1	5.4	5.4	4.2	5.8
N	148	550	173	130	1797	1503	4301

Table 6.3: Causes of visual disability among working age population according to different background characteristics in India, 2002

Background Charecteristics	*Causes*														
	Sore eyes during the 1st month of life	*Sore eyes after one month*	*Severe Diarrhoea before the age of six years*	*Cataract*	*Glaucoma*	*Corneal Opacity*	*Other eye diseases*	*Small pox*	*Burns*	*Injury other than burns*	*Medical/ surgical Inter-vention*	*Old age*	*Other reasons*	*Not known*	*Total*
1	2	3	4	5	6	7	8	9	10	11	12	13	14	15	16
Place of residence															
Rural	77.8	68.4	59.3	63.5	64.9	61.2	66.3	69.0	65.2	64.6	44.8	68.9	65.6	74.5	66.1
Urban	22.2	31.6	40.7	36.5	35.1	38.8	33.7	31.0	34.8	35.4	55.2	31.1	34.4	25.5	33.9
Sex															
Male	44.4	73.7	54.2	43.3	47.0	57.6	52.5	57.1	52.2	74.4	47.9	38.9	50.7	49.5	52.4
Female	55.6	26.3	45.8	56.7	53.0	42.4	47.5	42.9	47.8	25.6	52.1	61.1	49.3	50.5	47.6
Age Group															
15-29	33.3	39.5	40.7	3.4	11.9	20.0	19.0	23.6	26.1	22.4	14.6	1.1	25.5	21.6	18.2
30-44	33.3	23.7	27.1	14.9	22.4	34.1	23.8	34.0	30.4	35.0	31.3	1.1	25.5	25.0	24.5
45-59	33.3	36.8	32.2	81.7	65.7	45.9	57.2	42.4	43.5	42.7	54.2	97.8	49.0	53.4	57.3

(Contd...)

1	2	3	4	5	6	7	8	9	10	11	12	13	14	15	16
Caste															
ST/SC	22.2	47.4	35.6	36.5	32.1	28.2	34.0	30.5	26.1	31.3	27.1	43.3	29.9	33.7	33.3
OBCs	22.2	21.1	32.2	36.5	36.6	38.8	33.4	39.4	34.8	30.9	40.6	26.7	35.4	40.1	35.4
Others	55.6	31.6	32.2	26.9	31.3	32.9	32.6	30.0	39.1	37.8	32.3	30.0	34.7	26.2	31.1
Educational Level															
Illiterate	88.9	73.7	74.6	65.1	60.4	47.1	59.0	80.3	34.8	46.1	52.1	77.8	54.8	67.2	61.6
Lit. up to Middle	11.1	21.1	20.3	29.1	28.4	36.5	29.9	13.8	56.5	38.8	33.3	21.1	32.3	25.3	28.8
Secondary & above	0.0	5.3	5.1	5.8	11.2	16.5	11.1	5.9	8.7	15.1	14.6	1.1	12.9	7.5	9.7
Hhd. Avg. MCE															
<3000	66.7	71.1	57.6	67.1	63.4	50.6	66.3	65.0	73.9	61.4	63.5	65.6	63.9	72.4	65.8
3000-6000	22.2	23.7	40.7	28.4	32.1	43.5	29.4	34.0	21.7	32.1	27.1	33.3	29.9	24.8	29.9
6000+	11.1	5.3	1.7	4.6	4.5	5.9	4.2	1.0	4.3	6.5	9.4	1.1	6.1	2.9	4.4
N	9	38	59	416	134	85	710	203	23	246	96	90	294	416	2819

Table 6.4: Causes of hearing disability among working age population according to different background characteristics in India, 2002

Background Charecteristics	*Causes*										
	German measles/ rubella	*Noise induced hearing loss*	*Ear discharge*	*Other illness*	*Burns*	*Injury other then burns*	*Medical/ surgical intervention*	*Old age*	*Other reasons*	*Not known*	*Total*
1	*2*	*3*	*4*	*5*	*6*	*7*	*8*	*9*	*10*	*11*	*12*
Place of residence											
Rural	44.4	60.0	71.3	68.3	72.7	56.8	61.3	58.2	62.4	75.8	68.1
Urban	55.6	40.0	28.7	31.7	27.3	43.2	38.7	41.8	37.6	24.2	31.9
Sex											
Male	55.6	61.3	56.8	48.3	63.6	54.1	46.7	35.8	47.2	50.5	50.9
Female	44.4	38.8	43.2	51.7	36.4	45.9	53.3	64.2	52.8	49.5	49.1
Age Group											
15-29	27.8	20.0	31.1	24.2	27.3	23.6	21.3	0.0	13.6	19.9	22.7
30-44	33.3	32.5	29.7	31.7	45.5	36.4	33.3	1.5	25.7	28.8	29.8
45-59	38.9	47.5	39.2	44.0	27.3	40.0	45.3	98.5	60.7	51.3	47.5
Caste											
ST/SC	41.7	25.0	31.3	35.7	27.3	27.7	18.7	40.3	32.8	37.3	33.7
OBCs	36.1	41.3	39.8	35.3	27.3	43.2	49.3	26.9	33.1	30.9	35.8
Others	22.2	33.8	28.9	29.0	45.5	29.1	32.0	32.8	34.2	31.8	30.5

(Contd...)

1	2	3	4	5	6	7	8	9	10	11	12
Educational Level											
Illiterate	61.1	43.8	48.9	51.4	18.2	42.3	34.7	59.7	45.8	58.5	50.7
Lit. upto Middle	33.3	42.5	40.2	39.8	63.6	45.5	44.0	38.8	43.2	34.4	39.7
Secondary & above	5.6	13.8	10.9	8.8	18.2	12.3	21.3	1.5	11.0	7.2	9.6
Hhd. Avg. MCE											
<3000	52.8	56.3	65.8	61.3	63.6	57.7	57.3	64.2	58.5	68.3	62.9
3000-6000	44.4	36.3	29.4	33.8	27.3	36.8	36.0	29.9	36.4	28.8	32.5
6000+	2.8	7.5	4.8	4.7	9.1	5.5	6.7	6.0	5.1	2.9	4.6
N	36	80	599	961	11	220	75	67	354	658	3061

Table 6.5: Causes of speech disability among working age population according to different background characteristics in India, 2002

Background Charecteristics	*Causes*											
	Hearing impairment	*Voice disorder*	*Cleft palate/ lip*	*Paralysis*	*Mental illness/ retardation*	*Other illness*	*Burns*	*Injury other than burns*	*Medical/ Surgical Intervention*	*Other reasons*	*Not known*	*Total*
1	*2*	*3*	*4*	*5*	*6*	*7*	*8*	*9*	*10*	*11*	*12*	*13*
Place of residence												
Rural	80.0	58.8	45.0	49.5	53.1	52.8	53.8	49.4	46.2	56.1	63.7	55.0
Urban	20.0	41.2	55.0	50.5	46.9	47.2	46.2	50.6	53.8	43.9	36.3	45.0
Sex												
Male	57.5	69.1	65.0	68.7	57.3	62.1	38.5	85.7	69.2	62.1	67.8	65.8
Female	42.5	30.9	35.0	31.3	42.7	37.9	61.5	14.3	30.8	37.9	32.2	34.2
Age Group												
15-29	55.0	63.9	40.0	18.1	69.8	49.4	53.8	40.3	38.5	37.9	51.4	45.9
30-44	32.5	18.6	25.0	24.7	18.8	29.0	23.1	33.8	23.1	22.7	35.6	27.0
45-59	12.5	17.5	35.0	57.1	11.5	21.6	23.1	26.0	38.5	39.4	13.0	27.1
Caste												
ST/SC	25.0	23.7	21.1	31.3	27.1	27.9	46.2	27.3	19.2	33.3	28.8	28.2
OBCs	37.5	38.1	36.8	35.2	35.4	37.5	15.4	33.8	50.0	33.3	36.3	36.3
Others	37.5	38.1	42.1	33.5	37.5	34.6	38.5	39.0	30.8	33.3	34.9	35.5

(Contd...)

1	2	3	4	5	6	7	8	9	10	11	12	13
Educational Level												
Illiterate	67.5	51.5	50.0	47.8	72.9	55.4	53.8	37.7	34.6	50.0	62.3	54.5
Lit. upto Middle	30.0	36.1	40.0	38.5	25.0	34.2	38.5	46.8	50.0	39.4	29.5	35.2
Secondary & above	2.5	12.4	10.0	13.7	2.1	10.4	7.7	15.6	15.4	10.6	8.2	10.3
Hhd. Avg. MCE												
<3000	70.0	47.4	55.0	50.5	55.2	51.7	69.2	51.9	42.3	53.0	64.4	54.0
3000-6000	30.0	48.5	45.0	42.9	36.5	39.4	30.8	37.7	42.3	40.9	28.8	38.8
6000+	0.0	4.1	0.0	6.6	8.3	8.9	0.0	10.4	15.4	6.1	6.8	7.2
N	40	97	20	182	96	269	13	77	26	66	147	1033

Table 6.6: Causes of locomotors disability among working age population according to different background characteristics in India, 2002

Background Charecteristics	*Causes*																
	Cerebral Palsy	*Polio*	*Leprosy cured*	*Leprosy not cured*	*Stroke*	*Arthritis*	*Cardio-respiratory*	*Cancer*	*Tuber-culosis*	*Other illness*	*Burns*	*Injury other than Burns*	*Medical/ Surgical inter-vention*	*Old age*	*Other reasons*	*Not known*	*Total*
1	*2*	*3*	*4*	*5*	*6*	*7*	*8*	*9*	*10*	*11*	*12*	*13*	*14*	*15*	*16*	*17*	*18*
Place of residence																	
Rural	60.7	58.4	53.2	70.8	57.2	57.7	65.3	69.1	63.2	58.1	63.0	58.3	54.0	73.0	65.4	69.5	59.4
Urban	39.3	41.6	46.8	29.2	42.8	42.3	34.7	30.9	36.8	41.9	37.0	41.7	46.0	27.0	34.6	30.5	40.6
Sex																	
Male	64.5	64.3	69.5	66.7	67.4	44.4	69.4	65.5	70.6	59.8	62.5	80.4	63.6	37.8	64.9	61.5	67.8
Female	35.5	35.7	30.5	33.3	32.6	55.6	30.6	34.5	29.4	40.2	37.5	19.6	36.4	62.2	35.1	38.5	32.2
Age Group																	
15-29	25.0	68.5	7.1	7.8	13.8	11.4	14.3	21.8	27.9	34.8	38.2	27.2	44.2	2.7	27.6	31.9	40.5
30-44	29.1	21.6	35.7	29.2	25.0	26.3	26.5	23.6	39.7	28.6	38.2	37.0	26.9	5.4	30.8	32.2	29.0
45-59	45.9	10.0	57.1	63.0	61.2	62.3	59.2	54.5	32.4	36.6	23.6	35.8	28.9	91.9	41.7	35.9	30.5
Caste																	
ST/SC	24.3	25.8	36.4	42.9	26.2	27.8	26.5	27.3	27.9	31.3	31.1	28.2	29.1	51.4	33.1	30.5	28.3
OBCs	39.6	44.0	42.9	41.6	39.2	37.4	28.6	40.0	29.4	36.1	34.9	36.2	36.2	29.7	33.6	34.1	38.8
Others	36.1	30.2	20.8	15.5	34.6	34.8	44.9	32.7	42.6	32.7	34.0	35.6	34.7	18.9	33.3	35.4	32.9

(Contd...)

1	2	3	4	5	6	7	8	9	10	11	12	13	14	15	16	17	18
Educational Level																	
Illiterate	46.7	25.6	66.9	67.1	42.9	50.5	34.7	40.0	27.9	39.4	38.9	33.0	27.8	75.7	39.9	49.9	34.6
Lit. upto Middle	38.0	46.6	27.9	28.8	39.4	35.0	46.9	45.5	61.8	43.3	45.8	46.4	48.9	21.6	44.5	35.6	44.3
Secondary and above	15.3	27.9	5.2	4.1	17.6	14.5	18.4	14.5	10.3	17.3	15.3	20.6	23.3	2.7	15.6	14.5	21.1
Hhd. Avg. MCE																	
<3000	56.6	52.1	75.3	83.1	53.3	58.2	49.0	52.7	77.9	57.3	64.4	55.2	50.7	75.7	62.8	63.2	55.9
3000-6000	33.4	40.2	22.1	15.5	38.7	33.6	34.7	41.8	16.2	35.1	32.5	38.2	40.2	21.6	31.8	31.2	37.0
6000+	9.9	7.7	2.6	1.4	8.0	8.2	16.3	5.5	5.9	7.6	3.1	6.6	9.1	2.7	5.4	5.7	7.0
N	392	5701	154	219	1009	414	49	55	68	2220	424	4977	450	37	852	844	17865

Results from Table 6.4 describes that the various causes of hearing disability are also significantly associated with different back ground characteristics of disabled persons. Other illness (31 per cent) is the main cause of hearing disability among working age population in India. Ear discharge (20 per cent), other reasons (10 per cent) and injury then than burns (7 per cent) are the other major causes of hearing disability among working age population. Burns/injury that caused hearing problems are mostly due to home accidents (55 per cent). Other illness and ear discharge causes of hearing disabilities are high among rural residents, older working age population (45-59) years, ST/SC, OBCs, illiterate and lower economic status household groups. Female has 3 per cent higher percentage of other illness causes than male, but in case of ear discharge cause male have 14 per cent higher than female counter parts.

Results from Table 6.5 illustrates that there is a significant association between speech disability and different background characteristics in India. Generalization of some causes of speech disability like cleft plate/lip, burns and old age etc. are little problematic as there is very few numbers of cases at all India level. How ever other causes have considerable number of cases from which we can make some elaborative interpretation. Results from the table show that other illness (26 per cent), paralysis (18 per cent), voice disorder (9 per cent) and mental illness/retardation (9 per cent) are the major causes of speech disability among working age population in India. Burns/injury that caused speech problems, most of the cases are due to home accidents (49 per cent) and transport accidents (18 per cent). Other illness cause is significantly higher among rural residents, male, younger working age population (15-29) years, OBCs, illiterate and lower income group. Where as paralysis cause of speech disability is significantly higher among male, older working age population (45-59) years, OBCs, illiterate and lower income group population.

Similarly, results from Table 6.6 depict that various causes of locomotor diability are significantly associated with different background characteristics. Results show that polio (32 per cent) is the major cause of having locomotor disability among working age population in India. Injury other than burns (28 per cent), other illness (13 per cent), stroke (6 per cent), medical surgical intervention, burns and arthritis (3 per cent each) are the other major causes of locomotor disability. Burns/injury that caused locomotor disability is mostly due to transport accidents (31 per cent), home accidents (28 per cent), agricultural field and other worksite accidents (13 per cent each) and industries accidents (5 per cent) respectively. As per causes of other disability Polio is also showing significantly highest among rural residents, male, younger working age group (15-29) years and OBCs caste categories. Surprisingly, polio causes of locomotor disability are more among literate up to middle class educational attainment than illiterate and secondary and above educational group. Leprosy not cured, old age, cancer, cardio-respiratory disease, tuberculosis, burns and cerebral palsy causes of locomotor disability are highly prevalent (more than 60 per cent) among rural resident. Except, Arthritis and old age causes of disability all other causes of locomotor disability are significantly higher among males. Between different causes of locomotor disability, injury other than burns cause is showing that, more than 80 per cent of male are suffering from this cause while females are showing only 20 per cent. Although, OBCs are more prone of having different causes of locomotor disability, but cardio respiratory disease (45 per cent) and tuberculosis (43 per cent) cause are showing significantly higher among other general caste. Results from the table 7 indicates that cerebral palsy, leprosy, stroke and arthritis causes of locomotor disability significantly more among illiterate; where as polio, cardio-respiratory disease, cancer, tuberculosis, burns and medical/surgical intervention causes are highly occurring among literate up to middle class locomotor disabled. More than 75 per cent of locomotor disability among low avg. MCE group is due to leprosy, tuberculosis and old age problems. Among the older working age group (45-59), more than 60 per cent locomotor disability is due to stroke, arthritis, cardio-respiratory disease, cancer, leprosy and old age problems. However other illness and injury other than burns cause of locomotor disability are quite high among middle working age group (30-44). At the same time higher percentage of locomotor disability among younger working age group (15-29) is due to polio, burns, other illness and medical/surgical intervention causes.

IMPACT OF DISABILITY ON WORKING POPULATION

The bi-variate results in Table 6.7 illustrate the percentage distribution of working age disabled persons who changed or loosed their works due to onset of disability according to different background characteristics in India. Results from the table show that the disabled persons, who changed or loosed their works are significantly associated with their different socio-economic and demographic characteristics. More than 62 per cent of working age persons have changed or loosed their works after onset of different types of disabilities in India. 66 per cent of (45-59) working age disabled persons have changed or loosed their work due to on set of disability; while comparing for the corresponding age groups (30-34) and (15-29) it is 60 and 58 per cent respectively. OBCs caste disabled persons showing relatively higher percentage (4 and 6 per cent respectively) in changing or loosing works due to on set of disabilities as compared to ST/SC and other caste persons. How ever educational attainment among disabled persons is not showing significant differences in changing or loosing of works due to onset of disability. But illiterate are showing higher percentage in loosing or changing of works than other educational groups. Further, changed or loosed of works due to on set of disabilities is quite high among low avg. MCE group (64 per cent) as compared to (3000-6000) and 6000+ avg. MCE group with 61 and 55 per cent respectively. The results indicate, 68 per cent of persons have changed or loosed their work due to onset of disability, who are living without spouse as compared to disabled person living with spouse and other members (61 per cent) and living alone (53 per cent) respectively. One of the important finding of the study is that onset of different types of disabilities such as hearing/speech, visual, mental, locomotor and multiple disability, the changed or loosed of work are 18, 71, 83, 66 and 66 per cent respectively. Again the results explain that there is higher differential exists in loosed or changed of work according to extent of the disability. Severely disabled persons in loosed or changed of work are turn out to be 87 per cent compared to moderate (75 per cent) and mild/others (50 per cent) respectively. The results also show that most of the disabled persons except north eastern regions, more than 60 per cent have loosed or changed their works as the on set of disability.

Table 6.7: Percentage distribution of persons who are working before on set of disability and have changed or loosed their works due to on set of disability according to different back ground characteristics, India, 2002.

Background Characteristics	*Percentage change/ loss work due to on set of disability*	*N*
1	*2*	*3*
Place of residence		
Rural	62.5	9863
Urban	62.2	4572
Sex		
Male	62.2	10203
Female	62.9	4232
Age		
15-29	57.9	2567
30-44	60.0	4982
45-59	65.9	6886
Caste		
ST/SC	61.6	4735
OBCs	65.7	5136
Others	59.7	4561
Education		
Illiterate	63.6	6771
Lit. up to Middle	62.4	5676
Secondary & Above	58.6	1979
Avgerage MCE of HHd		
< 3000	63.7	9340
3000-6000	60.9	4416
6000+	54.6	679

(Contd...)

1	2	3
Living arrangements		
Alone	52.8	470
With spouse and other members	60.8	9682
Without spouse but with other members	67.2	4282
Extent of disability		
Mild/others	50.3	8640
Moderate	74.7	2518
Severe	86.6	1377
Disability type		
Hearing/Speech	17.6	2040
Mental	83.4	2224
Multiple	66.1	760
Locomotor	66.0	7825
Visual	71.3	1586
Region		
Southern	64.7	2919
Northern	63.5	1948
Central	65.6	2877
Eastern	60.9	3498
North-esatern	47.7	1448
Western	67.3	1745
Total	**62.3**	**14473**

The results from the multivariate analysis (Table 6.8) suggest that sex, working age groups, caste, educational attainment, avg. MCE of household, living arrangements, living in which geographical region, extent of disability and type of disabilities are significantly determining the changed or loosed of work due to onset of disabilities with their standard errors, among the working age population in India. Although bi-variate analysis shows that there is no differential exist between male and female in loosed or changed of works due to onset of disabilities. But the multivariate analysis shows that loosed or changed of works due to onset of disability is significantly lower (12 per cent) among male as reference to female. People staying in urban place are 9 per cent less likely that they changed or loosed their work as compared to rural counter parts.

Table 6.8: Logistic regression for factors associated with changed or loosed of works due to on set of disability in India, 2002

Background Characteristics	*Exp (B)*	*S.E.*
1	*2*	*3*
Place of residence		
Rural ®		
Urban	0.91*	0.047
Sex		
Female ®		
Male	0.88*	0.050
Working age group		
15-29 ®		
30-44	1.21***	0.063
45-59	1.77***	0.062
Caste		
ST/Sc ®		
Others	0.87***	0.053
OBCs	1.03	0.051
Education		
Illiterate ®		
Up to middle	1.00	0.049
Secondary & above	0.75***	0.069
Avg. MCE of household		
<3000 ®		
3000-6000	0.86***	0.049
6000+	0.60***	0.100
Living arrangements		
Without spouse but with other members ®		
Alone	0.47***	0.123
With spouse and other members	0.75***	0.051
Extent of disability		
Severe ®		
Moderate	0.48***	0.097
Mild/others	0.20***	0.087
Types of disability		
Hearing/Speech ®		
Mental	19.68***	0.159
Multiple	7.38***	0.101
Locomotor	8.38***	0.066
Visual	7.80***	0.085

(Contd...)

1	2	3
Region		
Southern ®		
Northern	0.94	0.074
Central	0.91	0.065
Eastern	0.82***	0.063
North-eastern	0.47***	0.085
Western	1.17**	0.076
Constant	1.20	

Note: *** (1% level of significance), ** (5% level of significance), * (10% level of significance)

Dependent variable: 0= No Loss or change of work, 1= Loss or change of work due to on set of disability.

Disabled persons in older working age groups (30-44) and (45-59) are 21 and 77 per cent respectively more likely to lossed or changed of works as compared to younger working age group (15-29). Odds of loosing or changing works are significantly lower (13 per cent) among other castes as reference to ST/SC population as the on set of disability. Whereas secondary and above educated person have 25 per cent less chances that they will loosed or changed works due to onset of disabilities as compared to illiterate disabled. Other results from the Table 8 indicate that (3000-6000) and 6000+ avg. MCE group disabled have 14 and 40 per cent significantly less chances that they would loss or change work as the onset of disability as reference to lower avg. MCE (<3000) people. Obviously, it may be possible that higher income group can afford for better medical treatment, can accommodate aid/appliances very easily and other necessities for avoiding or assistance for disabilities, so that there is a less chances that they can loosed or changed works. Among working age population who are living alone, with spouse and other members the odds of loosing or changing the works due to onset of disability is significantly less (53 and 25 per cent respectively) as compared to who are living with out spouse. The results gain importance when the types of disability are significantly determining the loosing or changing of works among disabled person in India. The odds of loosing or changing works are significantly higher (20, 7, 8 and 8 times) among mental, multiple, locomotor and visual disabilities respectively as referred to hearing/speech disability. Here one explanation needed is that the chances of loosing or changing work, as the on set of multiple disabilities is same as locomotor disability. The reason could be that multiple disability is only consists of physical disabilities (hearing, visual, speech and locomotor) and from the in depth analysis it can be explain that most of the persons in multiple disability are from speech, hearing problems). Further, the chances of loosed or changed of work are significantly lower (around 80 and 52 per cent) among mild and moderate extent of disability as compared to severely disabled working age persons. Again regional variation depicts that eastern and north eastern regions disabled people are 18 and 53 per cent less likely in loosing or changing of work as the on set of disability as compared to southern region person. But western region people are 18 per cent more likely to loosed or changed their work as the on set of disability as referred to southern region. Summarily, the loosing or changing of works due to disability among working age population is not only determine by types of disabilities, but also by the different background characteristics, the disabled person is associated with.

SUMMARY AND CONCLUSION

It is evident from the study that among the various types of disabilities, locomotor and mental are the main prevalent disabilities among working age population of India. Disabilities are highly prevalent among rural residents, low-income groups, illiterates, OBCs and ST/SCs populations. Plausible reasons may be that poverty, low nutritional level, they can't afford for better medical treatment, can't accommodate aid/appliances very easily and other necessities for avoiding or assistance for disabilities, and also may not be aware of the medical facilities, aids available for the treatment or they may not go for the early diagnosis of the disabilities. The study also reveals that locomotor and speech disabilities are high among younger working age population (i.e.15-29 years), where as hearing and visual problems are high among older working age population (i.e. 45-59 years). But mental problems are high among middle working age population (i.e. 30-44 years).

As per the causes of disabilities are concerned, Polio, injury, other illness, arthritis and stroke are found to be the most vital causes of physical immobility among working age population in India while serious illness during childhood, head injury in childhood, heredity and pregnancy and birth related causes are significantly associated with mental disability. Eye diseases and Cataract are found to be the most significant causes for visual disability. The main reason, which caused hearing problems among working age populations, is other illness, ear discharge and injury. Other illness, paralysis, voice disorder and mental illness/retardation are making the significant impact for causing speech problems. It is also clear from the study that the most vulnerable cause of different disabilities; burns/injuries is mostly due to transport accident, home accidents and working in manual activities.

The interesting finding of the study is that more than 62 per cent of people have either changed or loosed their works due to onset of disability. The chances of loosing or changing of works is significantly determine by sex of the person, place of residence, age group, which caste they belongs, educational attainment, economic status of household, living arrangements of the person geographical region they living, the most important predictor are the on set of the types of disability and how severe extent they are. The chances of loosing or changing of works is significantly high for the on set of mental, visual and locomotor disability.

The study highlights the main causes of all forms of disabilities which causing serious problems among the working age population of the country. The onset of different types of disabilities, which caused to loose works among the working population, is a major economic burden for many families and himself/herself is a social burden as well. Their rehabilitations and coping problems are also a major concerned for the governments. This study will also enable policy makers to implement preventive and precautionary steps to control on set of disability among working age population. At the same time it is also necessary for the govt. and programmers to develop better medical facilities and infrastructures for rural and low economic status people so that govt. can rectify the problems from the grass root level. It is also evident that to save disabled persons as well as their family from economic dilution we need to have a national network of vocational training centres for imparting knowledge and skill which will help them to remain economically active. This study can contribute to a certain extent to the programmers, policy makers for the effective policy and programme management of country for disabled. This study can also open the path for the researchers for further research on disabilities among working age population in India.

REFERENCES

Altman, B., 2001. "Definition, Model, Classification and Application", In: G. Albrecht (eds) *Handbook of Disability Studies*, Sage Publications, California.

Crimmins, Eileen M., Sandy L. Reynolds, and Yasuhiko Saito, 1999. Trends in Health and Ability to Work Among the Older Working-Age Population. *Journal of Gerontology: Social Sciences*, 54: 531-540.

Daly, Mary C. and John Bound, 1996. Worker Adaptation and Employer Accommodation, Following the Onset of a Health Impairment. *Journal of Gerontology: Social Sciences*, 518 (2): 553-560.

Favreault, M. and Douglas Wolf. 2002. *"Supplimental Security Income and Living Arrangements."* In: Toder *et. al. Modelling Income in the Near Term-revised Projection of Retirement Income Through 2020 for the 1931-60 Birth Cohorts*. Project Report. Urban Institute, Washington, D.C.

Habeck, Rochelle V., H. Allan Hunt and Brett Vantol, 1998. Work-place Factors Associated with Preventing and Managing Work Disability. *Rehabilitation Counseling Bulletin*, 42: 98-139.

Harper, Malcom and Momm, Will, 1986. *Self Employment for Disabled People: Experience from Africa and Asia*. International Labour Organisation, Geneva.

Hayward, Mark D., William R. Grady, Melissa A. Hardy, and David Sommers, 1989. Occupational Influences on Retirement, Disability and Death. *Demography*, 26: 393-409.

Kapteyan, A., 2004. Measuring Disability, *PAA – 2004 Annual meeting Programme*, Session 142-144, April 1-3, pp. 28-65.

Kramarow, E. A and Elsie Pamak, 2004. Alternate Definitions of Disability: Implications of increasing inclusiveness, *PAA 2004 Annual meeting program*, session 142-144, April 1-3, pp. 66-71.

Krishna, V.V, B.S.V. Dutt and K.H. Rao, 2001. *Disabled Persons*. Discovery Publishing House, New Delhi.

La Plante, M.P., 1993. Prevalence of Work Disability – US, 1990. *JAMA*, 270: 1921.

Loprest, Pamela, Kalman Rupp, and Steven H. Sandell, 1995. Gender, Disability and Employment in the Health and Retirement Study. *The Journal of Human Resources*, 30: 5293-5318.

Mutt, H.A., Parsons, P.E., and Harlon, W.R., 1996. *Disability, Utilization and Costs Associated with Musculoskeletal Conditions*. National Medical Care Utilization and Expenditure Survey, Series C, 5, DHHS Pub. 86-20405.

NSSO, 2003. *Disabled Persons in India*, NSS 58th Round (July-December-2002). Report No. 485. Ministry of Statistics and Programme Implementation. Government of India.

Stace, Sheila, 1986. Vocational Rehabilitation for Women with Disabilities, ILO, Geneva.

Verbrugge, Lois M., 1985. Gender and Health: An Update in Hypotheses and Evidence. *Journal of Health and Social Behaviour*, 26(3): 156-182.

Waidmann, Timothy. 2002. *Options for Projecting Job Demands and Health Status*. In Toder et. al. Modeling Income in the Near term-revised Projections of Retirement Income Through 2020 for the 1931-60 Birth Cohorts. Project Report. Urban Institute,Washington, D.C.

WHO, 1980. *International Classification of Impairments, Disabilities and Handicaps;* A Manual of Classification Relating to the Consequences of Disease, World Health Organisation, Geneva.

World Bank, 1993. *World Development Report 1993: Investing in Health*. Oxford University Press, New York.

7

Urbanization in Selected States of India *1981-2001*

Mr. Anadi Charan Sethi
Dr. Rajiva Prasad

INTRODUCTION

Urbanization is a process of transformation from traditional rural economies to modern industrial one. It is a process of switching from spread out pattern of human settlement to one of concentration in urban centers (Davis, 1965). It is also closely related to industrial revolution and associated with economic development. It is a long-term process. Urban areas are usually thought to be centers of business, commerce and industry. Earlier in the United States history, urban areas were far outnumbered by rural areas. It has been experienced by all developed nations in their transition from an agrarian to an industrial society. Different urbanization levels reflect differencing degree of economic development.

India is usually thought of a country where both the level and pace of urbanization are low. At the time of independence, the level of urbanization was very low almost in all the states of India. The urban population in India was found to be concentrated in few big cities. States such as Maharashtra, West Bengal and Tamil Nadu are having high level of urbanization than many other States of India. This is due to the type of development that occurred in theses states some 50 years ago. The port cities such as Mumbai, Chennai, and Kolkata, which were set up during colonial regime are dominating the urban scene and other metropolises of India. The onset of modern and universal process of urbanization is relatively a recent phenomenon in India. It is at the acceleration stage of the process of urbanization.

REVIEW OF LITERATURE

Davis (1965) in his popular concept argued that the rural urban migration is the prime cause of rapid urbanization in several countries. It was the population boom that caused overwhelming growth of the cities and not the rural urban migration. The theories, which assume a relatively homogeneous economic system, which exits in the city, are not adequate in explaining the patterns of economic activities that occurs in the Asian cities. The prominent economic zones found in the cities are (i) the part of the earlier centers of the economic activities in colonial areas, which retains its supremacy as one of the facial of the earlier cities and (ii) Out side the city boundary some intensive market gardening, which has been supplier of the agricultural goods to the city market.

Rapid population growth in cities of developing countries and their ever growth of population size is seen as out come of heavy influences of rural migrants to the cities, which had been pushed from the agricultural field, rather than pulled by the urban non agricultural sector. Since the Asian cities were mainly formed under colonial power, the space relation could not have formed at their extent. He opined that the basic problem of colonial urbanization is the parasitic nature of great cities, which were formed mainly as the linkages between colonial and the native places. These cities did not have any surrounding zones, even after the independences. Urbanization trend in these countries went on over depending on the metropolitan economies. It has already been found that the unequal economic growth between rural and urban areas, lead to a huge movement of rural migrants to the cities. Sovani (1966) observed that the India's urbanization is often termed as over urbanization, pseudo-urbanization. The big cities attained inordinately large population size leading to virtually collapse in the urban services and it has been followed by the basic problem in the field of housing, slum, infrastructure, and quality of life.

Though some studies have been made in assessing the levels and trends of urbanizations in states of India, there are few studies focusing on the growth of cities in states of India. Till 1991, there were three hundred urban agglomerations in India. However, the number of urban agglomeration has increased to 393 by 2001. While some attempt had already been made in understanding the growth process and the level of urbanization in the four metropolitan cities, there is no study focusing on growth of newly emerged megalopolis. Accordingly, this article attempts to understand the growth and pattern in urbanization as well as reasons for migration in 10 urban agglomerations of India, namely: Ahmedabad, Bangalore, Bhopal, Chennai, Greater Mumbai, Hyderabad, Kolkata, Lucknow, Patna and the national capital Delhi. The rational of selecting these 10 urban agglomerations are that they are representing the geographical sphere of the country. The parent states of these ten urban agglomerations are also included in the present study in order to know what is happening in these states as a whole.

OBJECTIVES

1. To examine the levels of urbanization in selected states of India during the period of 1981-2001.
2. To study the growth of urban population in selected cities of India.
3. To study the reasons for migration to the selected states and cities of India.

SOME CONCEPTS

Urbanization is the relative increase in the number of people living in places designed as urban. It is the result of changes that takes place in the economy as well as in the technologies that are used. Urbanization affects every aspects of social life. Urbanization in the demographic senses is an increase in the proportion of the urban population to the total population over a period of time.

The Indian census adopted the concept of urban areas from the 1961. According to 2001 census, an area with the following characteristics has been defined as urban:

(i) Having a minimum population of 5000,

(ii) At least 75% of male population engaged in non-agricultural sector,

(iii) The population density being at least 400 persons per sq km.

Urban population grows mainly because of natural increase, rural to urban migration; some areas are classified as urban due to annexation or reclassification, classified as urban.

Urbanization takes places due to concentration of population engaged in non-agriculture occupations. The main reason for urbanization is industrialization vis-à-vis modernization.

DATA SOURCES

Different volumes of Census of India 1971, 1981, 1991 and 2001.

Selection of states and cities: In this paper, 10 major states have been selected. From each of the state only one city has been selected. While selecting the states due to consideration was given to its population size and location such as north, south, east and west and level of development.

METHODOLOGY

Some indices have been calculated:

1. Per cent urban

It is the simplest and the most commonly used measure of the level of urbanization. It refers to the number of persons living in urban localities for each 100 people living in the country,

It is calculated as:

PU=U/P*100

PU= Per cent urban

U = Urban population of a specified area.

P = Total population of a specified area.

2. Tempo of Urbanization

The tempo of urbanization refers to the change in the level of urbanization over a specified period of time.

$T_{re} = 1/n*\ln (PU^{t+n}/PU^{t})*100$

PU^{t+n} = Per cent of population urban at time t+n.

PU^{t} = Per cent of population urban at time t.

3. Urban Rural Ratio

The urban rural ratio measures the number of city dwellers per rural inhabitant.

It is calculated as:

UR=U/R*100

UR= Urban rural ratio of a specified area.

U = Total urban population of a specified area.

R = Total rural population of a specified areas.

4. Rank Size Rule

It is believed that there exits a regularity between the size of a city and its rank. The rank size rule indicates the relationship between size of the cities and their ranks.

$$Z = \frac{\left[\Sigma \ln \frac{C_1}{C_k} * \ln(K)\right]}{\sum \left[\ln(K)\right]^2}$$

C_k= is the city ranked in place k from the largest to smallest city in population size.

C_1= is the population of the largest city.

k = Rank order.

Z= Constant of the city index distribution.

5. Primacy Index

The primacy index shows the dominance of the largest city with respect to the second largest city, or subsequent cities. The four city Primacy Index is calculated as follows

$PI_4 = C_1/C_2+C_3+C_4$

PI_4 = Four city Primacy Index

C_1 = It is the population of the largest city.

C_2 to C_4= Population of second, third and fourth ranked cities.

DISCUSSION

The growth rate of India and selected States for the period 1971-1981, 1981-1991 1991-2001 is presented in Table 7.1. Among the selected States, the growth rate of population was highest in Gujarat and lowest in Tamil Nadu in 1971-81. However in 1991-2001, the growth rate of population was highest in Delhi followed by Bihar. The possible reason for higher growth rate in Delhi may be due to migration while that in Bihar may be due to natural growth rate. The growth rate of urban population was highest in the state of West Bengal followed by Madhya Pradesh during 1991-01. It was lowest in the State of Andhra Pradesh.

Table 7.2 shows the level of urbanization and urban-rural ratio in selected States of India for the period 1981-2001. The per cent urban has increased from 23.31 per cent in 1981 to 27.82 per cent in 2001 for the country. However, there is a variation in the rate of increase in level of urbanization among the selected States of India. Except Bihar, Madhya Pradesh and Uttar Pradesh, all other selected States have higher level of urbanization, than the national average and it is same during 1981-2001. States such as Bihar, Madhya Pradesh, and Uttar Pradesh have lower level of urbanization and the increase is comparatively less than to other

Table 7.1: Decennial Growth Rate of India & Selected States, 1971-2001

State/India	Decennial Growth Rate					
	Total population			*Urban Population*		
	1971-1981	*1981-1991*	*1991-2001*	*1971-1981*	*1981-1991*	*1991-2001*
INDIA	25.05	23.23	21.83	46.41	35.09	32.60
Andhra Pradesh	23.10	24.16	14.62	48.62	43.08	16.46
Bihar	24.06	23.54	27.29	54.76	30.21	29.27
Delhi	53.00	51.45	47.02	50.65	29.62	29.15
Gujarat	27.67	21.19	22.66	56.03	44.89	31.38
Karnataka	26.75	21.12	17.51	39.99	38.87	34.57
Madhya Pradesh	25.27	26.84	22.67	27.98	19.59	44.06
Maharashtra	24.54	25.73	22.73	60.62	38.73	33.01
Tamil Nadu	17.50	15.39	25.16	31.73	29.49	19.88
Uttar Pradesh	25.49	25.48	25.57	41.42	34.38	32.88
West Bengal	23.17	24.73	17.77	58.16	46.87	52.34

States of India during the period 1981-2001. In developed States like Maharashtra, Tamil Nadu and Gujarat the level of urbanization has increased considerably over the decade. The level of urbanization is highest in Delhi (93.18 per cent) followed by Tamil Nadu (44.04 per cent) and lowest in Bihar in 2001. Similarly the urban rural ratio showed that it is high in Delhi. The possible reason is that the rural population is very small. Among other States, the urban-rural ratio is higher in Tamil Nadu followed by Maharashtra. In general, the states where the level of urbanization is high, the urban-rural ratio is high.

It has already been mentioned that growth of urbanization is very much associated with high in flux of migrants. The percentage share of migrants to total population is given in Table 7.3. Among all selected States, the percentage of migrants was highest in the state of Delhi followed by Maharashtra in 1981. The pattern has continued even in 2001. The percentage of migrants has been high in Delhi followed by Gujarat in 2001. However, this proportion has been low in the less developed states of Bihar and Uttar Pradesh.

It is a well known fact that the process of migration is associated with various pull and push factors. The various reasons for migration according to census of India are marriage, education, employment, family moved, moved with household, business, natural calamities and others. As such Table 7.4 presents the reasons for migration in selected states of India in the period of 1981-2001. Among the various reasons employment is one of the main reasons for migration to Delhi. Here it is clearly indicate that male and female separately describe. It is found that in 1981 about 47 per cent male migrants to Delhi were for employment purpose which has increased to 57 per cent in 2001. In case of Gujarat, the proportion of migrants for employment reason in 1981 was 39 per cent, which has declined to 23 per cent in 2001. It may also be observed that about 31 per cent migrated for employment purpose in Uttar Pradesh in 1981, which declined to 19 per cent in 2001. Marriage has been found as one of the prime reasons for migration in the some of the States. Female migration is high as comparable to male. In 1981, more than

Table 7.2: Level of Urbanization and Urban-Rural ratio in India and selected states, 1981-2001

State/India	*Percent Urban*			*Urban-Rural Ratio*		
	1981	*1991*	*2001*	*1981*	*1991*	*2001*
INDIA	23.31	25.73	27.82	30.40	34.64	38.54
Andhra Pradesh	23.32	26.87	27.30	30.41	36.75	37.56
Bihar	12.47	13.35	13.37	14.25	15.13	15.40
Delhi	92.73	89.93	93.18	1275.57	892.67	1366.09
Gujarat	31.10	34.49	37.36	45.14	52.64	59.64
Karnataka	28.89	30.92	33.99	40.63	44.76	51.48
Madhya Pradesh	20.29	23.18	24.82	25.45	30.17	33.02
Maharashtra	35.03	38.69	42.43	53.92	63.11	73.69
Tamil Nadu	32.95	38.26	44.04	49.15	61.98	78.70
Uttar Pradesh	17.95	19.84	20.78	21.88	24.76	26.61
West Bengal	26.47	27.48	27.97	36.00	37.89	38.84

86 per cent migrants in Uttar Pradesh and Bihar were for marriage as compared to only 0.4 per cent in Delhi. In 2001 also marriage has continued to be one of the main reasons for migration in many of the States. In case of Maharashtra, about 36 per cent migrants reported migration due to marriage. There are large variation in the others category as reasons for migration among the selected States. The others category includes migration due to natural calamities and business purpose. It is found that about 49 per cent in Tamil Nadu reported others as reason of migration followed by Andhra Pradesh 34 per cent in 2001.

Table 7.5 presents the per cent of urban population in the selected states and urban agglomerations. It is observed that the parent States for the cities like Bangalore, Bhopal, Delhi and Patna have a larger proportion of urban population in their respective states. Bangalore constitutes about 27 per cent of States urban population in 1981, which increased to 32 per cent in 2001. Similar pattern is observed in the cities such as Kolkata and Greater Mumbai. It is interesting to note that Kolkata constitutes more than 50 per cent of urban population in the State of West Bengal.

Table 7.6 shows that the annual exponential growth of selected metropolitan urban agglomerations and cities of India in 1981-2001. It is found that all these cities as well as urban agglomerations have experienced significant growth rate during 1981-91 as well as 1991-01. During 1981-91, the exponential growth rate was highest in Lucknow followed by Ahmedabad. In 1991-2001, the exponential growth rate was 4.85 per cent in Bangalore and 0.43 per cent in Kolkata.

Table 7.7 presents the percentage share of migrants in selected cities of India during the decade of 1981-2001. In 1981, the percentage share of migrants to total population was more than 52 per cent in Delhi and Greater Mumbai. However, in 2001 higher percentage of migrants were in Ahmedabad followed by Bangalore, Bhopal and Delhi.

Table 7.3: **Percentage Share of Migrants to Total Population of Selected States, 1981-2001**

States/UT	*1981*	*1991*	*2001*
Andhra Pradesh	32.03	29.51	30.79
Bihar	28.93	24.93	24.68
Delhi	48.05	39.52	43.42
Gujarat	33.75	33.08	37.93
Karnataka	32.07	29.87	31.33
Madhya Pradesh	34.35	32.75	30.19
Maharashtra	42.63	32.26	43.06
Tamil Nadu	28.98	24.04	25.36
Uttar Pradesh	24.48	21.39	24.80
West Bengal	29.77	26.25	31.30

Table 7.4: Reason for migration States 1981-2001

States	*Employment*						*Education*						*Family moved/Moved with household*					
	1981		*1991*		*2001*		*1981*		*1991*		*2001*		*1981*		*1991*		*2001*	
	M	*F*	*M*	*F*	*M*	*F*	*M*	*F*	*M*	*F*	*M*	*F*	*M*	*F*	*M*	*F*	*M*	*F*
0	*1*	*2*	*3*	*4*	*5*	*6*	*7*	*8*	*9*	*10*	*11*	*12*	*13*	*14*	*15*	*16*	*17*	*18*
AP	16.3	1.6	31.5	4.5	24.2	2.2	7.4	1.5	7.4	1.3	3.7	0.8	38.8	20.5	25.3	13.4	16.0	12.2
Bih	38.5	0.8	32.8	0.5	17.0	0.5	8.7	0.5	7.8	0.4	3.1	0.1	27.2	5.6	21.3	2.9	15.1	3.3
Delhi	47.0	4.7	51.6	2.9	57.0	4.1	2.9	1.7	1.8	0.8	1.9	0.6	34.7	49.4	29.4	48.6	22.7	47.3
Guj	39.6	3.6	24.2	2.1	23.9	1.2	5.0	1.1	4.2	1.0	2.2	0.6	25.5	15.6	22.7	12.9	19.0	15.0
Karn	31.8	3.9	26.2	2.8	28.1	2.6	7.2	1.5	6.5	1.2	4.4	0.9	27.5	18.8	24.8	14.6	14.5	11.2
MP	35.8	2.7	24.1	1.6	36.1	1.6	5.5	0.8	5.3	1.3	3.7	0.4	33.1	15.8	20.3	14.8	24.6	10.9
TN	35.9	2.9	28.8	1.6	37.2	2.7	4.6	1.3	5.2	0.8	2.6	0.7	31.4	20.8	30.7	12.0	17.7	16.9
WB	27.6	1.7	31.9	4.3	18.8	3.1	3.2	0.6	4.5	1.5	1.8	0.9	30.9	15.5	24.7	15.0	14.8	12.6
Mah	29.9	1.8	23.8	0.6	19.9	0.8	5.9	1.2	4.4	0.4	1.9	0.1	23.3	18.4	24.6	4.6	15.5	5.4
UP	31.2	0.8	22.3	1.4	19.8	1.2	5.8	0.4	3.1	0.5	1.8	0.2	30.0	6.3	28.8	11.0	25.0	12.2

(Contd…)

Table 7.4 (Contd...)

	Marriage						Others					
	1981		1991		2001		1981		1991		2001	
	M	F	M	F	M	F	M	F	M	F	M	F
0	19	20	21	22	23	24	25	26	27	28	29	30
AP	4.2	64.3	3.7	67.7	3.2	59.7	33.4	1.2	32.1	13.0	53.0	25.1
Bih	5.0	89.4	10.4	93.2	6.0	87.1	20.6	3.7	27.7	2.9	58.9	9.0
Delhi	0.4	31.1	0.5	40.6	0.3	34.0	15.0	13.2	16.6	7.2	18.1	14.0
Guj	1.5	68.9	3.0	71.3	1.1	65.7	28.5	10.6	46.0	12.7	53.9	17.6
Karn	2.2	60.7	2.8	65.5	2.4	63.2	31.2	15.0	39.7	15.8	50.6	22.2
MP	4.1	73.0	1.2	62.4	2.9	77.1	21.6	7.6	49.0	19.9	32.8	10.1
TN	2.3	64.1	3.9	77.8	0.7	59.1	25.9	1.1	31.4	7.9	41.8	20.6
WB	2.0	67.9	3.8	63.0	2.3	43.9	36.3	14.4	35.1	16.2	62.2	39.5
Mah	1.2	6.0	9.1	88.9	3.7	79.9	39.7	19.1	38.0	5.5	59.1	13.7
UP	4.4	86.6	3.2	74.8	2.3	70.0	28.5	5.9	42.6	12.3	51.1	16.4

Table 7.5: Percentage share of selected Urban Agglomeration's population to total population of respective states in India, 1981-2001

Sl. No.	*Urban Agglomeration*	*State/Union territory**	*Percentage Share in Total Urban Population*		
			1981	*1991*	*2001*
1.	Ahmedabad	Gujarat	24.03	23.28	23.90
2.	Bangalore	Karnataka	27.23	29.50	31.74
3.	Bhopal	Madhya Pradesh	6.34	6.92	9.11
4.	Chennai	Tamil Nadu	26.89	28.18	23.87
5.	Delhi	Delhi *	92.10	99.38	99.78
6.	G. Mumbai	Maharashtra	37.48	41.22	39.99
7.	Hyderabad	Andhra Pradesh	20.39	24.03	27.59
8.	Kolkata	West Bengal	63.64	58.62	58.88
9.	Lucknow	Uttar Pradesh	5.66	5.94	6.56
10.	Patna	Bihar	10.54	9.67	19.56

Table 7.6: Annual exponential growth of selected metropolitan urban agglomeration and cities of India, 1981-2001

Sl. No.	*Urban Agglomeration/City*	*Exponential Growth Rate of Cities*		*Exponential Growth Rate of UAs*	
		1981-1991	*1991-2001*	*1981-1991*	*1991-2001*
1.	Ahmedabad	3.50	2.02	2.58	3.16
2.	Bangalore	0.66	4.85	3.36	3.33
3.	Bhopal	4.59	2.99	4.60	3.14
4.	Chennai	1.50	1.05	2.23	2.02
5.	Delhi	2.93	3.14	3.80	4.30
6.	Greater Mumbai	1.86	1.84	4.22	2.68
7.	Hyderabad	3.08	1.69	5.20	2.94
8.	Kolkata	2.88	0.43	1.72	1.90
9.	Lucknow	5.75	3.27	4.88	3.22
10.	Patna	1.70	4.07	1.80	4.34

Table 7.7: Percentage share of migrants in selected cities of India, 1981-2001

Urban Agglomeration	*1981*	*1991*	*2001*
Ahmedabad	37.86	33.82	48.20
Bangalore	37.62	29.00	44.64
Bhopal	NA	40.06	44.30
Chennai	34.47	27.94	24.52
Delhi	52.17	39.29	43.10
G Mumbai	51.46	35.29	23.68
Hyderabad	19.93	26.24	21.09
Kolkota	31.28	23.98	28.29
Lucknow	27.44	28.32	45.20
Patna	NA	30.65	26.89

Table 7.8 shows the reasons for migration to selected cities of India in 1981-2001.In 1981 Mumbai had the highest number of migrants male for employment purposes and lowest in the Hyderabad. In female case highest is in Bangalore and followed by Hyderabad. Compared to 1981 census, in 1991 Delhi and Hyderabad has been getting more number of migrants. The five cities which have been growing due to employment reasons are Bhopal, Delhi, Lucknow, Patna and Mumbai. In case of education in 1981, Lucknow had highest number of migrants and Kolkata the lowest. Compared to 1981-1991, in 1991 more people have migrated to Chennai and Kolkata for education purpose. In 2001 in many cities, proportion of migrants for educational purpose has declined.

In case of family moved Delhi has highest number of migrants male and female where as Mumbai has the lowest. Compared to 1981 there is a decline in all the cities except Lucknow. Almost same picture has been observed in 2001, except Ahmedabad, Lucknow and Patna. The marriage migration is another reason for migration in 1981. The highest number of marriage migration is in Lucknow where as in 2001 all the cities have increased due to marriage migration.

Table 7.9 shows the Rank Size Rule and Primacy Index for the selected states of India. It has been found that there exists regularity between the size of a city and its rank. Rank size rule indicates the relationship between the size of the cities and their ranks. The greater the value of the index, the greater is the concentration of population in the largest cities relative to the smallest cities. It is evident from the table that Maharashtra, Bihar and Tamil Nadu had higher value of *Z* in 1981, i.e there was higher concentration of population in the largest cities such Mumbai, Patna and Chennai. In case of 1991 census the states having highest value of *z*, were Maharashtra, Bihar, and Karnataka. In other words, there has been tremendous increase in population of Bangalore (Karnataka) during 1981-91. The census 2001 presents a different picture where Patna has been replaced by Ahmedabad. It is interesting to note that the value of *z* has been decreasing in Bihar which indicates that population has been spreading to other cities (not only in Patna) and the

Table 7.8: Reason for migration in selected Cities, 1981-2001

UAs	*Employment*						*Education*						*Family moved/ Moved with household*					
	1981		*1991*		*2001*		*1981*		*1991*		*2001*		*1981*		*1991*		*2001*	
	M	*F*	*M*	*F*	*M*	*F*	*M*	*F*	*M*	*F*	*M*	*F*	*M*	*F*	*M*	*F*	*M*	*F*
0	*1*	*2*	*3*	*4*	*5*	*6*	*7*	*8*	*9*	*10*	*11*	*12*	*13*	*14*	*15*	*16*	*17*	*18*
Ahmedabad	49.4	5.8	34.6	4.7	31.6	1.9	4.2	2.2	3.0	1.3	1.3	0.4	20.9	29.8	19.5	23.0	19.3	30.1
Bangalore	50.7	6.3	49.0	6.2	46.1	7.2	7.6	3.9	6.7	2.3	4.3	1.7	22.2	36.0	22.5	33.2	12.8	23.4
Bhopal	NA	NA	50.9	5.1	51.3	4.8	NA	NA	6.0	2.0	4.7	1.3	NA	NA	24.8	34.1	21.5	35.7
Chennai	50.2	4.9	47.2	7.1	35.2	5.9	3.7	1.6	4.1	2.0	2.4	1.2	27.7	38.6	26.8	34.1	16.9	23.3
Delhi	47.0	4.7	52.4	2.9	57.2	4.2	2.9	1.7	1.9	0.8	2.0	0.7	34.7	49.4	28.4	49.2	22.3	47.5
Greater Mumbai	61.7	4.7	46.5	3.5	59.6	3.7	6.6	3.7	4.8	2.2	2.1	0.7	16.0	36.7	17.1	28.3	12.6	25.6
Hyderabad	43.7	5.3	43.9	8.6	40.5	7.0	6.6	3.7	5.3	2.0	3.6	1.5	25.1	66.4	26.9	38.8	14.6	29.7
Kolkata	43.0	4.1	36.0	3.7	33.3	3.1	3.4	1.3	2.9	0.9	2.2	0.5	22.1	32.4	25.4	26.6	22.4	27.8
Lucknow	45.8	5.0	38.3	2.8	40.1	3.9	10.8	4.0	8.8	2.5	5.3	1.3	21.8	29.9	25.5	29.3	21.1	37.5
Patna	NA	NA	32.6	2.4	36.3	2.8	NA	NA	12.9	3.2	9.6	1.6	NA	NA	23.7	16.7	21.6	30.6

(Contd…)

Table 7.8 (Contd...)

	Marriage						*Others*					
	1981		*1991*		*2001*		*1981*		*1991*		*2001*	
	M	*F*	*M*	*F*	*M*	*F*	*M*	*F*	*M*	*F*	*M*	*F*
0	*19*	*20*	*21*	*22*	*23*	*24*	*25*	*26*	*27*	*28*	*29*	*30*
Ahmedabad	0.5	43.3	2.0	49.4	0.4	37.2	24.9	18.9	41.0	21.6	47.4	30.5
Bangalore	0.8	37.5	1.0	42.6	0.8	33.5	17.9	16.3	20.7	15.7	36.0	34.2
Bhopal	NA	NA	1.0	48.4	0.4	41.5	NA	NA	17.3	10.4	22.2	16.7
Chennai	0.6	38.5	1.2	41.6	1.3	25.2	17.9	16.4	20.8	15.3	44.3	44.4
Delhi	0.4	31.1	0.5	39.4	0.3	33.1	15.0	13.2	16.8	7.6	18.3	14.6
Greater Mumbai	0.5	36.7	0.9	45.4	0.4	45.7	15.2	18.3	30.7	20.6	25.4	24.3
Hyderabad	0.8	31.3	0.7	33.7	0.5	20.9	23.9	17.6	23.2	16.9	40.8	40.9
Kolkata	0.4	33.0	1.6	47.2	0.6	37.6	31.1	29.1	34.1	21.5	41.6	30.9
Lucknow	2.0	47.9	2.4	53.5	0.4	27.9	19.7	13.2	25.0	11.9	33.1	29.4
Patna	NA	NA	4.8	71.2	0.6	42.4	NA	NA	25.9	6.5	32.0	22.6

value of z has been increasing in Madhya Pradesh i.e. concentration of population has increased in Bhopal. It can be observed from Table 7.9 that the value of rank size rule for Maharashtra has increased over time, i.e. concentration of population to the largest city, Mumbai has been increasing. City primacy index is computed for these selected states. The primacy index for Maharashtra indicates that concentration of population in Mumbai has increased over time where as in all over states and cities there has been fluctuation.

Table 7.9: Rank size rule and primacy index

STATES	*RANK SIZE RULE*			*PRIMACY INDEX*		
	1981	*1991*	*2001*	*1981*	*1991*	*2001*
Andhra Pradesh	0.156	0.093	0.141	0.355	0.355	0.373
Bihar	0.971	0.811	0.277	0.378	0.869	0.437
Gujarat	0.429	1.277	0.596	0.357	0.547	0.493
Karnataka	0.451	0.513	0.712	0.579	0.635	0.653
Madhya Pradesh	0.058	0.082	0.275	0.331	0.358	0.429
Maharashtra	0.702	0.677	0.874	0.846	0.783	0.954
Tamil Nadu	0.546	0.278	0.364	0.460	0.385	0.478
Uttar Pradesh	0.399	0.054	0.153	0.348	0.337	0.360
West Bengal	0.212	0.235	0.194	0.395	0.388	0.379

CONCLUSION

From the above discussion, it is found that in the developed states like Maharashtra, Tamil Nadu, Gujarat and Karnataka level of urbanization is high compared to other states during the period 1981-2001. Maharashtra stands out as a prominent migrants receiving state in India. There is also high concentration of population in the certain cities such as Mumbai, Bangalore, Ahmedabad, and Bhopal, which are growing at a faster rate. If this trend continues, these cities will be over populated. It is felt there is a need to develop some more cities, which could attracts migrants from rural areas or less developed states. This will help in reducing the impact on basic amenities available in these cities, Proper planning and establishment of new urban areas/ centers will able to redirect the migration flow which is currently to some selected cities. There is a need for the redirection of investment in order to develop a strong economic base for small and medium cities in these selected states of India. Developmental planning should also emphasize on development of newly annexed urban areas.

REFERENCES

Census of India: Provisional Population Total, Rural, Urban Distribution of Population 2001 of Andhra Pradesh, Bihar, Delhi, Gujarat, Karnataka, Madhya Pradesh, Maharashtra, Tamil Nadu, Uttar Pradesh, West Bengal.

Census of India (2001): "Final Population Totals and Migration Table Soft Copy".

Crook, N and Dyson, Tim (1981): "Urbanization in India-Result of the 1981 Census," *Population and Development Review*, Vol. 8 (1), pp. 145-157.

Davis, K (1965): *Scientific American* Article September. Vol. 213, No. 3.

Jain, M.K (1994): *Urbanization: An Analysis of Census and Ancillary Data*, New Delhi Book Well Publication.

Rajan, S,I.(1986): "Level and Trends of Urbanization in India: A Comparative Study of Tamil Nadu" *Nagarlok*, Vol. 8. No (3), July-September, pp. 21-35.

Ramachandaran, R. (1989): *Urbanization and Urban System in India-1989*. Oxford University Press. Delhi, pp. 75-90.

Patil, R.L (1993): "The Process of Urbanization in India, 1971-1991". *The Journal of Family Welfare*, Vol. 39, No (1), March 1993, pp. 44-51.

Sovani, N.V (1966): *Urbanization and Urban India*, pp. 33-40, Asia Publishing House. New Delhi.

8

Socio-cultural and Demographic Aspects of India's Population

Issues and Challenges for Sustainable Settlements

Harihar Sahoo
Manas Ranjan Pradhan

INTRODUCTION

India is situated at the southern extremity of the Asian continent at the head of the Indian Ocean and flanked by high mountain ranges on three sides. It is a country inhabited by people of diverse race, religion, language and customs. Social institution of caste provides a common cultural idiom to all Indians. The institution is so pervasive that it cuts across even religious boundaries. Every Indian irrespective of his religion finds himself in a universe of caste. Similarly in the Indian social setting, the form joint family is used in the sense of extended family. It has been considered one among the main pillars supporting the Hindu society. Women during the Vedic period occupied an exalted position and they enjoyed a fair amount of personal freedom and equal rights with men. Various factors like westernization, industrialization, urbanization, modern education etc are regarded as the factors responsible for the breaking down of the unique culture of Indian society. Demographically, India, is the second most populous country in the world where 1028 million population resides in 31,31,866 sq. kms. The share of the child population in the age group 0-6 comprises around 16 per cent; density of population is 324 persons per sq kms, and the sex ratio is 933 in 2001(Census 2001). The sex ratio among the child population (0-6) in India has declined by 18 points i.e. from 945 in 1991 to 927 in 2001.

Sustainability i.e. fulfillment of the needs of the present without compromising the ability of the future generations to meet their needs has become a key word in the 21st century. India is on the way of rapid socio-economic change. In view of the emphasis on science and technology, the quest for urban life style and economic development, sustainability in each sector has caught the attention of not only the policy makers but also the researcher's interest in the field. Human settlement plays a crucial role in achieving sustainable development both locally and nationally. Sustainable development can be ensured through planned management of settlements including the mobilization of resources used in the construction, operation and maintenance, the provision of services to meet the need of citizens and most importantly in the treatment, recovery and recycling of their by-product (Gurumukhi, 2001). Sustainable settlement will function as whole living systems, demonstrating quality lifestyle practices that enhance the quality of the surrounding natural environment. It will help people to move between, enabling productive expression of their inherent nature. Participants will live in an environmentally-enhancing and ethical manner and contribute skills, resources, knowledge and inspiration to the broader community. In particular, the specific elements of sustainable settlement are:

- Land-use and ecology;
- Resource management;
- Environmental rehabilitation;
- Employment creation;
- Community development;
- Application of appropriate technology;

- Architecture and built environment;
- Personal development and Healing; and
- Ethical business practice.

Sustainable human settlement promotes to the improvement of social, economic and environmental quality of human settlements and the living and working environments of all people. Human behavior is largely a product of the socio-cultural milieu into which human beings are settled and socialized. The success of any developmental programmes largely depends on behavior and the prevalent culture of the society. Therefore there is an urgent need to understand the socio-cultural and demographic contexts for the effective implementation of certain developmental programmes and policies.

SOCIO-CULTURAL AND DEMOGRAPHIC ASPECTS

Literacy

Literacy is one of the important indicators of social development, which affects cultural and demographic behavior of the society. In India, a person is considered "literate" if he can read and write with understanding.

Table 8.1: Trend of Literacy in India by Sex since 1901

Census Year	*Literacy rate**			*Crude literacy rate*		
	Total	*Male*	*Female*	*Total*	*Male*	*Female*
1901	5.35	9.83	0.69	5.35	9.83	0.69
1911	5.92	10.56	1.05	5.92	10.56	1.05
1921	7.16	12.21	1.81	7.16	12.21	1.81
1931	9.50	15.59	2.93	9.50	15.59	2.93
1941	16.10	24.90	7.30	16.10	24.90	7.30
1951	16.67	24.95	7.93	16.67	24.95	7.93
1961	24.02	34.44	12.95	24.02	34.44	12.95
1971	29.46	39.45	18.72	29.45	39.45	18.72
1981	36.23	46.89	24.82	36.23	46.89	24.82
1991	52.00	64.12	39.35	42.84	52.74	32.17
2001	65.40	75.95	54.21	55.30	64.13	45.84

Source: *Census of India.

It is clear from the Table 1.1 that there is a remarkable increase in literacy in the decade 1931-41 followed by a decade of almost stagnant growth. Before independence, education was confined generally to urban areas and the more affluent and higher classes took to it. They were probably encouraged by the employers both Governmental and others for they naturally preferred persons with basic intelligence. In the post-independence period, there has been more rapid growth of literacy. In the case of males it has grown from mere 25 per cent in 1951 to 39 per cent in 1971 and 76 per cent in 2001. In case of females literacy rate has increased itself from a plain 8 per cent in 1951 to 19 per cent in 1971 and 54 per cent in 2001. Because of the definitional changes it would not hold a clear picture when we compare it with different years. Therefore crude literacy rate have been computed for different years. It reflects that there is remarkable differences have been found among male and female with regard to literacy. Again the gender disparities have been declining from census to census. After independence facilities for higher, scientific and technical education has increased to a very large extent. Education has been made compulsory and also free to certain level and there has also been adult literacy drive.

POPULATION AND URBANIZATION IN INDIA

Table 8.2 reflects that trend of urbanization from 1901 to 2001, where the number of towns/UAs has more than doubled from 1811 in 1901 to 4378 in 2001. There was steady increase in the number of towns till 1951 and a sharp decline during the 1951-61 due to the stringent definition in 1961, many urban places were declassified. The total population increased 4.3 times between 1901-2001 while, the urban population increased nearly 11 times during the same period. The percentage of urban population to the total population of India increased 2.5 times from 10.8 per cent in 1901 to 27.7 per cent in 2001. The percentage variation during 1901-31 was slow but after this, urban population recorded a very high growth rate since 1951. The annual average exponential growth rate increased steadily over the decades but it started declining from 3.8 per cent in 1971-81 to 3 per cent in 1981-91 and further to 2.7 per cent in 1991-2001.

Table 8.2: Trend of Urbanization in India since 1901

Census year	*No. of Uas/Towns*	*Total Pop. (in million)*	*Urban Pop. (in million)*	*Growth rate*		*Per cent of Urban Pop.*	*No. of million plus cities*	*Pop. in m.cities (in million)*	*Per cent of pop. in million cities to*	
				Decennial	*Annual*				*Total pop.*	*Urban pop.*
1901	1811	238.4	25.8	–	–	10.84	1	1.51	0.63	5.85
1911	1754	252.1	25.9	0.35	0.03	10.29	2	2.76	1.09	10.66
1921	1894	251.3	28	8.27	0.79	11.18	2	3.13	1.24	11.18
1931	2017	279	33.4	19.12	1.75	11.99	2	3.41	1.22	10.21
1941	2190	318.7	44.1	31.97	2.77	13.86	2	5.31	1.66	12.04
1951	2795	361.1	62.4	41.42	3.45	17.29	5	11.75	3.25	18.81
1961	2270	439.2	78.9	26.41	2.34	17.97	7	18.1	4.12	22.93
1971	2476	548.2	109.1	38.23	3.21	19.91	9	27.83	5.08	25.51
1981	3245	688.3	159.4	46.14	3.83	23.34	12	42.12	6.16	26.41
1991	3696	844.3	217.1	36.19	3.09	25.72	23	70.66	8.37	32.54
2001	4378	1027	285.3	31.2	2.7	27.78	35	105.58	10.28	37

Source: Census of India 1991, Provisional population totals; Rural-Urban distribution, Paper 2 of 1991, pp. 13, 22,23,30,38 and Census of India 2001, Provisional Population totals, Paper 1 of 2001.

Another important feature of the present trend of urbanization is the increase of the relative share of million plus cities. According to 2001 census, there were 35 million plus UAs/ Cities. In 1901, there was only one city, i.e., Calcutta. It remained two (Kolkata and Mumbai) from 1901 to 1941. Then afterwards the number of such cities grew rapidly. About 37 per cent of the total urban population as per 2001 census lives in million plus UAs/Cities.

MARITAL STATUS

The study of marital status is important in a country like India because of several reasons. Since in many societies reproduction takes place only in wedlock, so it is an important factor affecting fertility. The other related factors like the proportion of persons who never married, proportion of females in the reproductive age group, the age at marriage, the proportion of those whose marriages have been dissolved either by death or divorce and their age at the time of the dissolution of marriage etc are of immense important. The data available suggest that there have been a steady upgrading of the age of marriage. There has been increasing tendencies on the part of upper class people to get married at a higher age than before. Among educated males and females, there has also been a tendency to remain unmarried or get married at a late age. This is proved with Table 8.3.

Table 8.3: Percentage distribution of females in India by marital status, 1951-91

Year	*10-14*		*15-44*		
	Never Married	*Currently Married*	*Never Married*	*Currently Married*	*Widowed and divorced*
1951	69.0	30.3	8.22	82.81	8.97
1961	80.5	19.3	7.44	85.81	6.75
1971	88.2	11.7	11.00	84.5	4.5
1981	93.4	6.6	15.36	80.48	3.6
1991	95.4	4.5	17.81	79.48	2.71
2001	98.3	1.6	30.93	67.07	2.01

Source: 1. *Census of India*, 1951, Vol. 1, A-II

2. *Census of India*, 1961, Vol. 1, Part II-C (i)
3. *Census of India*, 1971, Series 1, Part II special (Mimeographed)
4. *Census of India*, 1991, Series 1, Part IV A-C Series.

The incidence of child marriage, of course still persists in India, which is in a declining trend. The percentage of never married women has increased and that of widows, divorced and separated women has decreased. Decline in male mortality rates and the improvement in life expectancy may be attributed to decrease in the percentage of widows.

RELIGIOUS COMPOSITION

India is a secular State without any State religion, but its population practices a number of different religious faiths. Societal customs and practices influenced by religion not only influence fertility behavior in a country like India but also a range of socio-cultural and political environment to an extent.

It is observed from Table 8.4 that the percentage of Muslims, Christians and Sikhs have been increased from 1901 to 1941. But in 1951 census, the percentage of Muslims declined to nearly 10 per cent and that of Hindus increased by nearly 15 per cent. This was mainly because of movement of people to Pakistan according to their religious affinity. Later censuses reflect increase in percentages of Muslims in India's population.

CASTE AND FAMILY

India is a diversified society. Social institutions like the caste and the joint family, which is found throughout the length and breadth of the country, is going to decline its rigidity and role. These castes and sub-castes are hierarchical in nature i.e. the caste, which is at the bottom treated as backward and untouchable. The constitution has mentioned certain characteristics like literacy, poverty, exploitation of labor, non-representation in services and untouchables by which these backward castes are to be identified. The constitution also empowers the state to investigate the conditions of this backwardness and make special provisions for their uplift. There are three broad divisions, namely Scheduled Castes and Scheduled Tribes and Other Backward Classes have been recognized by the constitution. Table 8.5 clearly reflects that the percentage share of Scheduled tribe is increasing since very beginning.

Table 8.4: Percentage distribution of persons professing different religions in India since 1901

Religions	*1901*	*1911*	*1921*	*1931*	*1941*	*1951*	*1961*	*1971*	*1981*	*1991*	*2001*
Hindu	72.87	71.68	70.73	70.67	69.46	84.98	83.51	82.7	82.64	82.41	80.46
Muslim	21.88	22.38	23.23	23.48	24.47	9.91	10.7	11.21	11.35	11.67	13.43
Christian	0.98	1.21	1.46	1.77	1.91	2.35	2.44	2.6	2.43	2.32	2.34
Sikh	0.77	1.00	1.06	1.28	1.46	1.74	1.79	1.89	1.79	1.99	1.87
Buddhist	0.1	0.11	0.12	0.13	0.12	0.05	1.73	0.7	0.7	0.77	0.77
Jain	0.47	0.41	0.39	0.37	0.37	0.45	0.46	0.47	0.48	0.41	0.41
Others*	2.93	3.21	3.01	2.3	2.41	0.52	0.34	0.4	0.42	0.38	0.65
Not Stated	–	–	–	–	–	–	0.03	0.01	0.01	0.05	0.07
Total	100	100	100	100	100	100	100	100	100	100	100

* Include Zoroastrians, Jews etc.

Source: 1. Up to 1941 Kingsley Davis, *Population of India and Pakistan*, New York: Russell and Kursell, 1951, P. 175.

2. *Census of India*, 1961, Paper No. II of 1963, Religion, PP. IV-V
3. *Census of India*, 1971, Series 1, Paper 2of 1972, Religion, PP. 2-4
4. *Census of India*, 1981, Paper No. 4of 1984, Household Population by religion of head of household, Series 1, India and census of India, 2001.

Table 8.5: Per cent distribution of SC and ST in India since 1901

Year	*1901*	*1911*	*1921*	*1931*	*1941*	*1951*	*1961*	*1971*	*1981*	*1991*	*2001*
SC	–	–	–	–	–	–	14.67	14.6	15.75	16.48	16.2
ST	2.88	3.11	2.91	2.26	2.26	6.25	6.86	6.94	7.76	8.08	8.2

Source: Census of India, 1901, 1921, 1931, 1971, 1991and 2001.

Indian joint family system, which is rich in family values, norms are in a decline. Various factors may be referred as the factors playing the role. Nuclear family is replacing rapidly the joint families in India.

AGE STRUCTURE

The classification of population by age has considerable iterant from socio-economic and demographic point of view. It is essential for determining the proportion of working population to the non-working population i.e. for knowing the dependency load. Again to understand the future trends in population growth, it is essential not only to know the crude rate of natural increase but also to study the variation of births and deaths in different age groups. The age structure shows a slight change from 1921 to 1971 (Table 8.6). In 1921, the proportion of children under 15 and that of old persons of 65 and above were 39.0 and 2.5 per cent respectively. Even after 50 years, there has been no significant change in these proportions. In 1971, these proportions had slightly increased to 42.1 and 2.8 per cent respectively. In 1981, the proportion of children reduced to 39.7 per cent while that of elderly (65+) 4.0 per cent increased over the decade. The similar trend also continued in case of 1991 and 2001 census. This means that Indian population has been slightly younger as compared to developed countries. The principal reason for relatively high birth rate leading to the larger proportion in the age group 0-14, which is gradually decreasing.

Table 8.6: Percentage distribution of population of India in broad age groups, 1901-2001

Age Group	*1901*	*1911*	*1921*	*1931*	*1951**	*1961**	*1971**	*1981*	*1991*	*2001*
0-14	38.5	38.45	39.05	40.02	37.45	41.08	42.1	39.70	37.77	35.35
15-44	46.6	46.69	45.82	46.35	45.99	44.01	43.52	43.35	44.90	46.08
45-64	–	12.47	12.64	11.46	12.97	11.99	11.62	13.00	13.07	13.53
65+	–	2.39	2.49	2.17	3.59	2.92	2.76	3.95	4.27	5.04
All ages	100	100	100	100	100	100	100	100	100	100

* Percentages based on adjusted figures

Sources:
1. Up to 1951, UN, The aging of the Population and its Economic and Social Implications, Population Studies, No. 26, 1956, P. 114.
2. For 1961, Census of India, Paper No. 2 of 1963, Age tables, Part II, P. 35.
3. Census of India, 1971, Series 1, India, Miscellaneous Studies, Paper 2 of 1974, Age and Life Tables (One per cent sample), pp. 8-9.
4. For 1981 and 1991, able 2.09, Occasional Paper No 2 of 1992, PP 98-99 and Census of India, 2001.

DENSITY OF POPULATION

Density of population figure indicates the man-land ratio. India does not either rank among countries with a very high man-land ratio or among those with a very low man-land ratio. Here man has found ample opportunity in course of centuries to migrate from less favorable to more favorable spots. It is clear from the table that there is an increasing trend of man-land ratio. The density was 117 in 1951, which has increased to 324 in 2001 (Table 8.7).

Table 8.7: Distribution of population by density and sex ratio since 1901

Census Year	*Density per sq. kms.*	*Sex ratio (Female per 1000 males)*			*Child Sex ratio (0-6)*
		Rural	*Urban*	*Total*	
1901	77	979	910	972	–
1911	82	975	872	964	–
1921	81	970	846	955	–
1931	90	966	838	950	–
1941	103	965	831	945	–
1951	117	965	860	946	–
1961	142	963	845	941	976
1971	177	949	858	930	964
1981	216	951	879	934	962
1991	267	938	894	927	945
2001	324	946	901	933	927

Source: Census of India, 2001.

SEX RATIO

The distribution of population according to sex has vital economic bearings so far as it affects the labour supply through marriage and fecundity. Low sex ratio (scarcity of women) sometimes leads to prostitution and spread of vulnerable diseases from the industrial towns to the villages (Mamoria, 1981). India is one of the few countries with a deficit of females. The relative scarcity of women has been a striking feature of India's population throughout the whole of regular census history. There were 972 females per 1000 males in 1901, which has been declining and the overall extent of decline comes to 933 in 2001. The decade 1991-2001 showed a slight increase in the ratio (from 927 in 1991 to 933 in 2001). A great variation in sex ratio has been found in rural and urban population mainly due to the sex selective migration.

CHILD SEX RATIO (0-6)

The sex ratio for children upto age of six has gone down from 976 girls per 1000 boys in 1961 to 927 in 2001. The sharpest decline in sex ratio for the child population is reported from Himachal Pradesh, Punjab, Haryana, Gujarat, Uttaranchal, Maharashtra and Chandigarh where abortions of female fetus are known to be widely practiced.

FERTILITY RATE

The number of children she bears during her entire reproductive life indicates fertility of a woman. The number of birth has been an important bearing on the social conditions of a country. Besides social conditions, biological and cultural factors also influence in turn the number of births (Mamoria, 1981). It has been found that total fertility rate in India has been declined from 5.3 in 1970 to 3.8 in 1990 and finally to 3.1 in 2001. There is also a wide gap concerning fertility has been found in rural and urban areas. Similar pattern also persists in case of General Fertility Rate. In spite of a declining trend in fertility levels, India still has the distinction of having high birth rate in comparison to the developed countries (Table 8.8).

Table 8.8: Total Fertility Rate (TFR) and General Fertility Rate (GFR) for India (1970 to 1998)

Year	*TFR*			*GFR*		
	Rural	*Urban*	*Total*	*Rural*	*Urban*	*Total*
1970	5.6	4.1	5.3	173.4	133.2	165.8
1980	4.7	3.4	4.4	144.9	111.4	137.9
1990	4.1	2.8	3.8	132.6	96.1	123.9
1992*	3.9	2.6	3.6	127.6	89.1	118.6
1993*	3.8	2.8	3.5	125.2	93.5	116.6
1994*	3.8	2.7	3.5	128.6	89.7	118.3
1995*	3.9	2.6	3.5	126.7	87.3	117.0
1996*	3.7	2.4	3.4	122.7	81.5	112.5
1997*	3.6	2.4	3.3	119.5	80.7	109.9
1998	3.5	2.4	3.2	115.2	79.2	106.5
2001#	3.4	2.3	3.1	108.6	74.4	99.5

Note: *: Excludes Jammu & Kashmir.

Source: *Women and Men in India 2001*, Ministry of Statistics and Programme Implementation, Govt. of India.

\# SRS Statistical Report, 2001, RGI, New Delhi.

BIRTH RATE

On the basis of the surveys it may be observed that an Indian women gives birth to an average of 6 to 8 children, if she enjoys a continuous married life till the end of her reproductive period, i.e. for about 30 years, between the ages 15 to 45 (RGI: 1968). It is observed that the birth rate in India has been declining from the very beginning. Variation in birth rate has been found in case of rural and urban areas. It is higher in rural areas. Birth rate has been declined sharply from 49.2 in 1901-11 to 41.7 in 1951-61 and finally to 25.0 in 2002 (Table 8.9).

Table 8.9: Crude Birth Rates and Crude Death Rates in Rural/Urban Areas in India

Year	*Crude Birth Rates*			*Crude Death Rates*		
	Rural	*Urban*	*Combined*	*Rural*	*Urban*	*Combined*
1901-1911	–	–	49.2	–	–	42.6
1911-1921	–	–	48.1	–	–	47.2
1921-1931	–	–	46.4	–	–	36.3
1931-1941	–	–	45.2	–	–	31.2
1941-1951	–	–	39.9	–	–	27.4
1951-1961	–	–	41.7	–	–	22.8
1961-1971#	–	–	41.2	–	–	19.0
1971-1981	–	–	37.2	–	–	15.0
1971	38.9	30.1	36.9	16.4	9.7	14.9
1976	35.8	28.4	34.4	16.3	9.5	15.0
1981	35.6	27	33.9	13.7	7.8	12.5
1986	34.2	27.1	32.6	12.2	7.6	11.1
1991*	30.9	24.3	29.5	10.6	7.1	9.8
1996*	29.3	21.6	27.5	9.7	6.5	9.0
2001*	27.1	20.3	25.4	9.1	6.3	8.4
2002*	26.6	19.9	25.0	8.7	6.1	8.1

Note: The Aggregated Estimates for (1971-1976) India Exclude Bihar and West Bengal.

\# Rural Urban Breakup Prior to 1971 not available.

* 1991 & 1996: Exclude Jammu & Kashmir.

1991: Exclude Mizoram.

2001 & 2002: Exclude Nagaland (Rural).

Source: *Health Information of India 2002*, Ministry of Health and Family Welfare, Govt. of India.

DEATH RATE

During the 19th and early part of 20th century, the death rate in India was quite high. After 1920, there has been a progressive decline in the death rates. During 1891-1901, the deaths caused by famines, during 1901-11 by plague, during 1911-21 by influenza epidemic have been stressed as some of the reasons for the heavy toll of people. After 1951, a large number of health improvement programmes, such as control of malaria, filariasis, tuberculosis, leprosy, veneral diseases were undertaken. In addition development of better communication system helped in decline in death rate from 42.6 in 1901-11 to 22.8 in 1951-61 and finally to 8.1 in 2002 (Table 8.9). The rural urban differential in death rate has been gradually declining because of various avenues installed in rural areas.

INFANT MORTALITY RATE

In India, the infant mortality rate is still high, even though it has declined sharply during the last 50 years. It was 146 in 1951 and 134 in 1971 and after that, it has declined to a considerable extent from 104 in 1981 to 80 in 1991 and 66 in 2001. The decline in infant mortality has been attributed to the improvement in standard of living, better control of communicable diseases, better obstetric and health care services and expansion of maternal and child welfare services (Table 8.10).

Table 8.10: Infant Mortality Rate in India since 1951

Year	*Female*	*Male*	*Persons*
1951	138	153	146
1961	128.8	130	129
1971	135	130	134
1981	104	104	104
1991	80	81	80
2001	68	64	66

Source: Annual Report 2002-03, Department of Women and Child Development, Ministry of Human Resource Development, Government of India and *India Yearbook 2003*, Manpower Profile & Family Welfare Programme in India 2001,Department of family Welfare, Ministry of Health and Family Welfare, Government of India.

EXPECTATION OF LIFE AT BIRTH

It seems that there is an increase in expectation of life with the progressive decline in the death rate. Expectation of life at birth was 22.9 years during 1901-11, which became improved to 41.3 during 1951-61, and finally 62.9 during 1996-2001. More organized efforts have been made to attack epidemics and also with the introduction of improved health and sanitary conditions especially in rural areas, provision of pure water supply, increasing use of antibiotic wonder drugs, B.C.G., D.P.T. etc. all lead to decline in death rate with the improvement in health standard (Table 8.11).

Table 8.11: Expectation of Life at Birth by Sex since 1901-11

Year	*Female*	*Male*	*Combined*
1901-11	23.3	22.6	22.9
1911-21	20.9	19.4	20.1
1921-31	26.6	26.9	26.8
1931-41	31.4	32.1	31.8
1941-51	31.7	32.4	32.1
1951-61	40.6	41.9	41.3
1961-71	44.7	46.4	45.6
1970-75	49	50.5	49.7
1976-80	52.1	52.5	52.3
1981-85	55.7	55.4	55.4
1986-90	58.1	57.7	57.7
1991-95	60.9	59.7	60.3
1996-2001	62.36	63.39	62.9

Note: Figures for 1901-11 to 1961-71 are based on Census Actuarial Reports and for1970-75 onwards on the basis of estimated from Sample Registration System.

Source: Agricultural Research, *Data Book 2002* and *Compendium of Environment Statistics, 2000,* Central Statistical Organization, Ministry of Statistics and Programme Implementation, Government of India.

ISSUES

- Increasing concentration of population in million plus cities has a direct threat on the per-capita availability of infrastructures.
- Rapid increase in slum population, which are glossily congested, unhygienic for human habitation.
- Growing population poses a threat to limited resources, that the current rate of growth will lead to forests be disappeared, water supplies be exhausted, the hole in the ozone layer expanded and so on.
- The preference for sons has lead to discrimination against the girl child and lower female literacy, sex selective abortion, higher mortality levels for females in all ages up to the age of 45.
- Indiscriminate growth of industrial and chemical plants in urban centers.
- Urbanization and its consequences to health of the urban poor.
- Nutrition related problems like malnutrition complicated by increasing chemical use and adulteration of food.
- Health problems of the aged.
- Pollution related diseases including allergies, asthma and other hazards.

KEY CONCERNS

- Linking the provision of facilities to urban slum dwellers with their observance of the small family norms.
- Ensure safe water supply.
- Social mobilization for the effective utilization of health services.
- Emphasis on operational and action research.
- Gainful employment opportunities especially to the girls and the modification of the role of women.

- Development of population education.
- Provision of social security.

CONCLUSION

From the above discussion it is abundantly clear that, India is in a deplorable stage, where the concentration of population in large million plus cities has been increasing rapidly making the imbalances of age-sex structure. Information on marital status shows that the proportion of never married is increasing. In spite of the fact that, constitution of India provides for free and compulsory education for all children until they complete the age of 14 years, still a large chunk are debarred from it. Such situation is very worst in rural areas. Declining sex ratio especially child sex ratio is another problem which shows a relative scarcity of women in India. In India this high fertility may be taken as due to greater number of remarried widows among them and less strict observance of abstinence and religious celibacy besides adherence of people to large family norms. Though the decline in fertility and mortality at the national level is in its incipient stage, India still suffers from high fertility and mortality (especially infant and maternal) in comparison to developed countries.

Above all there is no doubt that rapid growth of population with large-scale migration and subsequent effect on water, energy, housing and other infrastructures are the basic problems of human settlements particularly in urban areas. It deteriorates the already deteriorated service delivery systems in the towns or cities that continue to grow in a haphazard fashion. Despite the introduction of National Housing Policy, 1994 with the objective of providing adequate shelter for all, the need of adequate housing in urban areas and for vulnerable groups the housing problem still persists, resulting in pressure on urban services and infrastructure. Increasing population pressure on land and infrastructure and the associated high costs have made proper housing inaccessible to the poorer segments of the population and have caused a growth of slums and squatter settlements. Sustainable settlement is to be based on technical cooperation, partnerships among the public, private and community groups, with special consideration for women, indigenous people, the elderly and the disabled. The first step in attaining sustainable settlements in urban areas is to reduce the pressure on cities resulting from migration from rural areas, by providing infrastructure and development opportunities there. Legislation regarding migration, resource mobilization and effective service delivery systems seems to be some of the effective steps for sustainability of the settlements as well as all round development of the country.

REFERENCES

Ali, Almas. 2005 '*Population and Health Challenges in Orissa*', Paper Presented at the National Seminar on Population Challenges and Health Needs in Orissa, Bhubaneswar.

Behera, M and A K Mitra (1996); 'The Standard of Living in India: An Attempt Towards Inter-Regional Study', *Indian Journal of Regional Science*, Vol. 38 (2).

Census of India, 2001, *India*, Series-1, Final Population Totals.

Census of India, 2001, *India*, Series-22, Provisional Population Totals, Paper 1 of 2001.

Gurumukhi, K.T. (2001). "Sustainable Development of Urban Settlements: Indian Context". In: Ravinder Singh Sandhu, Sorup Singh Minhas and Jasmat Singh Sandhu (Eds) '*Sustainable Human Settlements: The Asian Experience*'. Rawat Publications, 2001.

Madan, G.R., 1990, *Indian Social Problems; Social Disorganization and Reconstruction*, Volume-1, Allied Publishers Ltd., New Delhi.

Mamoria, C.B. (1981), Social Problems and Social Disorganization in India, Kitab Mahal, Allahabad.

Premi, M.K., Rananama A. and Bambawale Usha, 1983, *An introduction to Social Demography*, Vikas Publishing House Pvt. Ltd., Delhi.

Registrar General of India (1968), *Registration of Births and Deaths in India* Paper Presented at ECAFE Seminar on Civil Registration and Vital Statistics, Copenhagen, August, 1968, p. 20.

9

Gender Differentials in Disability Free Life Expectancy in India

Sangram Kishor Patel

INTRODUCTION

Health status of a population is a significant indicator of human development. Indicators such as different death rates or life expectancy are used to measure health status of a population. At the similar times it is also clear from the various studies that we cannot come to a conclusion about the health status of a population by taking into account the death rates or life expectancy alone. Health programmes and activities today include a variety of public efforts directed to wards both fatal and non-fatal heath out comes. There has been considerable interest in recent years in development of summary indices of health that reflect information on living population's morbidity/ disability level as well as on the level of mortality. In the past two decades, considerable international effort has been put into the development of summary measures of population health that integrate information on mortality and non-fatal health outcomes and international policy interest in such indicators is increasing (Preston, 1993; Vande *et al.*, 1996; Barendregt *et al.*, 1998; Field *et al.*, 1998; World Bank, 1993; Murray *et al.*, 1996, Mathers *et al.*, 2000). Generally, the summary measures divided into two groups namely health gaps (DALY etc.) and health expectancy (DFLE etc.).

The concept of combining population health state prevalence data with mortality data in a life table to generate estimates of expected years of life in various health states was first proposed in USA in the 1960s (Sanders, 1964) and developed in the 1970s (Sullivan, 1966, 1971). However, Sullivan has outlined the methods for using these measures with survey data available for the United States population and has noted the problems and draw backs of such techniques. Disability free life expectancy (DFLE) was calculated for a number of countries during the 1980s and an international research work, the Network on health expectancy (Re'seau Espe'rance de Vieen Sante' or REVES) was established in 1989 (Mathers and Robine, 1993). The objectives of REVES are to promote the use of health expectancy as an indicator of health and as a tool for health planning. DFLE taking care of both fatal as well as non-fatal health outcomes. Because of its potential influence on international and national resource allocation decisions, DFLE is now considered as one of the important summary measure. This type of analysis or measurement is underutilized despite the fact that it is very powerful and has fundamental policy implications (Murray, *et al.*, 1999).

NEED FOR THE STUDY

So far research on disability and health expectancy (Disability Free Life Expectancy) is very limited and focused mainly to developed countries. However WHO has made some estimate for the health expectancies of some of the developing countries including India, but these health expectancies are not available for different disabilities or for extent of disabilities in gender differentials term. After International Year of Disabled (IYD) – 1981, focused has been given to disability studies and research. Thereafter, worldwide very few studies are available which can contribute to the gender differentials in disability as well as health expectancy. In India, these types of research are scarce and there is no literature available till date which can demonstrate the gender differentials in influence of different types of disabilities on life expectancy. So it's an urgent need to explore the gender differentials of different types of disability free life expectancy as well as the severity of disability on life expectancy. NSS-58th round data on disabled persons provides information about basic socio-economic and demographic characteristics of disabled persons with different types of disabilities and extent of disability. This study is an attempt in this direction that certainly raises some researchable issues and further understanding the gender differentials in different types of disabilities free life expectancies in India is an important step for the policy and programme points of view. Because it is necessary to know the numbers of years or times both the sex are spending with and without disability in India.

OBJECTIVES

The basic objectives of the study are as follows:

1. To examine the disability free life expectancy (DFLE) by age and sex in India.
2. To examine the gender differentials in different types of disability free life expectancy at birth in India.
3. To examine gender differentials in extent of disability free life expectancy at birth in India.

METHODOLOGY

For the purpose of the study, bivariate analysis, life table technique, Sullivan's method and descriptive statistics (e.g. standard error) have been used for the analysis.

Sullivan's Method (Developed by D. Sullivan in 1971)

Health expectancy calculated by Sullivan's method is the number of remaining years, at a particular age, that an individual can expect to live in a healthy state (however health may be defined). Disability-Free Life Expectancy (DFLE) is found by partitioning the person years lived in the interval into those lived with and without disability.

It can be formulated as,

Disability Free Life Expectancy

$$= DFLE_x = \frac{1}{l_x} \sum_{i=x}^{w} (1 - prev_x) * L_x \text{ and}$$

Disability Life Expectancy

$$= DLE_x = \frac{1}{l_x} \sum_{i=x}^{w} prev_x * L_x$$

where, l_x is the number of survivors at age x in the hypothetical life table cohort.

L_x is the number of years of life lived by the life table cohort between ages x and $x + 1$.

$prev_x$ is the prevalence of disability between ages x and $x+1$ in the population.

Calculation of standard error for disability free life expectancy

In general variance can be calculated as

$$S^2 (prev_x) = \frac{prev_x * (1 - prev_x)}{N_x}$$

Where N_x is the number of persons in the age interval $[x, x+n]$ participating in the prevalence survey.

Hence the variances of $DFLE_x$ can be approximated by

$$S^2 (DFLE_x) = \frac{1}{l_x^2} \sum_{x=o}^{w} L_x^2 S^2 (1 - prev_x) = \frac{1}{l_x^2} \sum_{x=0}^{w} L_x^2 \frac{prev_x (1 - prev_x)}{N_x}$$

So, the standard error can be

$$S (DFLE_x) = \sqrt{\frac{1}{l_x^2} \sum_{x=0}^{w} L_x^2 \frac{prev_x (1 - prev_x)}{N_x}}$$

DATA SOURCES

The data for this study is the survey of disabled persons in India conducted at the national level by the National Sample Survey Organisation (NSSO), in its 58th round of survey during the year 2002. The study consider five types of disabilities – mental, visual, hearing, speech and locomotor. We have adopted the NSSO (2002) definition for these disabilities and to make the paper self-contained, the operational definition of disability is briefly spelled out here as "A disability is any restriction or lack (resulting from an impairment) of ability to perform an activity in the manner or within the range considered normal for a human being".

Types of Disabilities

Mental, visual, hearing, speech, locomotor and multiple cases are likely to exhibit differences by sex and age. Sex is an important factor, which can induce disability considering the practice of discriminating treatment towards women and wide gap in occupational patterns between male and female. The extent of disability can be classified as severe (can not able to do the daily activities even with the help of aids or appliances), moderate (can able to do the daily activities only with the help of aids or appliances), and mild (can able to do the daily activities without the help of aid or appliances, not try for aids or appliances and aids or appliances not available). As the number of cases for disabled person not try for aids or appliances and appliances not available are very few, so that these cases were added with mild category.

For this study, the life tables of India were taken from SRS based abridged life tables (1999-2003)-2006 report.

RESULTS

Results from the Table 9.1 explain that India has life expectancy (with disability) of 63 years; where as life expectancy without any disability is 49 years. In other words at birth a person can expect to live with disability for around 14 years. It can also be find out from the result that at age 15 and 60 a person can expect to live without disability of 41 and 10 years respectively. It is also a well-known fact that biologically female are stronger than male. It can be observed from the results of life expectancy from the Table 9.1. Male has life expectancy of 62 years at birth as compared to female with 64 years. At the same time, it can also be clearly viewed from the results of life expectancy of other ages among both the sex. Results show that male has 46 years of disability free life expectancy at birth while female has 51years. In another way it can be expected that females are living less number of years with disability in their lives than males. National Sample Survey -2002, on disabled person (58th round) findings also reveals that males are more vulnerable to wards having different types of disabilities in their lives than females. The results of disability life expectancy (DLE) also show the similar pattern for age up to 44 years that males are spending more number of years in disability than females. But, surprisingly after the age 45 years the pattern showing differently that the disability life expectancy is highest among females than males. It can be interpreted that at later ages, females are spending more number of years in disability than their males counter parts.

Table 9.1: Life Expectancy (e_x), Disability Life expectancy (DLE), Disability Free Life Expectancy (DFLE) by Age and Sex, India, 2002

Age	*Total*			*Male*			*Female*		
	e_x	*DLE*	*DFLE*	e_x	*DLE*	*DFLE*	e_x	*DLE*	*DFLE*
1	2	3	4	5	6	7	8	9	10
00-01	62.7	14.1	48.6(0.045)	61.8	15.6	46.2(0.064)	63.5	12.6	51.0 (0.063)
01-04	66.3	15.2	51.1(0.048)	65.3	16.7	48.6(0.069)	67.2	13.5	53.7 (0.068)
05-09	64.5	15.4	49.2(0.050)	63.0	16.8	46.1(0.070)	66.2	13.8	52.4 (0.070)
10-14	60.1	14.9	45.2(0.049)	58.4	16.2	42.2(0.070)	61.8	13.4	48.4 (0.070)
15-19	55.4	14.1	41.3(0.049)	53.7	15.4	38.3(0.069)	57.1	12.8	44.3 (0.070)
20-24	50.8	13.4	37.5(0.049)	49.1	14.5	34.6(0.068)	52.7	12.2	40.4 (0.069)
25-29	46.4	12.7	33.7(0.048)	44.6	13.6	31.0(0.067)	48.3	11.7	36.6 (0.069)
30-34	42.0	12.0	30.0(0.047)	40.2	12.7	27.5(0.066)	43.9	11.2	32.6 (0.068)

(Contd...)

1	2	3	4	5	6	7	8	9	10
35-39	37.6	11.3	26.3(0.047)	35.8	11.9	24.0(0.065)	39.5	10.8	28.7 (0.068)
40-44	33.2	10.7	22.6(0.046)	31.5	11.0	20.5(0.063)	35.0	10.4	24.7 (0.067)
45-49	28.9	10.0	18.9(0.045)	27.4	10.2	17.2(0.062)	30.6	9.9	20.7 (0.066)
50-54	24.8	9.3	15.5(0.045)	23.4	9.3	14.0(0.061)	26.3	9.4	16.9 (0.065)
55-59	20.9	8.6	12.3(0.043)	19.6	8.5	11.2(0.059)	22.2	8.8	13.4 (0.064)
60-64	17.4	7.9	9.5(0.043)	16.3	7.6	8.7(0.057)	18.5	8.2	10.3 (0.063)
65-69	14.2	7.1	7.2(0.042)	13.3	6.7	6.6(0.056)	15.1	7.4	7.7 (0.063)
70+	11.5	6.2	5.2(0.043)	10.7	5.8	4.9(0.058)	12.1	6.5	5.5 (0.065)

Note: Figures in parentheses indicate standard error of DFLE.

Results from Table 9.2 show that among the different types of disability life expectancy, locomotor disability life expectancy is highest with 7 years at birth follows by visual, hearing and multiple each with 2 years, where as mental and speech each follows with 1 year. Among the males the locomotor, mental, visual, hearing, speech and multiple disability free life expectancy are 54, 60, 60, 60, 61 and 60 years respectively. Whereas among the females, these are with 51,62, 61, 62, 63, 59 and 62 years accordingly. One important finding coming out of this Table 9.2 is those females have high visual disability life expectancy at birth than males. Another way it can be explained that females are spending more time in visual disability as compared to males counterparts.

Results from the Table 9.3 explain that at birth a person can expect to live up to 61 years in sever disability free life expectancy. At the same time at birth a person can live 60 and 54 years respectively for moderate and mild disability free life expectancy. In terms of DLE, at birth a person can expect to live with severe, moderate and mild disability life expectancy of 2, 3 and 8 years respectively. Surprisingly, there is no gender differentials found in the severity disability life expectancy. Where as there is differentials exist in moderate and mild disability life expectancy among males and females. Males have 3 years of moderate disability life expectancy as compared to females with 2 years. Similarly, mild disability life expectancy is 9 years among males as compared to 7 years for females.

Table 9.2: Different Types of Disability Life Expectancy and Disability Free Life Expectancy at Birth by Sex, India, 2002

Types of Disability	*Total*			*Male*			*Female*		
		DLE	*DFLE*		*DLE*	*DFLE*		*DLE*	*DFLE*
Total	62.7	14.1	48.6 (0.045)	61.8	15.6	46.2(0.064)	63.5	12.6	51.0 (0.063)
Mental		1.4	61.3 (0.016)		1.7	60.2(0.023)		1.1	62.4 (0.021)
Visual		2.3	60.5 (0.023)		1.9	59.9(0.029)		2.6	60.9 (0.037)
Hearing		1.7	61.0 (0.021)		1.7	60.1(0.028)		1.7	61.8 (0.030)
Speech		0.6	62.2 (0.009)		0.7	61.2(0.014)		0.4	63.1 (0.012)
Locomotor		6.5	56.2 (0.034)		7.9	53.9(0.051)		5.1	58.5 (0.045)
Multiple		1.6	61.1 (0.036)		1.7	60.1(0.025)		1.6	62.0 (0.027)

Note: Figures in parentheses indicate standard error of DFLE.
e_0^x indicates Life expectancy at birth.

Table 9.3: Extent of Disability Life Expectancy and Disability Free Life Expectancy at birth by sex, India, 2002

Extent of Disability	*Total*			*Male*			*Female*		
	e_0^x	*DLE*	*DFLE*	e_0^x	*DLE*	*DFLE*	e_0^x	*DLE*	*DFLE*
Total	62.7	14.1	48.6(0.045)	61.8	15.6	46.2 (0.064)	63.5	12.6	51.0 (0.063)
Severe		2.0	60.7(0.021)		2.0	59.9 (0.028)		2.0	61.5 (0.032)
Moderate		2.6	60.2(0.024)		2.9	58.9 (0.035)		2.2	61.4 (0.034)
Mild		8.3	54.4(0.038)		9.3	52.5 (0.054)		7.3	56.2 (0.053)

Note: Figures in parentheses indicate standard error of DFLE.
e_0^x indicates Life expectancy at birth.

SUMMARY AND CONCLUSION

It can be summarize from the study that females have the highest life expectancy as well as disability free life expectancy at birth compared to males in India. In can also be concluded from the study that males are living more number of years with disability than females except at the later ages, although females have better life expectancy and disability free life expectancy. Locomotor and visual disabilities are the two vulnerable disabilities, by which it can be expected that a person will spend more number of disabled years at birth in India. Male are likely to live more number of years with different types of disabilities life expectancy at birth than females except for the visual disability. Severe disability life expectancy is equally prevalent among both the sex. It can also be pointed out from this study that in India one can expect to live fourteen numbers of years with disability at birth. It's a huge number of years in the whole life span of a person. From this one can easily concluded that India is lacking in better heath infrastructures, health facilities or the health facilities are not reaching to the grass root level as well as poverty is a major concerned. Although in India now things are changing, but it will take time to reach at the grass root level. So, the government and policy makers can think for better programmes and policies, which will be beneficial to the health of general population (mainly for poor). It is also a well known fact that certain disabilities can be prevented. Instead of living with the number of years with disabilities, people can contribute these numbers of years to the development of society and productivity of the nation. But the government and policy makers have to find out the solutions, so that certain disabilities can be eliminate from the nation. Thereafter one can think of a better, productive and healthy nation. It is in the sense that this study has some policy relevant and its showing some path for the future research in health expectancy in India.

REFERENCES

Barendregt, J.J., Bonneux L., Vander Mass P.J. (1998). "Health Expectancy: From a Population Health Indicator to a Tool for Policy Making". *Ageing and Health*, Vol. 10, pp. 242-58.

Field, M.J., and Gold G.M. (1998). *Summarizing Population Health: Direction for the Development and Application of Population Metrics*. Institute of Medicine, National Academy Press, Washington.

Mathers, C., and Robine, J.M. (1993). Health Expectancy Indicators: A Review of the Work of REVES to Date. In: J.M. Robine, C.D. Mathers, M.R. Bone and I. Romieu (eds.), *Calculation of Health Expectancies, Harmonization, Consensus Achived and Future Perspectives*. Colloque INSERM Vol. 226, John Libbey Eurotext and Les Editions INSERM, France.

Mathers, C.D., Vos, E.T, Stevenson, C.E., and Begg, S.J. (2000). "The Australian Burden of Disease Study: Measuring the Loss of Health from Diseases, Injuries and Risk Factors". *Medical Journal Australia;* Vol. 172(12), pp. 592-606.

Murray, C.L.J., and Lopez, A.D. (1996). *The Global Burden of Disease: A Comprehensive Assessment of Mortality and Disability from Diseases, Injuries and Risk Factors in 1990 and Projected to 2020*. Global Burden of Diseases and Injuries Series, Vol. 1, Havard University Press, Cambridge.

Murray, C.L.J., E. Gakidou and J. Frenk (1999). "Health Inequalities and Social Group Differences: What should we Measure"? *Bulletin of the World Health Organisation*, Vol. 77(7), pp. 537-543.

NSSO (2003). *Disabled Persons in India, NSS-58th Round* (July-December-2002). Report No. 485. Ministry of Statistics and Programme Implementation. Government of India.

Preston, S.H. (1993). "Health Indices As a Guide to Health Sector Planning: A Demographic Critique". In: Gribble J.N, Preston S.H, (eds), *The Epidemiological Transition. Policy and Planning Implications for Developing Countries*. National Academic Press, Washington DC, USA.

Sanders, B.S (1964). "Measuring Community Health Levels". *American Journal of Public Health;* Vol. 54, pp. 1063-1070.

SRS (2006). *SRS Based Abridged Life Tables 1999-2003, SRS Analytical Studies Report No. 2 of 2006*, Office of the Registrar General of India, New Delhi.

Sullivan, D.F. (1966). *Conceptual Problems in Developing An Index of Health*. US Public Health Series Publication Series No. 1000. Vital and Health Statistics Series 2. No. 17. National Center for Health Statistics.

Sullivan, D.F. (1971). "A Single Index of Mortality and Morbidity". *HSMHA Health Report*, Vol. 86, pp. 347-354.

Vandewater H.P., Perenboom R.J., and Boshuizen H.C. (1996). "Policy Revelence of the Health Expectancy Indicator: An Inventory of European Union Countries". *Health Policy;* Vol. 36, pp. 117-129.

World Bank (1993). *World Development Report 1993: Investing in Health*. Oxford University Press, New York.

10

Level and Differential of Unemployment among Youth in Rural Orissa and NREGP

Hrushikesh Tripathy
Arabinda Acharya
Uma Shankar Majhi

ABSTRACT

This chapter examines the level and differential of unemployment rate among youth in rural Orissa. The analysis carried out with the principal usual status variable of National Sample Survey data using bivariate and multivariate analysis. The finding of the study reveals that unemployment rate among youth in rural area is highest among female, better educated, never married, general category and richest quintile of the population. It also reveals that unemployment among youth (15-24) is higher as compared to all other broad age groups. Further an attempt has been made to appraisal of National Rural Employment Guarantee Programme (NREGP) in association of rural youth unemployment. The result suggests, being existed of the excellent programme (NREGP), one sixth (17%) of the youth in rural Orissa are unemployed. Therefore, there is need more government programme integrating quality aspects rather than quantity in rural area to make more transparency by which intended beneficiaries would be much benefited.

INTRODUCTION

India has celebrated her 60th years of the largest democracy with second fastest Gross Domestic Product (GDP) growth (around 9 per cent per annum) country in the world after China with large chunk of working population. Among the working population, majority of them are youth around one in every third (32 per cent) of the working population. But the Indian economy has had a tremendous change in its socio-economic, demographic and institutional structure in post liberalization era. After new economic reforms in 1991, the opening up our economy to the rest of the world has changed in terms of the growth in macroeconomic indicators like; GDP, PCI (per capita income) savings, investment both in terms of foreign direct investment (FDIs) and foreign institutional investments (FIIs) etc. Despite these achievements, millions of our peoples are facing poverty, unemployment, hungry, skeptical and insecure. The decline in the employment rate over the period due to some major changes; particularly, the disinvestment policies by various governments has decreased the job opportunities in public sector units but skilled and semi-skilled job opportunities have been increased in private sector units. The share of agricultural sector to the overall employment dropped from 61 per cent to 57 per cent and this trend is continuing. But the manufacturing sector's share increased marginally during this period, trade, hotel and restaurant sector contributed significantly higher to the overall employment than in earlier years. The other important sectors whose shares in employment have increased are transport, storage and communications apart from financial, insurance, real estate, business and community, social and personal services (GOI, 2004-05). However, keeping all the good and worrisome achievement facts in the mind the present study focuses on the relation between the economic reform and unemployment among the youth (age group 15-24) in rural Orissa. Further an attempt has been made to understand the level and differential of unemployment rate in various socio economic and demographic strata in rural Orissa.

Orissa is one of the poorest States in India. More than 80 per cent of the population is rural inhabitant and agriculture is their primary source of income. Although in Orissa population growth is minimized but health status of the people is below the accept level. According to latest report of census of India, three-fifths (63%) of the total population are literate in Orissa (Census, 2001). In addition to poor health status and low level of literacy half of the total population of the State living below poverty line. Poverty, hunger and starvation death in is not only well-known to State in the country but also in worldwide. Although the abiding role of the natural calamities such as super cyclone and flood in coastal region, drought and famine in western and southern region are vital reasons for sever poverty, unemployment, and starvation death in the state. Lack of Political will of leaders and political power of the people is another cause of current situation of the state. In addition to it, low economy performance and poor health status of the people causes low productivity and high unemployment in Orissa.

However, both Central and State governments have been trying to eradicate poverty and unemployment by several economic reforms and policy initiatives realizing right to work as a fundamental rights of every citizen. Realizing the fundamental rights, the Government of India declared the National Rural Employment Guarantee Programme (NREGP) in October 2005 to provide work and opportunity to rural people in the country. This programme is one of the most creative initiatives of government in the field of social policy. Under the Act, any adult who is willing to do casual labour at the minimum wage is entitled to be employed on local public works within 15 days. The National Rural Employment Guarantee Programme has potential to provide "big push" in India's regions of distress. It is the first tangible commitment to the poor that they can expect to earn a living wage without loss of dignity as a right. The government has a statutory obligation to provide employment to every household, but it unable to do so on providing unemployment allowances. It is true that this will not end either poverty or exploitation, but it is significant nevertheless and could mark the beginning of momentous of the rural poor.

It is a matter of fact that, introducing the programme actualization of employment has been increasing, the real wage rate increased sharply amongst casual labourers in rural Orissa. But the worrisome possible factor is an offset of public employment programmes and declining general prices in wage for rural labourers. Inter-state remittances around 6 per cent also those from abroad, could have possible the emergent configuration of declining poverty, increasing youth unemployment and declared growth at the State level noted that being unemployment as a "principal activity" over as long period was an ill-affordable luxury for rural males in the poor households. Analyzing the NSSO (National Sample Survey Organization) data, earlier study cited that, there is no significant association between incidence of poverty and usual status of unemployment rate and a significant positive relationship in terms of the person's day unemployment.

The United Nations defined young people as the persons between the ages of 15 and 24 years (United Nations, 2003). They constitute about one-fifth of world's population and estimated at almost 1.2 billion by 2006 (United Nations, 2003). This cohort is better educated, healthier and more urbanized than earlier generations. However, young people face many challenges today, particularly the economic and social uncertainty. According to the estimates of International Labour Organization (ILO), the young people between the ages of 15 and 24 comprise around 18 per cent of the world's population while it constitutes around 41 per cent of the unemployed (ILO, 2001). In addition, many young people continue to suffer from poverty, discrimination and inequality, and a large proportion lack access to proper education and health services (United Nations, 2003).

In Indian youth population constitutes about one-fifth of total population and estimated that 195 million in 2001. It is projected that the size of youth population will be about 195 million in 2001 and 240 million by 2011. The growth rate of youth population is faster as compared to any other age group. They are not a homogenous group with wide variation in educational, health and economic well-being. The more challenging is the increasing insecurity in the labour market. The slow growth rate of employment not only aggravates the overall unemployment but also the youth unemployment, particularly in post economic reform period in India. The National Sample Survey (NSS) organization usually collects data on the employment and unemployment in its quinquennial round. The first quinquennial survey on employment and unemployment situation in India was carried out in 27th round 1972-73 based on the recommendation of Dantawala Committee (*Planning Commission, 1970*). As of data, seven quinquennial rounds of employment and unemployment survey (27th round, 32nd round, 38th round, 43rd round, 50th round, 55th round, 60th round) has been completed. The definition and procedure used by the NSS is same in all rounds. The definition of the unemployment not only permits to compare with past data but also as well as the other countries of the world. In all these rounds, the persons are classified into three broad activity statuses namely, (i) working or employed, (ii) unemployed and (iii) not in the labour force.

These information's are collected using *three basic approaches* namely, usual status, current weekly status and current daily status:

(i) *Usual Status (US):* The reference period is 365 days preceding the date of survey.

(ii) *Current Weekly Status (CWS):* The reference period is 7 days preceding the date of survey.

(iii) *Current Daily status (CDS):* The reference is each day refers to the each day of seven days preceding the date of survey.

India accounts for a major chunk of Asia's unemployed. By 2001, there were 212 million young people in India, but only 23.6 per cent could be absorbed in the labour force. Simultaneously, there has been a marked decrease in the number of jobs from the organized sector (less than 10 per cent). As a result, the emphasis of job creation has shifted to the informal sector. As far as Orissa is concerned, growing educated unemployed youth is one of the burning issues in the State. According to 2001 census, 38.79 per cent of total population, which accounts 142.76 lakh, are total workers in Orissa. Out of the total number of workers, main workers account for 67.2 per cent. The main workers comprise of agricultural labourers (21.9 per cent), cultivators (35.8%), household industries workers (4.2 per cent) and other workers (38.1 per cent). When we calculate the unemployment figure in term of male and female population, the proportion of working population is to be kept in view which accounts currently 52.5 per cent of male population and 24.7 per cent of female population.

The total unemployment at the beginning of 2004-2005 was 9.97 lakhs. During the year, the additional labour force was 1.87 lakh while the employment generation was 1.94 lakh. So the unemployment expected by the end of the 2004-2005 will be of the order of 9.90 lakh. But the government has decided to set a target of providing employment opportunity to 3.19 lakh youths in the current fiscal. As per the Live Register (LR) maintained by employment exchanges in the State, there are 6.16 lakh applications from individuals categorized as 'educated'. Only 2,239 were placed in jobs in 2002-03. This is only the tip of the iceberg because not all job-seekers register with these exchanges. It is only in the case of the educated unemployed who make the effort to get themselves registered at employment exchanges that a reliable figure of unemployment can be reached. What about school or college dropouts who have never heard of employment exchanges or who are not eligible for any government job. In order to tackle the problem of unemployment, the Orissa Government attempted to address this problem in its Tenth Plan (2002-07) through self-employment schemes for around one crore people living below the poverty line. However, in 2002-03, only 1.33 lakh were employed on daily wages. In 2003-04, this number rose slightly to 1.68 lakh and expected employment generation during 2004-05 is about 1.94 lakh population (Mahapatra, 2005).

OBJECTIVES

The broad objective is to understand the levels and differentials in unemployment among youth in Orissa.

The specific objectives are:

- To examine the degree of difference of level of unemployment among youth and broad age groups in rural Orissa.
- To understand the differentiation of unemployment among youth in their socio-economic and demographic characteristics.
- An appraisal of NREGP in the context of youth unemployment in rural Orissa.

DATA AND METHODS

The 60th round of NSS Data (Schedule 10) is used for the analysis. The schedule 10 is given in 11 Blocks and six levels. Blocks 0, 1 and 2 are used to record identification of sample households and particulars of field operations. Block 3 is for recording the household characteristics along with information on Monthly Per capita Consumption Expenditure (MPCE). Block 4 is for recording the demographic information and unemployment by usual principal status for all members in the households. These blocks are used in the analysis. The analysis is carried out in STATA-10 software. The unemployed as defined in the principal usual status is used. The variables used in the analysis are age, sex, education, economic condition, caste, religion and MPCE. The following computation has been made youth unemployment rate. The bivariate and multivariate techniques are employed to carry out the analysis to examine the statistical significance differentials in unemployment by different background and predicted variable.

DISCUSSION

It is estimated that about one-fifth (18%) of the population are youth in the State. The trend is expected that it will continue up to 2011. It also estimated, one-third (32%) of the working population are youths in Orissa as well as in the country. Hence, it is a matter of grave concern to diversify these resources to productivity purpose rather than to turn down their fate as unemployment, hunger, social exclusion and poverty as well as chronic poverty.

The analysis is presented in different parts. In part one discussed the unemployment level by age and sex of youth. In the second two, it elucidates the differentials in unemployment by social groups such as caste and religion categories of youth. Third, it has been estimated the unemployment rate by the educational and marital status of youth population in rural Orissa. Fifth, it represents the unemployment rate by economic categories of youth in rural Orissa. Finally the multivariate analysis is carried out to test the statistical significance in unemployment among rural youth by the socio-economic and demographic characteristics.

Table 10.1: Differential of Unemployment among Youth and Broad Age group by Sex in Rural Orissa in 2004

Age Groups	*Total*	*Male*	*Female*
15-19	18.88	18.89	18.88
20-24	14.49	12.87	20.69
15-24	16.7	15.7	19.7
25-29	7.15	7.97	4.3
30-34	2.23	2.13	2.61
35-39	0.04	0.05	0
40-44	0	0	0
45-49	0.07	0.09	0
50-54	0.37	0.49	0
55+	0	0	0

The Table 10.1 shows the differentials in level of unemployment among youth and broad age group by sex in rural areas. The result reveals that in rural Orissa one in every sixth (17%) of youth is unemployed during the period of 2004. It is highest in the age group 15-19 (18.88 per cent) followed by 14.49 per cent in the age group 20-24. The unemployment among youth (15-24 years) is estimated 16.65%. It is observed that the unemployment rate is higher among the females (20.69) than males (12.87 per cent) in the age group of 20-24 years. It also shows the equal per cent (19%) of youth are unemployed in the age group 15-19. Further the result of the study shows the unemployment among youth (15-24) is higher among females (19.70 %) as compared to males (15.73). It may be due to increase of female education which results higher female youth unemployment and also increase of higher age at marriage which increases their number of days in the labour force.

Table 10.2: Unemployment among Youth in Rural Orissa by Social Groups in 2004

Social Groups	*Total*	*Male*	*Female*
Caste			
ST	9.88	15.35	0.06
SC	13.97	14.02	13.74
OBCs	18.11	15.11	30.3
General	32.42	21.1	93.63
Religion			
Hindu	17.23	16.07	21.26
Muslim	26.73	26.73	0
Christian	0.28	0.52	0
Others	0	0	0
Total	**16.65**	**15.73**	**19.7**

The differentials in unemployment by social groups, such as caste and religion are given in Table 10.2. It is found that the unemployment rate is 9.88 per cent among scheduled tribes (ST), 13.97 per cent among scheduled caste (SC), 18.11 per cent among other backward classes (OBCs) and 32.42 per cent among other caste groups. By sex wise differential result shows majority of female are unemployed as compared to male irrespective of their caste and also it is observed highest in the general caste (94% female as compared to 21% male). The reason may be in general category females are more conservative and cultural bound, also this groups are belongs to affluent families in the state. Similarly, differentials in unemployment among religious groups are 17.23 per cent Hindus, 26.73 per cent Muslims, and 0.28 per cent Christian. It is evidenced that unemployment rate is highest among the Muslims followed by Hindu. By analyzing religion wise sex differential of unemployment rate among youth, it was found 21.26 per cent of Hindu females are unemployed in comparison to 16% male. There is no evidence of unemployment among youth females in other religious groups except Hindus in rural Orissa.

Table 10.3: Unemployment among Youth in Rural Orissa by Educational and Marital Status in 2004

Social Categories	*Total*	*Male*	*Female*
General Education			
Below primary	3.32	0.8	6.72
Primary	17.71	17.28	19.99
Middle	24.62	19.49	58.16
Secondary	37.36	35.5	45.85
Higher secondary	100	100	.0.0
Graduate and above	50.81	34.63	82.68
Marital Status			
Never married	19.42	17.69	26.07
Ever Married	2.93	3.66	1.62
Total	**16.65**	**15.73**	**19.7**

Youth unemployment by educational level observed from Table 10.3. It is observed that increased educational level is increasing the unemployment rate among youth in rural Orissa except the higher secondary education group where (100 per cent) of the youths are unemployed. The trend of unemployment is increasing over the period in the rural Orissa. This is may be because of educational level increase which raise their aspiration for the better jobs and they are not getting the suitable job as per their educational level. In other hand the higher unemployment rate in the rural area is also due to lack of technical education and is being opted very less to them and not able to avail the facility like technical educational institute facility in the locality. Many researchers have set up the possible explanations for positive association between unemployment and the level of education. It may be that the young people with some education do not want to engage in low productivity, low income work in informal sectors. They want non-manual work, preferably in the organized sector. It is fact that they have some education means that their families have some capacity to support them (Ghose, 1999). Similarly an observation has been made by education wise sex differential, i.e. the rate of unemployment increases by increased educational status of youths and it is more among females compared to the males.

The unemployment status of youths by marital status is observed that those who are married among them the unemployment level is very low (2.93%) as compared to the never married (19.42%). It may be fact that ever married youths are more responsible because of their family burden and children than never married youths. Therefore, the ever married youths engaged more in work which results the lower level of unemployment.

Table 10.4: Differentials in Unemployment among Youths by Economic Status in Rural Orissa

Economic Categories	*Total*	*Male*	*Female*
MPCE (Monthly Per capita Consumption Exp.)			
Poorest quintile	12.88	14.35	8.77
Sec. poorest quintile	18.56	15.3	35.09
Middle quintile	31.6	28.44	53.31
Second Richest quintile	13.23	7.26	31.38
Richest quintile	36.73	6.7	90.4
Household Type			
Self-employed in non-agriculture/Self-employed	14.32	9.76	29.34
Agricultural labour/ regular wage/salary earning	10.88	14.26	2.25
Other labour/casual labour	7.59	7.61	7.48
Self employed in agriculture	22.4	21.43	26.09
Others	39.14	26.19	90.44
Total	**16.65**	**15.73**	**19.7**

The level of unemployment among youth by economic status is a critical indicator in understanding the economic viability of the nation that is shown in Table 10.4. To understand the economic status of the population NSS provides the two information one is MPCE (Monthly Per capita Consumption Expenditure) and other is household type. But former one has greater potential to understand the economic status of the population in comparison to later. It is a proxy of income of the household. Therefore, in the present study examines the level of unemployment by dividing MPCE into five quintiles, reflecting from the poorest to the richest population. The differentials of unemployment by MPCE shows that 12.88 per cent poorest quintile, 18.56 per cent second poorest quintile, 31.6 per cent middle quintile, 13.23 per cent second richest quintile and 36.73 per cent of youths among richest quintile are unemployed in rural Orissa. It reveals that unemployment rate increases among youth as economic status increases in the state. It may be pointed out that the youths belonging to affluent families do not want to be in workforce at early stage of the life. Similar, the pattern has been observed among females while analyzing the sex differential of unemployment. Also it was found by analyzing the household type information in rural Orissa. About two-fifth (39%) of youths are in job or employment in the other type of household followed by 22% self employed in agriculture, 14% employed in non agriculture and 10% are agriculture labourers.

Table 10.5: Result from the Multivariate Analysis of Unemployment among Youth in Rural Orissa

Name of Variables	*Odds Ratio*
1	2
Sex: Male®	1
Female	2.56*
Youth: 15-19 ®	1
20-24	0.71
Marital Status: Never Married) ®	1
Ever married	0.23**
Self-employed in non-agriculture/Self-employed®	1

(Contd...)

1	2
Agricultural labourer/regular wage/salary earning	1.24
Other labourer/casual labourer	0.87
Self employed in agriculture	1.98**
Others	3.48**
Caste: ST®	1
SC	0.83
OBC	0.96
General	1.69
Poorest quintile®	1
Second poorest quintile	1.08
Middle quintile	1.44
Second Richest quintile	0.5
Richest quintile	0.85
Religion: Hindu)	1
Muslim	0.86
Christian	0.02
General education	
Below Primary®	1
Primary	5.77*
Above Primary	10.9*

Note: Dependent variable is unemployment among youth.

®: Reference Category, *p<0.01, **P<0.05.

For the regression analysis the place of residence is excluded because the study has been taken only the rural samples focusing on the rural unemployment with regard to the NREGP. The results of the logistic regression by the background variables on youth unemployment are presented in Table 10.5. To understand the statistical significance differentials in unemployment, a logistic regression is employed. The dependent variable is employment status of youth which has been coded with '1' and '0' for unemployment and employment respectively. The dependent variables are sex, place of residence, age group (15-24), marital status educational level, MPCE, caste and religion.

The odds ratio of predicted variables is shown in Table 10.5. It may be seen that the odds of being unemployed for females is 2.56 as compared to the males and it is statistically significant. It is observed that in rural Orissa female youths are more than twice likely to be unemployed as compared to males. Similarly the other independent variables like; sex, marital status, household type, and education status of youths shows a significant relationship with the unemployment rate. But the variable such as caste, religion, and MPCE does not show any significant relationship with unemployment.

CONCLUSION

Youths have been recognized as "the most vital section of the community". Among the several problems, the youths of Orissa have been facing the unemployment problem and life of an unemployed youth is very miserable in all aspects. They are in tremendous pressure from all direction. The reality of employment opportunity is a question of the usefulness of youth's life. The problem lies with the high expectation of the family member and the society, who always nag him without knowing the mental tensions of the youth concerned and the situation around him. The educated youth rushes after tuition for his livelihood forgetting almost all-important aspects of his life and getting less chance to think for the society and for himself too. Obviously the problem of youth unemployment has been recognized as an aspect of national unemployment problem. Educated youths have no stable and durable employment at all. An unemployed youth takes a long time to find work and secures it at an inadequate remuneration. Though, Orissa has plenty of natural resources and a large pool of labor, still lack and unable to invite potential entrepreneurs. At the same time, the state ranks poorly on all socio-economic indicators, with nearly half of its population are living below the poverty line. Education, healthcare, infrastructure development, agriculture and industrial growth are all in poor shape, while infant and maternal mortality rates are high. The government needs to do a whole lot of brainstorm on tools of reduction of unemployment (through job and self-employment) and creation of job (through entrepreneurship). Keeping in mind, government started a scheme like 'Swarnajayanti Gram Swarojgar Yojana (SGSY)', which is sponsored by Government of India and the State with 3:1 ratio funding to establish micro-enterprises and this scheme emphasizes Self-Help Groups (SHGs). In 2001, the government has implemented Sampoorna Grameen Rozgar Yojana (SGRY) on same proportion of resources sharing between Government of India and the State, which focuses on additional wage employment generating food security in rural areas. State Government has set up Employment Mission to work on a missionary zeal for creating employment opportunities in Orissa. The mission is networking now with private colleges and placement agencies to locate more and more job opportunities. The State government has also decided to promote technical education at all levels. To meet the target, Government started training programme for rural youths in BPL families through Prime Minister Rojgar Yojana (PMRY), urban youth is getting job opportunities which is likely to reduce poverty in long term. Keeping in view the growing unemployment problem, recently the government has decided to prepare a five-year perspective plan to provide sector-wise opportunities to the unemployed youths. The decision to this effect was taken at the steering committee meeting of the Employment Mission presided over by development commissioner of state. Besides that the steering committee meeting was decided to accord top priority in providing employment opportunity to the tribal youths in KBK (Kalahandi, Bolangir and Koraput) districts and entrust the information technology and agriculture departments to a key role in creating opportunities for the youths. It was decided that IT (Information Technology) kiosks would be set up on vacant government land in urban areas while the farm equipment would be made available at a subsidized rate to help rural youths. The committee is also decided to cultivate jatropha that can be used as bio-fuel, in these areas for which the Orissa Renewable Energy Development Agency (OREDA) would formulate a specific programme. The committee decided to request the banks to dispose of all pending applications with them under the Prime Minister's Rojgar Yojana (PMRY).

The NREGA is the first tangible commitment to the poor that they can expect to earn a living wage, without loss of dignity, and this as a right. The government has a statutory obligation to provide employment to every household, or it unable to do so, to provide an unemployment allowances. It is true that this will not end either poverty or exploitation, but it is significant nevertheless, and could mark the beginning of momentous enlarge in the lives of the rural poor. Thus according to several press reports, Orissa is the first state to place the name, age, job card numbers and other details of each job card holder on the net, and enable access to online records of muster rolls, works undertaken, with costs and bill numbers, this is a clear indication of transparent Management Information System (MIS). Orissa Rural Employment Guarantee Scheme (OREGS), the collector came up with some good suggestions such as the project complication actual should be written on backside of boards that have been put.

Finding of the Comptroller and Auditor General of India (CAG) audit report on NREGA shows, there is a complication if people are paid by piece rate rather than day-wage rate in terms of transparency, since on job card and muster rolls, days worked are only being entered and payments made. The objective of 100 days of employment was not achieved in any state. That apparently shows the audit report of CAG's findings. The highlighting of the report's find-ing reveals that only 3.2 per cent of registered households in the country have been provided work for 100 days (the minimum number of days of work to be provided under the Act). However, some states of India like to compared per district person day of employment and comparatively high in MP (1.6 Lakh households, 68 days), Orissa (0.7 Lakh household, 57 days), Chhattisgarh (1.7 Lakh household, 54 days), and Rajasthan (2 Lakh household,83 days). In West Bengal and Tamil Nadu although 3 Lakh & 1.2 Lakh household, they could do so only for 14 and 26 days, respectively (GOI, 2007).

However, despite the back drop of the NREGP, it is the holistic approach and also has greater potential of reducing the unemployment rate in general and youth unemployment rate in particular. In this association the study suggests that there should be more attention required in following avenue in rural Orissa then it would be generate demographic dividend rather than the anarchy (Chandrasekhar, *et al.*, 2006). The avenues are better educated group, female, never married, general caste and richest income quintile in the rural areas. In addition to the NREGP government has put small scale industries in the rural mass then somehow it can be expected that the unemployment rate especially among youths can be reduced. Another matter of concern is increasing the unemployment level by increasing education level of the person. So the increasing trend of unemployment rate among educated mass can be proscribed, if they broaden their horizon towards technical and self-reliance education rather than general education.

REFERENCES

Chandrasekhar, C.P. Ghosh, J. and Roychowdhury, A. (2006): "The Demographic Divend'and Young India's Economic Future", *Economic and Political Weekly* (Special Article), December.

Ghose, Ajit K., (1999): "Current Issues of Employment Policy in India", *Economic and Political Weekly*, September 4.

Government of India (2007),"*Performance Audit Report of NREGA Programme*" Comptroller and Audit General of India, Government of India, New Delhi.

(2001), "Census 2001, Registrar General of India", New Delhi.

Higgins, N.O. (2001): *Youth Unemployment and Employment Policy: A Global Perspectives,* ILO, Geneva.

ILO)2001): *Key Indicators of the Labour Market 2000-2001.*

Mahapatra, D. P. (2005): *Youth Unemployment: A Serious Concern of Orissa,* Ezine Articles, November, 25.

Makeham, P. (1980): *Youth Unemployment*, Department of Employment Research Paper, Herajesty's Stationary Office, London.

NSSO (2004), *Employment and Unemployment Situation In India,* NSS Report No. 506 (60/10/1).

NSSO (2004-05), *Employment and Unemployment Situation in India,* Various Round NSS Report, Planning Commission, Government of India.

Planning Commission (1970): *Report of the Committee of Experts of on Unemployment Estimates,* Government of India, New Delhi.

Pradhan, P. and Das, V.(2007): Illusions of Change, *Economic and Political Weekly*, August 11.

Visaria, P. (1998): *Unemployment among Youth in India, Level, Nature and Policy Implications*, ILO, Employment and Training Papers, 36, Institute of Economic Growth, New Delhi.

United Nations, (2003), *World Youth Report 2003*", United Nations, Publication Division Geneva.

11

Devastated Health Sector in Orissa
An Analysis

Dr. Sudhansu Sekhar Nayak
Mr. Rajib Lochan Panigrahy

INTRODUCTION

As a state of welfare India, Orissa State is under obligation to provide economical and efficient health services to its citizen. Although the health care system in the state has improved remarkably over the years, communicable and nutrition related diseases continue to be a major problem mostly in the tribal and backward regions as well as in the remote rural areas. Steps have been taken to bring adequate improvement in the health care system of the State especially in the rural and tribal areas and backward regions.

The main objectives of health sector programmes are as follows:

- To provide adequate qualitative preventive and curative health care services to the people.
- To reduce maternal and infant mortality rate and to improve maternal and child health.

- To ensure health care services to all, particularly to disadvantaged groups like Scheduled Tribes, Scheduled Castes, backward classes and women.
- To provide affordable quality health care through allopathic, homeopathic and ayurvedic systems of medicine.
- To impart training to doctors, nurses and other paramedical staff to upgrade their skill and knowledge.
- To ensure greater access to primary health care by providing medical institutions as close to the people as possible or through mobile health units, particularly in the under-served 3rd backward districts.
- To improve hospital services at primary, secondary and tertiary levels in terms of infrastructure, drugs and personnel.
- To eliminate diseases like polio and leprosy from the State and prevent and control other communicable diseases.
- To improve health care facilities in the KBK districts of the State in particular.

The State is committed to achieve the following monitorable targets set for Eleventh Plan:

- Reduce Infant Mortality Rate (IMR) to 37 Maternal Mortality Rate (MMR) to 1.19 per 1000 live birth and to reduce Fertility Rate to 2.1.
- Provide clean drinking water for all by 2009 and ensure that there are no slip backs by the end of Eleventh Plan.
- Reduce malnutrition among children in the age group 0-3 to half its present level and reduce anemia among women and girls by 50% by the end of Eleventh Plan.

As per the Registrar General of India sources, the estimated birth rate in Orissa lies much below the all India level as well as other bigger States. In 2007, the estimated birth rate in Orissa was 21.5 as against 23.1 at all India level. The birth rate in rural and urban Orissa stood at 22.4 and 16.1 respectively while at all India level it was 24.7 and 18.6 respectively. Highest birth rate has been recorded in Uttar Pradesh (29.5) followed by Bihar (29.4), Madhya Pradesh (28.5) and Rajasthan (27.9). Lowest birth rate was recorded in Kerala (14.7). As per the estimation of Central Bureau of Health Intelligence, Ministry of H. & F.W., GDI, the CBR (Crude Birth Rate) in Orissa will be reduced to 18.9 for thousand live birth during 2006-10 as against 21.3 at all India level.

The death rate in Orissa, during 2007 was highest among all the States and UTs, i.e., 9.2 as against 7.4 at all India level. Orissa occupied highest rank followed by Madhya Pradesh (8.7), Assam (8.6) and Uttar Pradesh (8.5). As per the estimation of CBHI, the CDR (Crude Death Rate) in Orissa will be reduced to 8.9 during 2006-10.

Though the *Infant Mortality Rate* (IMR), in Orissa has declined considerably from 83 in 2003 to 71 per thousand in 2007, it is still highest at all India level. The infant mortality rate in the rural Orissa was 73 while in urban Orissa it was 52. During 2007, the IMR at all India level stood at 55 and in Kerala it has been recorded as 13. The target of 11th Plan is to reduce the IMR to 37 as compared to 28 at all India level.

The high occurrence of IMR in Orissa is mainly due to three factors viz.:

(i) Poor availability of professional attendance at birth

(ii) High percentage of low birth weight babies and

(iii) Lack of professional pre and post-natal care.

About 64% of infant deaths are attributed to neonatal mortality. Premature deliveries results in 38.5% infant deaths. Pneumonia, respiratory infection, tetanus and diarrhea of new born are result in 34.1% infant deaths. Anemia, which is caused due to malnutrition, suffered by both pregnant mothers and infant, explains 8.1% infant death and 19.3% infant deaths occur for other causes. IMR Mission is being operated in the State with an object to expedite fast reduction in IMR. Besides, verbal autopsy has been made mandatory for each infant and child death. Table 11.1 shows the birth rate, death rate and infant mortality rate in Orissa and at all India level since 1981.

The Maternal Mortality Rate (MMR) in India during 2001-03 was 301 per 1,00,000 live births as against 358 in Orissa. It has been targeted to reduce the MMR to 100 at all India level and 1; 19 per thousand live births in Orissa by the end of Eleventh Plan period (2007-12). In order to achieve the goal, emphasis is being given on the following strategies:

- To increase ANC coverage ensuring at least three ANC checkup for 100% of pregnant women.
- To universalize registration of pregnancy or 100% antenatal registration.
- To increase institutional delivery up to 80%
- To increase delivery by trained personnel up to 100%
- To make health awareness on RTI/STI as well as on AIDS.

Life expectancy at birth has increased from 58.6 years for male and 58.7 years for female in 1999-2003 to 60.3 for male and 62.3 for female during 2001-05. As per the report of Technical Group on population projection, the projected level of expectation of life at birth in Orissa will be 64.3 for male and 67.3 for female during 2011-15 as against 67.3 for male 69.6 for female at all India level.

Natural Growth Rate (NGR) of Orissa during 2007 has marginal decreased and stood at 12.4 as against 15.7 at all India level. The nature growth rate in rural Orissa was 12.9 while in urban Orissa, it was 9.1. The corresponding figures for all India stood at 16.8 and *12.7* respectively.

In Orissa, the Decadal Growth Rate (DGR) of population during 1991-2001 was 15.94% as against the all India average of 21.34% as per 2001 Census. Thus the decadal growth rate target fixed for the decade 2001-2011 at the national level has already been realized in the state during the decade 1991*2001. The following initiatives will be continued to check the trend in the coming decade.

1. High use of contraception
   - *(i)* Advocacy on high use of contraception and reduction of birth rate to 33.2 as per 2002 SRS.

(ii) Effective contraceptive coverage by 75% of couples

(iii) Increased use of contraception among couple with less than two children.

(iv) Drop in illegal abortion

2. Use of family welfare methods, like sterilization.

ALLOPATHIC MEDICAL INSTITUTIONS

During the year 1951, medical and health care facilities created by the Government were available to the people through a network of 365 medical institutions with 3,112 hospital beds and 1,083 doctors with a doctor-population ratio of 1 : 13,500. By end of Dec. 2007, the facilities have been increased to 1,704 Government allopathic medical institutions in the State with 14,166 hospital beds and 5095 doctors as follows:

Table11.1: Beds available in Government Hospitals in 2007

SI. No	*Medical Institutions*	*Nos.*	*Beds*
1.	Medical College Hospitals	3	2861
2.	Dist. Headquarters Hospitals	32	3923
3.	Sub-Div. Hospitals	22	985
4.	Other Hospitals	124	2001
5.	CHCs	231	3520
6.	PHCs	114	726
7.	PHCS(New)	1164	150
8.	Mob. Health Units	14	–
9.	Sub-Health Centres	6688	–

Source: Directorate of Health Services, Orissa, Bhubaneswar.

Population served per medical institution being about 23,304 with area served per medical institution being 91 sq km by the end of 2007. The distribution of districts as per the indicator (medical institution per lakh population) reflects that Kandhamal district ranks at the top, i.e., with maximum no of institutions per lakh population followed by Malkangiri (8), Gajapati (6), Rayagada (6), Nayagarh (6), Sambalpur, Sonepur, Nawarangpur, Mayurbhanj, Koraput, Keonjhar, Kalahandi (5-each). The remaining districts have four such institutions per lakh of population.

Bed-population ratio is an important indicator of health-services. There were 14,166 hospital beds available in the State in Government medical institutions (allopathic) by the end of December 2007. During the year 2007, the bed-population ratio in the State was 1:2803. The bed-population ratio in Sambaipur district ranked the top with 1:887 followed by Cuttack 1:1317, Kandhamal 1:1745, Nayagarh 1:1844 and Jajpur district occupied the lowest rank, i.e., one bed for 7895 population.

State Government have taken special steps to provide better health care to rural people belonging to KBK districts. At present, 700 medical institutions are functioning in 118 tribal dominated blocks with 5,705 hospital beds.

AYURVEDIC AND HOMEOPATHIC INSTITUTIONS

State Government have taken steps for health care of the people by providing facilities under Indian System of Medicine and Homoeopathy. Chronic and complicated diseases such as paralysis, arthritis, liver disease, diabetes, asthma & tuberculosis etc. are being successfully treated with affordable cost through ISM & H process. By the end of 2007-08, there were 4829 registered Ayurvedic doctors in the state including 134 doctors registered during 2007-08. Similarly, there were 3685 registered Homeopathic doctors in the state by the end of 2007-08, including 147 homeopathic doctors registered during 2007-08. At present, 5 Ayurvedic Hospitals with 418 beds and 4 Homoeopathic Hospitals with 125 beds are also rendering health services in the State. Besides 619 Ayurvedic, 560 Homoeopathic and 9 Unani Dispensaries are providing health care services in the State. During 2007, about 153.23 lakh patients availed treatment facilities under these hospitals and dispensaries as against 154.74 lakh patients treated in 2006.

Three Government Ayurvedic Colleges and four Homeopathic Colleges have been imparting degree courses and producing 90 Ayurvedic and 100 Homeopathic graduate doctors every year. Post-graduate courses in five Ayurvedic and five Homeopathic disciplines are available in the state. Central assistance of Rs.325 lakhs have been availed to upgrade the status of Gopabandhu Ayurvedic Mahavidyalaya, Puri and Dr. Avirna Chandra Homeopathic Medical College and Hospital, Bhubaneswar as the 'State Model Institute[1]. Government Ayurvedic Pharmacy Colleges at Bolangir and Bhubaneswar have been modernized with the assistance of Government of India.

STATE HEALTH PROGRAMMES / PROJECTS

As per the National Health Policy, a number of Central Plan Schemes and Centrally Sponsored Plan Schemes are being implemented in the State to ensure better health care services at the primary and secondary levels. Besides, some State Plan schemes are also in operation. Some of these are highlighted below.

REVISED NATIONAL TUBERCULOSIS CONTROL PROGRAMME (RNTCP)

The Revised National Tuberculosis Control Programme (RNTCP) with Directly Observed Treatment Short course Strategy (DOTS) was implemented in the State with DANIDA support from 1996 to 2005. Global Funds for AIDS, Tuberculosis and Malaria (GRATM) support through Government of India is available from 2006 to 2010 to implement the said programme in the State. The objective of this programme is to achieve 70% case detection, 90% sputum conversion and 85% cure rate by the end of 2005. At present 104 sub-districts TB units and 545 Microscopy Centres are engaged in providing diagnosis and treatment services under the revised strategy.

Since inception of RNTCP till September 20-08, 2,99,728 patients have been detected and treated under DOTS. As on September 2008, annualized new sputum positive case detection rate was 67% against the national norm of 70%. Sputum conversion rate was 86% against the national norm 90%. The success rate of new smear positive case is 86%. Government of India provides anti T.B. drugs for patients treated free of cost under DOTS.

NATIONAL FILARIA CONTROL PROGRAMME (NFCP)

The National Filarial Control Programme, a Centrally-sponsored Plan scheme on a sharing pattern of 50 : 50 between the Centre and the State, is being implemented through a Filariasis Bureau comprising a research unit at Puri, 15 Filaria Control Units and 15 Filaria clinics in urban areas. The Filaria clinics conduct night blood survey in a confined area of 50,000 populations and undertake treatment to microfilaria carrier as well as to the diseased. 15.23 During the year 2007, 40127 blood slides were examined and 393 persons were clinically found positive by the concerned institutions. 2682 persons having microfilaria/ Filaria decease were treated. The microfilaria (MF) rate which was 1.13 in 2005 has decreased to 0.97 during 2007.

In order to achieve the national goal of eliminating Lymphatic Filariasis from the country by 2015, Mass Drug Administration (MDA) programme is being implemented in 20 districts of Orissa since 2004 with Govt. of India assistance. It has been decided to continue M.D.A. programme for the next five years and to include other districts in this programme.

NATIONAL PROGRAMME FOR CONTROL OF BLINDNESS (NPCB)

National Programme for Control of Blindness (NPCB), a World Bank assisted project, was introduced in the State since 1976, with an aim to reduce the prevalence of blindness from 1.4% to 0.3%. For this purpose, strengthening of Central Mobile Units, District Mobile Units, up gradation of Medical Colleges, training of Ophthalmic Surgeons and District Blindness Control Society (DECS) all over the State have been taken up. The available infrastructure includes 176 Dark Rooms, 28 nos. of 20-beded eye wards, 25 nos. of 10-beded eye wards and one 91-beded Referral Eye Hospital at S.C.B. Medical College Hospital, Cuttack. The Referral Eye Hospital at S.C.B. Medical College Hospital, Cuttack has been upgraded to Regional Institute of Ophthalmology with 30 numbers of vision centres and 56 numbers of O.T.s.

The World Bank assistance was received by the State from 1st April 1994 to 30th June 2002. Now the programme is continuing with 100% Central assistance.

During 2007-08, 95,690 cataract operations were performed as against 1,11,049 operations performed in 2006-07. During 2007-08 highest nos. of cataract operations were performed in Cuttack district (21474) followed by Ganjam district (7744). During 2006-07, the cataract operation rate was 286 per one lakh population in Orissa and ranked 18th position at national level as per survey made by Govt. of India.

Besides, school eye screening programme is also operating in the State. The achievement made under the programme during 2005-06 to 2007-08 is given in Table 11.2.

Table 11.2: Achievement under NPCB in Orissa

(in numbers)

Item	*2005-06*	*2006-07*	*2007-08*
Student screened	31 7897	359382	3,02,128
Students detected with refractive error	17662	18349	14,680
Free spectacles distributed	7965	9202	7355
Health worker trained	3734	–	–
No. of teachers	2222	–	–

Source: Directorate of Health Services, Orissa, Bhubaneswar.

EYE DONATION

Eye donation programme is being conducted in the state through three Government medical colleges and one private organization L.V. Prasad Eye Institute, Patia, Bhubaneswar. During 2007-08, against the target to collect 500 nos. of eyes; 92 eyes have been collected and 62 nos. were utilised.

NATIONAL IODINE DEFICIENCY DISORDER CONTROL PROGRAMME (NIDDCP)

Iodine is an essential Micronutrient with daily requirement of 100-150 micrograms which plays an important role in normal human growth and development. It has been widely recognized that deficiency of iodine not only contributes to goiter but also is an important risk factor for preventable mental retardation. It also affects reproductive functions and impaired child rearing ability. It has been assessed that about 2 billion people are at risk of Iodine Deficiency Disorder (IDD) in the World including 600 million people in South-East Asia region. In India, as many as 73 million people are suffering from IDD.

Hence to prevent IDD, the National Iodine Deficiency Disorders Control Programme (NIDDCP) is being implemented in the State since December, 1989 as a Centrally Sponsored Scheme with a goal to bring down goiter prevalence rate to below 10%. Use of common salt has been banned in the State from 18.10.2001. IDD Survey is being conducted in different districts since 1989. In our State, 15 districts surveyed so far shows endemicity (Goiter Prevalence Rate > 10%) in twelve districts. The districts Sundargarh and Cuttack are under resurvey during 2006-07 and the report has not yet been received. Year-wise IDD survey conducted in different districts are shown in Table 11.3.

Table 11.3: Year-wise IDD survey

Year of survey	*Name of the District*	*IDD prevalency rate*	*Survey conducted by*
1	*2*	*3*	*4*
1987	Sundargarh	33.5	DGHS, New Delhi
1989	Puri	19.34	-do-
1998	Cultack	21.61	-do-
1999	Keonjhar	14.9	-do-
2001	Nuapada	14,4	VSSMC, Burla, SBP
2001	Balasore	0.83	5CB Med. College, Cuttack
1995-99	Baragarh	10.8	RMRC, Bhubaneswar
2002	-do-(Resurvey)	7.66	V SS Med. College, Burla
2003-04	Ganjam	15.79	MKCG M.C., Berhampur

(Contd...)

1	2	3	4
2003-04	Kandhamal	27.79	MKCG M.C., Berhampur
2004	Gajapati	21.15	-do-
2004	Bolangir	8.57	VSS M.C., Burla
2005-06	Sambalpur	10.04	-do-
2006	Koraput	22.39	MKCG M.C., Berhampur
2006	Jagatsinghpur	3.08	SCB Med. College, CTC
2006	Rayagada	19.7	MKCG M.C., Berhampur
2006	Sundargarh (Re survey)	NR	CGS Team DGHS New Delhi

Source: Directorate of Health Services. Orissa, Bhubaneswar.

NATIONAL LEPROSY ELIMINATION PROGRAMME (NLEP)

The National Leprosy Elimination Programme (NLEP) is under implementation in the State since 1982-83. The programme is being supported by WHO, World Bank and international donor agencies such as Lepra India, HOINA and the German Leprosy Relief Association. The objective of the programme is to eliminate leprosy by detecting all the cases and bring them with "Multi Drug Therapy (MDT)". "Elimination of Leprosy" means to bring down the prevalence rate of leprosy to one (1) or below i.e. one case per 10,000 populations. Due to successful implementation of the programme in the State, the prevalence rate of leprosy which was 121.4 per 10,000 population in the year 1982-83 has come down to only 0.80 per 10,000 population by March, 2008 while at national level it has come down from 55 per 10,000 population to 0.78 per 10,000 population. By the end of March, 2008, 23 districts have achieved the elimination goal and the prevalence rate (PR) of the balance seven districts have decreased remarkably to 1-3 per 10,000 populations. The P.R. in Phulbani district is the lowest i.e. 0.29 while it is highest in Sonepur district 2.49. In 247 blocks out of 314 blocks of the State, Leprosy Elimination target has been achieved. Since beginning of this programme 9.78 lakh cases have been cured with MDT and now only 3283 cases of leprosy are on record in the State.

The "diagnosis and treatment" facilities of leprosy cases have been extended to all the peripheral health institutions including sub-centres. Re-constructive surgery facility has also been made available at the Leprosy Home and Hospitals, Cuttack, MKCG Medical College, Berhampur, V.S.S. Medical College, Burla and the Mission Hospital, Bargarh.

NATIONAL VECTOR BORNE DISEASE CONTROL PROGRAMME (NVBDCP)

Orissa has a high incidence of malaria with 20% of the total affected persons and about 40% of the death recorded in the country. The National , Anti-Malaria Programme (NAMP) renamed as National Vector Borne Disease Control Programme (NVBDCP) is being implemented in the State since 1953. During 2007, 49.45 lakh blood slides were examined of which about 3.71 lakh were found positive. The percentage of positive falciparum is recorded as 86.89 per cent.

This problem is more alarming in tribal areas (158 blocks) which contribute 70% cases of the State. The State Government have targeted to bring down malaria death to 50% of the current level by 2010. The Enhanced Malaria Control Project (EMCP), assisted by World Bank, is in operation in hyper endemic areas since 1997-98 covering 240 blocks spread over 26 districts. This programme will be extended to all the 30 districts during the current fiscal year.

NATIONAL RURAL HEALTH MISSION

The National Rural Health Mission (NRHM) a flagship endeavour was launched in the state in June, 2005. It is one of the largest health programmes in the State in the past 54 years and aims at improving the access to and availability of quality health services to the under privileged like the women and children, especially the rural poor.

The important objectives of NRHM are:

- Reduction of child and maternal mortality.
- Prevention and control of communicable/non-communicable diseases, including locally endemic diseases.

- Revitalization of local health tradition and mainstream Ayurvedic Unani Naturopathy, Siddha and Homeopathy (AYUSH).
- Population stabilization, gender and demographic balance.
- Access to integrated comprehensive primary health care.

ACCREDITED SOCIAL HEALTH ACTIVIST (ASHA)

An 'ASHA' is a volunteer who works as an interface between the community and the public health system and is accountable to the Panchayat. An ASHA has been deployed in every village of population 1000 and above to provide basic health services to rural population. They have been trained to discharge their duties and responsibilities with the help of local Mahila Swasthya Sangha, Youth Club, ANM etc. Besides, they have also been provided with a medicine kit for treatment of cold, cough, first aid and have got the knowledge of their uses. At present, 34,324 numbers of ASHAs have been deployed.

With an aim to mainstreaming the conventional method of treatment, 'AYUSH' doctors have been engaged in block PHC/CMC. They are treating the OPD patients and distributing medicines. At present 250 AYUSH doctors have been engaged in the state and 54 more are in selection process.

In order to ensure better management of health services, *Rogi Kalyan Samiti* have been constituted in all the District Headquarter Hospitals, Sub-Divisional Hospitals, Block CHC/PHC/PHC (New). The main aim of this Samity is to provide better health services through people's participation, improving the standard of health institutions, peace keeping and necessary clearing arrangements.

VILLAGE HEALTH AND SANITATION COMMITTEES

The main responsibilities of this committee is to aware the rural people regarding maternal and child health services, family welfare services, etc. Besides, people are being made aware on various programmes viz. Malaria, Leprosy, TB, Blindness control etc. 'Janani Surakhya Yojana' is being implemented in the state from August, 2006 with an objective to reduce overall maternal mortality ratio, infant mortality rate, and to increase institutional delivery.

REPRODUCTIVE AND CHILD HEALTH (RCH) PROGRAMME

The Reproductive and Child Health (RCH), a 100% centrally assisted programme, is being implemented in the State. The Phase-I of this programme was carried out for a period of 5 years from 1997-98 to 2002-03. The total cost of the programme was Rs.119.75 crore including Rs.15.00 crore for Kalahandi sub-project.

The reproductive and child health programme, Ph-ll is an ongoing programme and major component of NRHM, with the objective of improving the Reproductive health of men, women and children. The main objective of the programme is to reduce the maternal, child mortality and morbidity. A programme management unit has been set up in the state and the district level to provide support for implementation of NRHM activities in the state.

PANCHA BYADHI CHIKITSA

Five major diseases namely malaria, leprosy, diarrhea, acute respiratory infections and scabies called *"Panchavyadhi"* contribute about 70% of the patient load in the primary health institutions and affect a large number of poor people. Orissa accounts for about one third of malaria death 'in India. The State Government launched the Panchavyadhi scheme in July, 2001 to provide free treatment including free medicines for the above five diseases. The scheme is very beneficial to all the poorer sections. Government is contemplating to extend the scope of this Panchavyadhi scheme to other common diseases.

NATIONAL AIDS CONTROL PROGRAMME

National AIDS control Programme is being implemented through National AIDS Control Organisation (NACO), New Delhi under M.H. & F.W., Government of India with support of World Bank and DFID funds. State AIDS Control Societies, an autonomous organization, have been formed in each State for smooth implementation of the programme.

National AIDS Control Programme, Ph-l (1992-1999) was implemented in the State under Director, Health Services. NACP

- Ph - II programme was implemented in the State through Orissa State Health & Family Welfare Society till 13.07.2004 and there after by Orissa State AIDS Control Society (OSACS) with an objective to reduce the spread of HIV infection in the State and to detect, reduce and control the spread of HIV infection.

National AIDS Control Programme (NACP) Ph-III (2007-12) has been launched from 6th July, 2007. The overall goal of NACP, Ph-lll is to halt and reverse the epidemic in India over the next 5 years by integrating programmes for prevention, care, support and treatment. This will be achieved through a four pronged strategy:

1. Prevention of new infections in high risk groups and general population through:
   - Saturation coverage of high risk groups with TIs.
   - Scaled up interventions in the general populations.
2. Providing greater care, support and treatment to a large number of PLHAs.
3. Strengthening the infrastructure systems and human resources in prevention care, support and treatment programmes at the district, state and national level.
4. Strengthening the nationwide strategic information management system.

HIV/AIDS SCENARIO

The scenario is as follows:

- Orissa is low prevalent state but highly vulnerable to HIV/AIDS.
- AIDS was first identified in the united state of America in 1981.
- First care of AIDS in India was identified in 1986 in Chennai and in Orissa it was identified in 1993 in Nayagarh district.
- Till October, 2008, 11156 nos were living with HIV/AIDS as detailed below:

Particulars			No. of cases as on Oct. 2008
1.	Counselled	:	522233
2.	Screened	:	219981
3.	HIV + VE		
	(i) Total	:	11156
	(ii) Male	:	7115 (63.78%)
	(iii) Female	:	4041 (36.22%)
4.	AIDS cases	:	1032
5.	Death due to AIDS	:	815
6.	Percentage of HIV + ve Person in the age group 25-39 (up to Dec. 07)	:	64.7
7.	Percentage of Sexual Transmission cases, Total cases (up to Sept, 08)	:	82.9

- Ganjam district has been recorded as the highest AIDS affected district with 370 cases followed by Cuttack district 111 numbers. Both the districts constitute 46.6% of the total AIDS cases as on 31st October 2008.
- By the end of October, 2008 total 850 death due to AIDS has been recorded out of which 300 cases has been recorded in Ganjam district followed by Kendrapara (68) and Puri (63).

ACTIVITIES UNDERTAKEN BY OSACS

The following activities have been taken:

1. OSACS has established 129 Integrated Counselling and Testing Centers (ICTC) at all District Headquarters Hospitals and some of the Sub-Divisional Hospitals for counselling and blood testing of persons to know their HIV Status free of cost.
2. To provide services to High Risk Groups i.e. Female Sex Workers (FSW), Inject Drug Users (IDU), Men having Sex with Men (MSM) and Migrant Labourers, 23 Targeted Intervention projects are functioning covering 22 districts of the State, where the above targeted populations are being provided services for practicing safe behaviors, availing STI/RTI treatment, behaviour change activities, Condom

Promotion Activities, providing enabling environment and empowering the people living with HIV/AIDS (PLHA) through community mobilization.

3. To provide support to People Living with HIV/AIDS the State Government have included the PLHAs under Madhubabu Pension Yojana. They are provided with Rs. 200 pension per month. The money is sent to their address by post, ensuring non-disclosure of identify. Till October 2008, 9214 PLHAs have been included in the scheme. This is one of the leading initiatives taken by any state in the country.

4. While going for CD4 testing and ART treatment, PLHAs are being reimbursed minimum transportation cost at district branches of Indian Red Cross Society in the State. This is also, one of the leading initiatives taken by any state in the country.

5. Extensive Village Level HIV/AIDS awareness campaign has been completed in 17 districts, where information on HIV/AIDS have been disseminated through street plays, folk media in 14,187 villages of 3,749 GPs and 67 nos. of ULBs covering 188 Blocks. This year Extensive Integrated Village Level Awareness Campaigns will be implemented in 11 most prevalent districts of the State.

6. Four Community Care Centers (CCC) at Koraput, Berhampur, Cuttagk and Bhubaneswar have been set up for providing low cost community care to the people living with HIV/AIDS in the state. Facilities of treatment and care are also available to 10 nos. of PLHAs for a period of 5-15 days in these centers.

7. Anti-Retro Viral Therapy (ART) medicine is being provided free of cost to PLHAs to fead a healthy life which is generally preceded by CD4 testing and counseling. Three ART centers have been set up in three Government medical colleges to provide ART treatment.

8. Two CD4 blood testing centres have been setup at MKCG Medical College, Berhampur and VSS Medical College, Burla for HIV + ve persons to know the CD4 count status free of cost.

9. Capacity building and counselling facilities have been provided to the PLHAs in three Drop-in-Centers established by OSACS at Cuttack, Bhubaneswar and Berhampur. Two more Drop-in-Centers will be set up in Bolangir and Ganjam districts during the current year.
10. Four Blood Component Separation Units (BCSU) have been established at the blood banks of Capital Hospital, Bhubaneswar VSS Medical College, Burla, MKCG Medical College, Berhampur and DHH, Angul.
11. Out of the 77 licences Blood Banks, OSACS provides financial grants to 53 blood banks and HIV and HCV kits to 54 blood banks to provide safe blood and blood products to people living with HIV/AIDS.
12. For the first time in the State, Female Condoms for social marketing of condoms have been launched in March, 2007 at Malisahi, Bhubaneswar, "the CSW site for HIV/AIDS prevention programme", which is a measure step forward for empowering women to play effective role in HIV presentation in the state.

MOU WITH INDIAN OIL CORPORATION

A Memorandum Of Understanding (MOU) have been signed between OSACS and Indian Oil Corporation Ltd. (IOCL) in association with UNICEF, Orissa to create awareness on HIV and AIDS among the most vulnerable group of people within the State of Orissa, mostly the truckers. The MOU will cover IEC activities in 500 retain outlets (petrol pumps) of IOCL where IOCL will provide its infrastructure, manpower and distribution mechanism and OSACS will provide supports in terms of replication of IEC materials, design and develop new materials targeting HRGs, make available condom vending machines for Highway outlets etc., whereas UNICEF, Orissa will assist in better coordination between the partners and required technical support in terms of software development and monitoring and evaluation.

SCHOOL AIDS EDUCATION PROGRAMME (SAEP)

During 2005-06, OSACS had covered 2390 nos. of schools in ten districts under school AIDS Education programme. During 2006-07, as per the decision of National Aids Control Organization, New Delhi, the programme has been undertaken by department of School and Mass Education of the State with a view to covering all the government secondary and higher secondary schools, which includes formation of red ribbon clubs in the educational institutions. During 2007-08, NACO has approved to conduct the AEP in 1824 schools indicating that, the refresher Training Programme, Monitoring and Evaluation and Red Ribbon Club Activities are to be conducted.

MEDICAL EDUCATION AND TRAINING

There are three medical colleges with hospital facilities in the State. These colleges offer courses leading to MBBS, BDS degrees, Post-graduate and Post-doctoral courses in about 35 different disciplines. Besides, three medical colleges have also started functioning since 2006-07. There is one nursing college, one dental college, one pharmacy college, three Ayurvedic colleges and four homoeopathic colleges under Government sector in the State. The State Institute of Health and Family Welfare is functioning as the apex in service training institute with three functional units at the state level and cells/wings at district/block levels for imparting training support under various programmes. During 2004-05, one Nursing college and three Nursing schools have come up in private sector. Super specialized treatment is being provided in all the three Medical College Hospitals through ultra modern diagnostic and therapeutic equipments.

The S.C.B. Medical College Hospital has 1208 beds and is equipped with all type of modern instruments viz. heart-lung machine, equipment for open heart surgery, C.T. scan etc.

MKCG Medical College and Hospital, Berhampur and V.S.S. Medical College and Hospital, Burla are also well equipped with 881 and 772 hospital beds respectively.

For better treatment of heart patients and patients undergoing various surgical operation, it has been decided to establish two ICU, one at VSS medical college, Burla and other at MKCG medical college, Berhampur. It has been proposed to spent Rs.60.00 crore during 11th Five-year Plan period.

An out lay of Rs.5.00 crore has been provided in the Annual Plan 2008-09 for construction of new 50 PHCs @ Rs.10.00 lakh each. Besides, an amount of Rs.16,82 crore has also been provided for construction of essential building for the Government medical colleges and Capital Hospitals.

INTRODUCTION OF INFANT MORTALITY REDUCTION MISSION

The Infant Mortality Rate (IMR) is a key indicator of the general health status of a population. As per SRS report the IMR in Orissa was 97 per thousand live births during 1999. In order to reduce the IMR from 97 to 50 per thousand live births by 2010, Infant Mortality Reduction Mission was launched in the State on 15th August, 2001. The key activities include:

- Immunization in outreach inaccessible areas.
- Chemoprophylaxis against malaria during pregnancy.
- Institutional delivery to the pregnant women free of cost.
- Free treatment service for slum dwellers.
- Reimbursement of transport cost for institutional delivery.

Infant mortality rate has reduced from 97 per thousand live births in 1999 to 71 by the end of 2007.

INTEGRATED POPULATION AND DEVELOPMENT (IPD) PROJECT

Integrated Population and Development (IPD) Project is being implemented in the 4 districts of the State, namely Rayagada, Malkangiri, Nawarangpur and Koraput with assistance from United Nation's Fund for Population Activities (UNFPA). This project has all the components of the RCH programme and it aims at reducing maternal mortality and infant mortality as well as achieving population control and stabilization of population through education. The project includes components such as provision of new infrastructure (building for Sub-Centres), maintenance of old building, up-grading the skill of health personnel including doctors, female health workers, sub-technician etc. through training, provision of facilities in girls hostels and interest-free moped advance to ANMs.

REGIONAL SPINAL INJURY CENTRE (RSIC)

The RSIC is being functioning in the State since February 2001 with Government of India assistance for a period of 5 years. The center is functioning inside SCB medical college campus with 30 beds for the paralysis patients. Since inception, till date more than one lakh patients have been treated in this centre. The centre also provides supporting appliances to the patients prepared in the institution. Various training and awareness programmes are also being organized for the periphery doctors, medical and Para-medical staff as well as the NGOs. As per the commitment given to government of India, the state government proposes to have an outlay of Rs.55.00 lakh for 2008-09 for running of the centre out of the total provision Rs.3.00 crore for the Eleventh Five Year Plan.

DIAGNOSTIC CENTRES

The Eleventh Finance Commission have recommended for establishment of 8 diagnostic centres in the state during 2000-01 to 2003-04 with a cost of Rs. 3.00 crore per centre. Out of this Rs. 3.00 crore, Rs. 2.50 crore is earmarked for purchase of equipments and Rs. 0.50 crore towards construction of diagnostic centre building. Regional Diagnostic Centres started functioning at the three medical colleges and hospitals of the state and district head quarter's hospital at Koraput, Sundergarh, Mayurbhanj and Bhawanipatna and Capital Hospital, Bhubaneswar, have been duly equipped with diagnostic equipments.

RLTAP PROGRAMME IN KBK DISTRICT

The number of green card holders in the State as on 31st March, 2005 are functioning in 80 blocks of 8 KBK districts. Out of these 90 MHU, 39 are operational with Government vehicles while the remaining 51 Mobile Health Units (MHU) is operating with hired vehicles. Each MHU works with one Medical Officer, one Pharmacist, one Female Health worker, a Driver (for institutional van) and one Attendant. The MHU holds health camp in the remote and inaccessible areas for minimum 24 days in a month and supply medicines worth of Rs. 1000 per camp during their visit.

FAMILY WELFARE PROGRAMME

The Family Welfare Programme aims at stabilizing the population in order to accelerate the economic growth and is being implemented as a part of the National Population Control Programme. This has been introduced with full Central assistance covering both population control and maternal and child health services.

Under Family Welfare Programme, the strategy has been to motivate eligible couples to limit family size by adopting various family planning methods such as sterilization, contraception, IUD etc. The new technique for male sterilization, namely 'No Scalpel Vasectomy' (NSV) is being popularized with UNFPA assistance. The programme seeks to promote responsible parenthood with focus on the one child norm.

REFERENCES

Annual Reports, Ministry of Rural Development. 2006-07 & 07-08.

Economic Survey, Government of Orissa, Bhubaneswar, 2007-08 & 2008-09.

Himachalam, D. "Entrepreneurship Development in Small-Scale Sector", *Yojana*, Feb. 16-28, 1990.

Khanka, S.S. *Entrepreneurship Development*, S. Chand & Sons, New Delhi, 2007.

Orissa Review, Department of I & B, Orissa, Bhubaneswar.

Pandian, M. Soundara. "Micro Finance for Rural Entrepreneurs, Issues and Strategies", *Kurukshetra*, Sept. 2000.

Rani. C. and Raju, U.B. *A Trainer's Hand Book for Developing Enterprise Among Women*, Tata McGraw-Hill.

Saibaba, Rudra, *Fundamentals of Entrepreneurship*, Kalyani Publication, New Delhi, 2003.

Souvenir, National Seminar on Rural Entrepreneurship and Sustainable Development in Orissa", KBDAV College, Nirakarpur, Nov. 2007.

Statistical Hand Book, Department of Statisticts & Economics, Orissa, Bhubaneswar.

Swain, Alekh Ch. *Fundamentals of Entrepreneurship*, Himalaya Publishing House, New Delhi, 2007.

Uddin, Sami. *Entrepreneurship Development in India*, Mittal Publications, New Delhi, 1989.

12

Domestic Violence in Indian Society as Reported by NFHS-3

Dr. Aditya Kumar Patra*

Human rights and their preservation form the very basis of the human civilization. But the violation of Human Rights in its extreme form is seen in the form of violence against women. On the one hand the constitution of India guarantees 'equality of rights, freedom, opportunity and protection irrespective of sex, race, caste and creed' and on the other hand 'violence against women' is a burning issue of the present day Indian society. A society where half the population comprises of women can never achieve holistic growth if such type of events occurs very often.

Violence refers to 'force', whether overt or convert used to wrest from a women something that she does not want to give of her own free will and which causes her either physical injury or emotional trauma or both. Violence against women can be categorized as criminal violence (rape, abduction, murder, molestation, etc.), domestic violence (dowry death, wife beating, sexual abuse by kin, maltreatment by elderly women, etc.) and social violence (forcing wife/daughter-in-law to go for female foeticide, eve-teasing, etc.).

Crimes against women have been increasing over the years. The violence/crimes/atrocities against women occurred in and outside the family. Violence against women may be dowry harassment, eve-teasing, wife-beating or other incidents. Since the 1990s, there has been increasing concern about violence against women in general and domestic violence in particular. Violence of any kind has a detrimental impact on the economy through increased disability, medical costs and loss of labour hours. As women bear the burnt of domestic violence, they disproportionately bear the health and psychological burden as well. In Indian society women are socialized to accept, tolerate and even rationalize domestic violence. They remain silent about such ill experiences. Domestic violence is a situation of paradoxical in nature: victims are abused inside the most protected and secure environment – their own homes – and usually by the persons they trust most.

Domestic violence was recognized as a criminal offence in India in 1983. The offence chargeable under section 498 – A of the Indian Penal Code that relates to domestic violence is 'any act of cruelty by a husband (or his family) towards his wife'. After a decade-long process of consultations and revisions, a comprehensive domestic violence law, came in to operation since 2006 as *'Protection of Women from Domestic Violence Act, 2005'*. Key elements of the law include the prohibition of marital rape and the provision of protection and maintenance orders against husbands and partners who are emotionally, physically or economically abusive.

DOMESTIC VIOLENCE

Domestic violence is defined to include violence by spouses as well as by other household members. This includes: (1) violence by husbands and other family members on ever-married women; and (2) violence by any one including boyfriends on never married women. In NFHS-3 physical, sexual and emotional violence is measured using the following set of questions:

Does your husband ever do any of the following things to you:

- Slap you.
- Twist your arm and pull your hair.
- Push you, shake you, or throw something at you.
- Punch you with his fist or with something that could hurt you.
- Kick you, drag you or beat you up.
- Try to choke you or burn you on purpose.
- Threaten or attack you with a knife, gun, or any other weapon.
- Physically force you to have sexual intercourse with him even when you did not want to.
- Force you to perform any sexual acts you did not want to.
- Say or do something to humiliate you in front of others.
- Threaten to hurt or harm you or someone close to you.
- Insult you or make you feel bad about yourself.

(First 7 sets of acts are physical, next 2 sexual and last 3 relates to emotional violence.)

Table 12.1 represents the percentage of women who have experienced physical and sexual violence at any time since the age of 15 years. thirty-four per cent of all women age 15-49 have experienced physical violence at anytime since the age of 15 and 9 per cent of women have experienced sexual violence at some times during their life time.

By age the prevalence of physical violence is lowest at 21 per cent for women in the age group of 15-19 and 5 per cent of women in the said age group is reported having experience of sexual violence, the lowest rate among all age groups. Violence increases with the increase of age. However, the trend shows an opposite one in the age group of 40-49.

Table 12.1: Experience of Physical and Sexual Violence

Background Characteristics	*Percentage who have ever experienced Physical Violence since age 15*	*Percentage who have experienced Sexual Violence since age 15*	*Number of Women*
Age:			
15-19	20.7	4.5	16617
20-24	30.8	8.6	15427
25-29	38.1	10.2	13832
30-39	39.4	10.2	22542
40-49	37.7	8.5	15286
Residence:			
Urban	28.3	5.9	27371
Rural	36.1	9.7	56332
Education:			
No Education	44.3	12.1	34138
< 5 years completed	39.1	10.5	6600
5-7 years completed	32.4	8.1	12557
8-9 years completed	26.0	6.0	11700
10-11 years completed	21.3	3.7	8683
12 years or more	14.3	2.3	10023
Marital Status:			
Never Married	16.1	1.1	16477
Currently Married	37.4	10.1	62652
Married, *gauna* not	14.9	1.8	568
performed	37.9	9.7	2692
Widowed Divorced/ Separated/Deserted	66.1	24.6	1314
Total	33.5	8.5	83703

Source: National Family Health Survey, 2005-06, India Report, IIPS, Mumbai.

Percentage of women age 15-49 who have experienced physical violence since age 15 and ever experienced sexual violence, by background characteristics, India, 2005-06.

Rural women are more likely than their urban counterpart to have ever experienced both physical and sexual violence.

The prevalence of violence declines sharply with increase of education. forty-four per cent of women have experienced physical violence at sometime since the age of 15 and 12 per cent of women ever experienced sexual violence with no education. Theses proportions decline steadily with education.

Two-thirds of currently divorced, separated or deserted women have experienced physical violence and 25 per cent women of the said category have reported to have sexual violence.

Eighty-five per cent of ever-married women have experienced violence (both physical and sexual) at the hands of their husbands.

In India 35 per cent of women age 15-49 have experienced physical and sexual violence; this proportion is 40 per cent for ever-married women and 17 per cent for never married women. Both types of violence are higher in rural than in urban areas.

Women's experience of the different types of violence varies greatly by state. However, in all states physical violence alone tends to be the most common form of violence. Sexual violence rarely occurs without physical violence. The prevalence of any violence is least in Himachal Pradesh at 6 per cent and most in Bihar 56 per cent.

SPOUSAL VIOLENCE

Spousal violence is one of the most common forms of violence experienced by women in the age group of 15-49. *It refers to violence perpetrated by partners in a marital union*. Hence, violence perpetrated by the husbands is measured in more detail than violence caused by any other family members. NFHS-3 collected detailed information on the different types of violence: Physical, Sexual and Emotional, as detailed in the earlier paragraph. However, different types of violence are not mutually exclusive of each other. Hence, women may report different forms of violence simultaneously. Table 12.3 shows the percentage of ever-married women's report regarding different forms of spousal violence committed by their spouses.

Table 12.2: Experience of Different Forms of Violence

Percentage of women age 15-49 who have experienced different forms of violence by residence, age, marital status, and state, India, 2005-06.

Characteristics	*Physical Violence only*	*Sexual Violence only*	*Physical and Sexual Violence*	*Physical or Sexual Violence*
Age:				
15-19	18.0	1.8	2.7	22.5
20-24	24.7	2.4	6.2	33.2
25-29	29.7	1.9	8.4	39.9
30-39	30.8	1.7	8.5	41.1
40-49	30.5	1.3	7.2	39.0
Residence:				
Urban	23.5	1.1	4.8	29.4
Rural	28.5	2.1	7.6	38.3
Marital Status:				
Ever Married	29.7	2.1	8.3	40.1
Never Married	15.7	0.8	0.3	16.9
State:				
Andhra Pradesh	29.9	0.5	3.4	33.8
Assam	24.7	2.2	9.6	36.5
Bihar	38.9	2.9	13.8	55.6
Gujarat	20.7	2.2	4.8	27.8
Haryana	23.4	1.4	4.3	29.0
Karnataka	16.7	0.2	2.9	19.9
Kerela	12.6	1.3	3.4	17.3
Madhya Pradesh	37.0	1.4	8.4	46.8
Maharashtra	27.2	0.3	1.7	29.2
Orissa	24.5	3.5	8.2	36.2
Punjab	25.0	1.0	4.9	30.9
Rajasthan	27.5	4.6	12.6	44.6
Tamil Nadu	36.1	0.0	2.5	38.7
Uttar Pradesh	30.3	1.1	6.7	38.1
West Bengal	19.9	6.2	12.2	38.3
India	26.9	1.8	6.7	35.4

Source: National Family Health Survey, 2005-06, India Report, IIPS, Mumbai.

Table 12.3: Forms of Spousal Violence

Percentage of ever-married women age 15-49 who have experienced various forms of spousal violence, India, 2005-06.

	%
Physical Violence	
Any form of Physical Violence	35.1
Pushed her, shook her, or threw something at her	13.6
Slapped her	34.0
Twisted her arm or pulled her hair	15.4
Punched her with his fist or with something that could hurt her	10.9
Kicked her, dragged her, or beat her up	11.5
Tried to chock her or burn her on purpose	2.2
Threatened her or attacked her with a knife, gun, or any other weapon	1.2
Sexual Violence	
Any form of sexual violence	10.0
Physically forced her to have sexual intercourse even when she did not want	9.5
Forced to her to perform any sexual acts she did not want to	4.6
Emotional Violence	
Any form of emotional violence	15.8
Said or did something to humiliate her in front of others	13.1
Threatened to hurt or harm or someone close to her	5.4
Insulted her or made her feel bad about herself	8.2
Any form of physical and/or sexual violence	37.2
Any form of physical and sexual violence	7.9
Any form of physical and/or sexual and/or emotional violence	39.7
Any for of physical and sexual and emotional violence	4.2

Source: National Family Health Survey, 2005-06, India Report, IIPS, Mumbai.

Slapping is the most common form of physical violence. Thirty-four per cent of ever-married women being slapped by their husbands. The next most common form of physical violence is hair pulling and arms twisting (15 per cent).

Ten per cent of women report experiencing one or both types of sexual violence. Being physically forced to have sexual intercourse is more common than being forced to perform any other acts without their consent.

Sixteen per cent of ever-married women report having experienced emotional violence.

Around 40 per cent ever-married women experienced spousal physical, sexual or emotional violence and 4 per cent experience all three.

Large differentials exist by background characteristics in the proportions of women who experience different forms of spousal violence as shown in Table 12.4. *But the trend is more or less same as that of domestic violence.*

Table 12.4: Spousal Violence by Background Characteristics

Percentage of ever-married women age 15-49 by whether they have ever experienced different forms of violence committed by their spouses, India, 2005-06

Age	*Emotional*	*Physical*	*Sexual*	*P or S*	*E, P or S*
1	*2*	*3*	*4*	*5*	*6*
Age:					
15-19	12.5	25.3	13.1	30.8	33.9
20-24	14.4	32.3	10.5	35.2	37.6
25-29	16.3	36.3	10.4	38.2	40.6
30-39	16.5	37.3	10.1	39.0	41.5
40-49	16.5	35.7	8.2	37.1	39.9
Residence:					
Urban	13.4	29.1	7.3	30.4	32.7
Rural	16.9	37.7	11.2	40.2	42.9
Education:					
No Education	19.2	44.4	12.5	46.4	49.0
< 5 years completed	18.9	39.5	11.7	42.0	44.8
5-7 years completed	15.4	32.6	9.7	35.2	37.7
8-9 years completed	11.9	26.0	8.3	28.8	31.3
10-11 years completed	9.6	19.3	4.9	20.8	32.4
12 years or more	6.2	11.0	2.7	12.3	14.7

(Contd...)

1	2	3	4	5	6
Marital Status:					
Just Married	15.0	34.5	9.7	36.7	39.2
Widowed	16.7	35.0	9.5	36.6	38.1
Divorced/separated/deserted	50.6	62.3	24.4	63.5	68.4
Respondent's father beat her mother					
Yes	28.5	57.4	17.4	59.6	62.2
No	12.4	28.3	7.8	30.3	32.8

Source: National Family Health Survey, 2005-06, India Report, IIPS, Mumbai.

The fact that women whose mothers were beaten by their fathers are twice as likely to report all forms of violence as women whose mothers were not beaten by their father.

Why this Syndrome?

There are several reasons ascribed for this. In NFHS-3 data has been collected on the characteristics of the husband and the marriage to find the relationship with spousal violence (Table 12.5).

Table 12.5: Spousal violence by husbands characteristics

Percentage of ever-married women age 15-49 who have ever suffered any spousal violence.

Background characteristics	*Emotional*	*Physical*	*Sexual*	*Pl or S*	*E, P or S*
1	2	3	4	5	6
Husband's Education					
No Education	20.5	45.2	12.8	47.2	49.8
< 5 years completed	19.7	43.8	13.0	45.7	48.4
5-7 years completed	16.7	38.2	10.4	40.5	42.8
8-9 years completed	15.2	34.2	10.4	36.6	39.2
10-11 years completed	12.5	27.2	8.1	29.9	32.4
12 years or more	8.9	18.9	4.9	20.8	23.6
Spousal Education Difference					
Husband better educated	15.0	34.1	9.7	36.4	39.0
Wife better educated	14.5	29.7	9.0	31.9	34.4
Both equally educated	10.0	21.4	6.0	23.3	25.3
Neither educated	20.6	46.0	12.8	47.8	50.4

(Contd...)

1	2	3	4	5	6
Spousal age difference					
Wife older	16.1	34.6	8.0	36.9	40.9
Wife is same age	14.8	31.0	8.4	33.6	37.3
Wife 1-4 year younger	14.5	34.7	9.7	36.7	39.2
Wife 5-9 year younger	15.1	34.3	10.1	36.5	39.0
Wife 10+ year younger	15.8	34.9	9.2	37.1	39.6
Husband's alcohol consumption					
Does not drink	12.1	28.0	7.9	30.3	32.9
Drinks/never gets drunk	18.1	43.8	15.0	47.3	50.3
Gets drunk sometimes	20.5	46.8	11.6	48.5	50.6
Gets drunk very often	38.6	67.6	23.6	68.6	71.5

Source: National Family Health Survey, 2005-06, India Report, IIPS, Mumbai.

Increase in husband's education shows a clear negative association with prevalence of violence, but it has less of an effect on lowering the prevalence of violence than do increase in women's own education. The prevalence of spousal violence does not vary much with spousal age difference; however, it does vary greatly by spousal educational difference.

As commonsense goes 'alcohol addicted husbands' inflict more spousal violence. The NFHS empirical evidence supports this. However, the prevalence of spousal violence even among women whose husbands do not consume alcohol indicates that 'alcohol consumption' is not the only explanation for the occurrence of spousal violence.

TASKS AHEAD

Promulgation of law is not sufficient enough to counteract the visible/invisible domestic/spousal violence. Under no circumstance wife-beating (violence against women by their spouses) be justified referring to stereotyped roles of women. The notion of wife-beating is a symbol of manliness and its social acceptance should be countered by tooth and nail. The victims of women violence should have access to counseling so as to regenerate the confidence. The change of people's attitude is a must to have a lasting effect on reducing the extent of women violence. For this: (1) Launch an awareness campaign to make the invisible violent acts visible (2) Document and publicize the nature and extent of atrocities on women (3) Sensitize the community to the productive contribution of women to the society.

13

Pre-marital Sex and Condom Use among Indian Unmarried Men

Sabyasachi Behera

ABSTRACT

Youth and their sexual health was given priority in the International Conference on Population and Development (ICPD) held at Cairo in the year 1994. With all the attention that is currently focused on the various aspects on Indian youth, there is a surprising lack of information and the attempts that deal with, what is generally considered to be the dominant theme of youth, the psychological problems which come in the wake of sexual maturation. Sexual behaviour is an important determinant of both fertility patterns and the transmission of sexually transmitted infections. Information about sexual behaviour is essential to inform preventive strategies and to correct myths about what constitutes safe and unsafe activity. Talking about sex is treated as a taboo specially the country like India. The prevalence of risky sexual behaviour of men has been the primary focus. If unsafe sex were to cease most parts of the world would see a substantial drop in the number of new HIV infections. The consequences like unwanted pregnancy and sexually transmitted infections are the cause of pre marital sexual behaviour among the youths. The present chapter is based on the sample population of unmarried men based on the data NFHS, 2005-06. From the sample population 13.5% have had pre marital sexual experience and among them only about one third have used condom at their first sexual intercourse. So the major chunk of population is vulnerable towards RTI/STI and HIV/AIDS.

INTRODUCTION

Youth and their sexual health were given priority in the International Conference on Population and Development (ICPD) held at Cairo in the year 1994. More than half of the world population is under 25 years' age and over 1.5 million young people aged 10-24 years live in developing countries. These young people face serious health problems in modern times. With all the attention that is currently focused on the various aspects on Indian youth, there is a surprising lack of information and the attempts that deal with, what is generally considered to be the dominant theme of youth, the psychological problems which come in the wake of sexual maturation. Sexual behaviour is an important determinant of both fertility patterns and the transmission of sexually transmitted infections. Information about sexual behaviour is essential to inform preventive strategies and to correct myths about what constitutes safe and unsafe activity. Increased research in this area provides a historically unique opportunity to take stock of sexual behaviour and efforts to safeguard it, at the beginning of the 21st century. This paper analyses data from National Family Health Survey (NFHS) 2005-06 in India to answer the questions such as related to sexual behaviour of youth and the underlying factors which determines the practice of safe/unsafe sex. The regional diversity can shows how strong social influences make impact on sexual behaviour. No general approach to sexual health promotion will work anywhere. The selection of public health messages needs to be guided by epidemiological evidence rather than by myths and moral stances. The greatest challenge to sexual health promotion in almost all countries comes from opposition from conservative forces which harm reduction strategies. Sexuality is an essential part of human nature and its expression needs to be affirmed rather than denied. For a large part of developing nations, there is absence of any empirical information on health and sexuality needs of youths, the type of problems they face, the risky they encounter as adolescents or young adults and their sexual behaviour.

REVIEW OF LITERATURE

A study conducted by (Bhende,1993) in the slums of Mumbai, has found that half of the boys knew nothing about the married life, and so on. Pre-marital sex is considered as a taboo in India. Teenagers and young adults have always experimented with it. The past few years have perhaps seen an increasing trend towards greater experimentation by the youths in India (Ramasubban, 1992; Sehgal, 19992; Jain, 1994; Jejeebhoy, 1994). A number of studies have documented the prevalence of abortions among adolescents and the unmarried constituted the larger proportion (Jejeebhoy, 1994). Despite an increasing trend in sexual practices among youth contraceptive use was found to be very low (Wasta, 1994). Pre-marital sex has been increasing over time among youth, which is considered as risky behaviour (Reddy, 1993). A few studies were conducted among college students about their attitudes towards pre marital sex (Reddy, 1993). In the later part of the 20th century studies have concentrated on risky sexual behaviour and use of condom among the youths (Watsa,1994; Chitale,1992; Goparaju 1993; and Sethi *et al.* 1995). A study conducted (Gupta, 1978) in Kanpur has found that many people had perception that by holding hand and kissing leads to conception. A study conducted by (FPAI, 1992) reported that three out of four persons disapproved pre marital sex in Uttar Pradesh, Delhi, Haryana and Rajasthan among adolescents age 14 to 17. A few recent studies indicate that the practice of pre marital sex is not that common in both educated and uneducated and also in rural and urban population (Nag, 1996). A study (Sehgal, 1992) among the secondary going school boys, reported that 25% admitted to have had experienced sexual intercourse. A study in the Mumbai slum (Bhende, 1993) also suggested the presence of high level of sexual activity among the adolescents. Recent studies of sexuality in India show that pre marital sex is not as rare as generally believed to be

(Goparaju,1993; Bhende,1993) and that young people often lack adequate information in order to protect themselves from unwanted pregnancies and sexually transmitted infections.

RATIONAL BEHIND THE STUDY

Talking about sex is treated as a taboo specially the country like India. The prevalence of risky sexual behaviour of men has been the primary focus. The prevalence of sexual behaviours and characteristics varies greatly between countries and between regions. If unsafe sex were to cease most parts of the world would see a substantial drop in the number of new HIV infections. The consequences like unwanted pregnancy and sexually transmitted infections are the cause of pre marital sexual behaviour among the youths and not only the policy makers but also the researchers emphasize on the behaviour of those who indulge in pre marital sex. The policy makers and the researchers should give emphasize because the youths are the future of modern India. It is essential to protect the youths from unwanted sex, early child bearing, unwanted pregnancies, unsafe abortions, STD and HIV/AIDS.

RESEARCH QUESTIONS

From the available literature it is important that very few studies have examined sexuality and sexual behaviour among unmarried men in India. In the present study attempt to answer some of the question related to sexuality and sexual behaviour among the Indian unmarried men has been made. The questions are:

1. What are the determinants which lead to pre marital sex among Indian unmarried men?
2. Who are the vulnerable groups moving towards RTI/STI and HIV/AIDS.

HYPOTHESES

Based on the literature review and research work done earlier, some of the hypotheses are drawn which are given below:

- Pre-marital sex is high among them those with no education than those with higher education.

- Vulnerability to STI (use of condom) is higher among the urbanites than the rural people.
- Pre-marital sexual behaviour is high among those who are consume alcohol than those who do not consume.

OBJECTIVES

In broader sense, the present study attempts to understand the premarital sexual behaviour and its correlates among unmarried men.

Specifically the objectives of the current research are:

1. To study the premarital sexual behaviour among Indian unmarried men.
2. To understand the factors affecting the premarital sex among unmarried men.
3. To understand their vulnerability towards RTI/STI and HIV/AIDS.

DATA

For the present research work secondary data has been used. So for the analysis purpose data from National Family Health Survey (NFHS) 2005-06 have been utilized in this paper. The data provides information of 25382 Indian unmarried men of age 15-54.

METHODOLOGY

For the present study, both the bi-variate and multivariate analysis has been used. Bi-variate analysis has been done to understand the differentials in pre marital sexual behaviour of unmarried men by selected background variables such as; age, education, occupation, religion, caste, exposure to mass media, drinking alcohol, wealth index, type of family, type of residence and region. This analysis has been done by generating cross tabulations through SPSS 15.0 package. Further binary logistic regression analysis has been used to understand the factors responsible for pre marital sex. For this purpose pre marital sex has been taken as dependent variable with dichotomous categories. 0=no (not having pre marital sex) and 1=yes (have indulge in pre marital sex). Another set of multivariate logistic regression has been used by taking condom use at first sexual intercourse and last intercourse as dependent variable with dichotomous categories. 0=no (not used) and 1=yes (have used) to understand the vulnerability towards RTI/STI among those who have pre marital sex.

CONCEPTUAL FRAMEWORK

The present study attempts to study the pre marital sexual behaviour and the factors which affect it. It is important to understand and sexual behaviour of Indian unmarried men the individual level, the family level and the societal level. In at the individual level how the age, education, occupation, exposure to mass media, alcohol drinking, caste and the religion have apparent impact on pre marital sexual behaviour and their vulnerability towards RTI/STI and HIV/AIDS. At family level, and societal level, how it affects pre marital sex and their vulnerability towards RTI/STI and HIV/AIDS. The conceptual framework has been presented diagrammatically in the fig. 13.1.

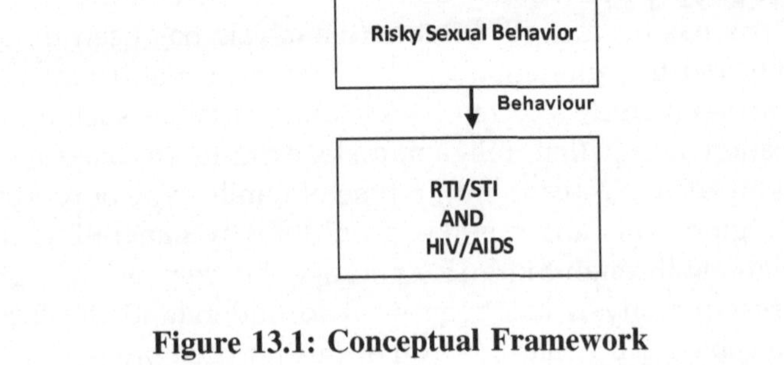

Figure 13.1: Conceptual Framework

RESULTS AND SALIENT FINDINGS

Determinants of Pre-marital Sex

Table 13.1 depicts the percentage of unmarried men involved in pre marital sex by selected background characteristics, India, 2005-06. The present research finds that the experience of pre marital sex among the unmarried men is higher (21%) in the 25+ age groups than the younger ages 15-19 and 20-24. As human being crosses ages from one stage to another stage that is from adolescents to youth, it is expected that sexual experience before marriage could be higher among grown up persons. A part from socio-economic status of the parents, maternal employment, marital disruption, income of the parents, may influence the teenager's sexual behaviours. Mass media communication may also play an important role because better exposed have more awareness about different health related problems and this may lead to use of preventive measures. People who are in early age groups are more prone to impulsive behaviour. Emotional instability and the use of sexual gratification treated as a means of relief. The peer pressure has its own impact on sexuality and sexual behaviour. The present study has found that pre-marital sex is more among the non- going school groups and among those who have completed primary education. It has also been found in earlier studies that pre-marital sex is more among the non-going school group is higher than those who had already completed basic education (Chauhan and Joshi, 2005). So again in case of education the pre marital sexual behaviour is more in the rural areas than in the urban areas. Earlier studies indicate however that the practice is not uncommon in both educated and uneducated among the youth Indians (Nag, 1996). The present study found that pre marital sexual behaviour is more among the working groups than the non-working groups. The involvement is more among them; the reasons might be they are away from the home. To get rid of stress they might be indulge in such type of activity. Peer pressure also plays a major role in sexual behaviour. Studies show that migration and sexual behaviour is highly co-related to each other. Sexual behaviour is more among the migrant workers and they are prone towards RTI/STI and HIV/AIDS. In case of caste the present study found that pre-marital sex is higher among the ST caste groups, then SC. The pre-marital sex is more among the ST population; the possible reasons may be they are more liberal, they are leaving in the hilly areas, so their movement is free from one place to another. It is also true in case of Sikh religion. Sikhs are more advanced than the other religion. In case of Hindus it shows only 13% indulge in pre marital sex. Hinduism considers premarital sex "not a good thing," similarly for the Muslim faith premarital sex is a "sin" (*Al-Shawish*). It is found in the present study that consumption of alcohol leads to more pre marital sexual behaviour. It has also been found in the earlier studies by (Satihal, 2002), (*et al.*). Exposure to mass media has its impact on pre-marital sex among Indian unmarried men. The present research work has found that the difference between those who are exposed and those who are not is negligible in case of experience of pre marital sex. The present research work found that pre marital sex is higher among the poorer section of the society. It has also been found in earlier studies by several researchers. It is higher in the rural areas than in the urban areas. It has been found that in the richest section only 10% of the sample populations have indulged in pre marital sex and it is higher in the rural areas than in the urban areas. The possible reasons may be they have higher education, their style of living and awareness of pros and cons of pre marital sex. In the non-nuclear family nearly 16% have involved in pre marital sex as where it is only 11% in the nuclear family. To see the regional variation in pre marital sex, about one fifth among unmarried men of the Central region population have experienced pre marital sex, which is highest among all the regions. The possible reasons may be sex with the future spouse, because in the central region Gauna still exists in the society. Pre marital sex is lowest among the Southern regions possibly due to higher educational level.

Table 13.1: Percentage of unmarried men and involvement in premarital sex any time before the survey by selected background characteristics, India, 2005-06

Background Characteristics	*Numbers*	*Involvement in PMS*		
		Rural	*Urban*	*Total**
1	*2*	*3*	*4*	*5*
Age in years				
15-19	12635	9.9	6.5	8.6 (1092)
20-24	8086	19.5	14.3	17.0 (1378)
25+	4661	22.6	18.9	20.7 (967)
Education				
No Education	1964	19.0	18.0	18.7 (367)
Primary	2872	17.2	16.6	17.0 (489)
Secondary	16916	13.7	11.5	12.8 (2162)
Higher	3622	13.7	10.3	11.5 (417)
Religion				
Hindu	20461	14.8	11.8	13.6 (2773)
Muslim	3378	11.4	11.3	11.4 (384)
Christian	609	12.6	12.7	12.7 (77)
Sikh	522	26.1	25.4	25.9 (135)
Others	412	20.4	12.1	16.3 (67)
Caste				
SC	4631	19.4	16.0	18.0 (835)
ST	1644	20.0	20.2	20.1 (330)
OBC	9698	12.9	9.9	11.7 (1138)
Others	8517	13.0	11.7	12.3 (1049)
Occupation				
Non-Working	8712	6.9	5.3	6.2 (539)
Working	16670	18.5	15.8	17.4 (2897)
Drink Alcohol				
No	20382	10.3	6.9	8.9 (1813)
Yes	5000	33.1	31.7	32.5 (1624)

(Contd...)

1	2	3	4	5
Exposure to Mass Media				
No	2859	12.8	15.3	13.2 (378)
Yes	22523	15.1	11.8	13.6 (3059)
Wealth Index				
Poorest	2791	16.3	18.8	16.4 (457)
Poorer	3994	17.0	14.2	16.6 (665)
Middle	5206	14.1	13.3	13.9 (722)
Richer	6301	12.8	13.0	12.9 (814)
Richest	7090	12.3	10.6	11.0 (779)
Type of Family				
Nuclear	12386	12.7	9.7	11.3 (1404)
Non-Nuclear	12132	16	14.5	15.4 (1869)
Region				
North	3724	13.3	16.5	14.7 (549)
Central	5785	21.6	16.3	19.6 (1136)
East	4826	11.7	8.6	10.6 (512)
North-East	1225	13.2	13.6	13.3 (163)
West	4311	15.7	12.4	13.8 (597)
South	5511	10.3	6.8	8.7 (481)
Total	25382	14.7	12.0	13.5 (3437)

* Total may not add due to missing cases.

VULNERABILITY TOWARDS RTI/STI

Table 13.2 shows the percentage of unmarried men who have used condom in the first sexual intercourse by selected background characteristics, based on the information from NFHS, 2005-06. The STD is reportedly the third major communicable diseases group in India, after Malaria and Tuberculosis. On the whole Condom used in the first sexual intercourse is nearly 31% thereby suggesting that the major chunk among the sample population have not been using condom at the time of sexual intercourse. In other words we can say that those who have not been using condom, they are more vulnerable towards RTI/STI and HIV/AIDS. The condom use is less among teenagers in age 15-19 than the other two age groups. However, among unmarried males age 20-24 and 25+, the use of condom at the first sexual intercourse is relatively high (34%). The difference in urban and rural areas in condom use is around 20%. Condom use is less in the rural areas perhaps due to non availability and accessibility of condoms. Other studies suggested that most sexual encounters are unplanned, takes place in sugarcane and public toilets. (Satihal, 2002, *et al.*). There is growing tendency among youth to indulge in sexual behaviour and experimentation with different type of partners and the use of condom is less. Earlier studies by (Wasta, 1994) has found that despite an increasing trend in sexual practices among youth, contraceptive use was found very low. As educational level increases the use of condom is also increasing. In the rural areas the use of condom is increasing as educational level increases and it is lowest among no educational groups and highest among the higher educational groups, but in case of urban areas it shows some variation that condom use is more in the no educational groups than those who have completed primary education. In case of secondary and higher education, use of condom is slightly different in urban areas, but the concern about the adolescent reproductive health, which is exists both in developed and developing countries. In the developing world, however, the high proportion of unwanted pregnancies, the level of morbidity and mortality, the number of unsafe abortions and the growing incidence of STDs/AIDS reveal a higher vulnerability of adolescent and youth in the area of sexual and reproductive health. This is aggravated by the deficiencies in the channels of sexual education. Over all by occupation there is slight difference in the use of condom among those who are working and those who are not working. But when we look at the condom use by residence then we see a variation in the use of condom. That is in the urban areas the condom use is more than the rural areas. The difference is coming around 20% in the working sector and where as the difference is nearly about 22% in the non-working sector. Condom use is less among the ST population than the other caste groups. Again it is different for urban and rural areas. It is higher in the urban areas than in the rural areas. The condom use is highest among 'Others'; it is coming around 41% as where it is 27% for SC and 25% for the OBC caste groups. By religion, the percentage of condom use is less among the Hindus than the other religions but it is higher in the urban areas than in the rural areas, where as in case of Sikh the condom use is slightly more in the rural areas than in the urban areas, the difference is only 1%. The results suggested that those who consume alcohol are using condom more than who are not drinking alcohol. Though they are drinking they are more aware about the use of condom than those who have not consumed. Here, also we can see that the use of condom is higher in the urban areas than in the rural areas. Exposure to mass media has a greater impact on the use of condom among the unmarried men. It is all most double among those who are exposed to mass media (32%) than those who are not exposed to any sort of mass media communication (16%). The results suggest impact of mass media on the use of condom which is higher in the urban areas than in the rural areas. Those who are staying in the nuclear family condom use is higher than those who are staying in the non-nuclear family and it is higher in the urban areas than in the rural areas. In the western region use of condom is highest (48%) than in other regions. The use of condom is lowest in the central region where the prevalence of pre marital sex is highest. Except the northern region the use of condom is more in the urban areas than in the rural areas. The difference between the rural and urban area shows that, the rural people are more vulnerable towards RTI/STI and HIV/AIDS.

Table 13.3 shows the percentage of sexual experience and condom use in the last twelve months. The present research work found among adolescents sexual behaviour is higher but the use of condom is less among them, where as condom use is higher among the youths who indulge in sexual activity in last twelve months. Those who have completed secondary education condom and sexual experience are higher followed by the higher educational group. By religion condom use is higher among the Hindus where as Sikhs are more involved in sexual behaviour. By caste who are in the 'Others' category they are less vulnerable to RTI/STI in comparison to other caste groups. Those who are working use of condom are much higher than those who are not working. Those who are exposed to mass media condom use are higher (94%) than those who are not exposed. In case of alcohol consumption sexual behaviour and condom use is higher than those who do not consumed. In the richest quintile condom use is higher than the other economic category of wealth index. In case family those who are in the non-nuclear family they are less vulnerable to RTI/STI. The urbanites are using more condom than the rural people.

Table 13.2: Percentage of condom used in first sexual intercourse any time before the survey among unmarried men in India, 2005-06

Background characteristics	*Percentage of condom used*		
	Rural	*Urban*	*Total **
1	2	3	4
Age in years			
15-19	16.8	37.6	22.7 (248)
20-24	26.0	46.5	34.2 (470)
25+	25.7	43.8	34.1 (329)
Education			
No Education	12.4	29.7	16.7 (61)
Primary	15.8	23.4	18.2 (89)
Secondary	25.7	47.0	33.6 (726)
Higher	27.7	50.0	40.5 (169)
Religion			
Hindu	20.8	42.0	28.4 (786)
Muslim	24.7	49.5	37.2 (143)
Christian	28.2	47.4	36.4 (28)
Sikh	42.7	41.3	42.2 (57)
Others	42.9	58.3	48.5 (32)
Caste			
SC	22.5	37.2	27.4 (229)
ST	17.5	29.9	20.3 (67)
OBC	18.3	39.4	25.3 (288)
Others	31.0	50.2	40.8 (426)

(Contd...)

1	2	3	4
Occupation			
Non-Working	19.2	42.9	28.4 (153)
Working	23.2	43.6	30.9 (893)
Drink Alcohol			
No	21.2	39.6	27.3 (494)
Yes	24.3	46.9	34.0 (552)
Exposure to Mass Media			
No	14.2	25.0	16.4 (62)
Yes	24.0	44.5	32.2 (984)
Wealth Index			
Poorest	12.6	35.7	14.0 (64)
Poorer	16.5	24.6	17.3 (115)
Middle	21.3	31.8	23.8 (171)
Richer	35.3	39.7	37.7 (306)
Richest	42.8	52.4	50.1 (390)
Type of Family			
Nuclear	24.5	45.6	32.5 (456)
Non-Nuclear	21.3	42.2	29.6 (552)
Region			
North	35.2	35.6	35.4 (193)
Central	14.5	29.4	19.1 (217)
East	17.5	60.5	30.3 (155)
North-East	20.5	37.0	25.2 (41)
West	35.5	60.0	48.1 (286)
South	26.9	41.9	32.2 (154)
Total	22.6	43.5	30.5 (1046)

* Total may not add due to missing case.

Table 13.4 gives the results of odds ratio for sexual experience and use of condom in the last twelve months. The last two age groups are less likely to indulge in sexual behaviour than the reference age group 15-19.

Table 13.3: Percentage of sexual experience and use of condom in last Twelve months, 2005-06

Background characteristics	*Percentage (PMS)*	*Percentage (Condom)*
1	*2*	*3*
Age in years		
15-19	79.1(864)	28.3(203)
20-24	72.2(995)	41.4(297)
25+	61.6(590)	30.4(218)
Education		
No Education	72.0(265)	7.2(52)
Primary	66.5(325)	7.9(57)
Secondary	72.7(1571)	69.4(500)
Higher	68.6(286)	15.4(111)
Religion		
Hindu	71.0(1969)	75.8(545)
Muslim	70.1(269)	12.9(93)
Christian	66.7(52)	2.4(17)
Sikh	81.5(110)	6.3(45)
Others	73.1(49)	2.6(19)
Caste		
SC	72.8(608)	23.7(165)
ST	73.0(241)	6.6(46)
OBC	69.6(792)	25.6(178)
Others	71.7(751)	44.1(307)
Occupation		
Non-Working	71.1(383)	16.3(117)
Working	71.3(2065)	83.7(602)
Drink Alcohol		
No	68.0(1232)	43.7(314)
Yes	74.9(1216)	56.3(404)
Exposure to Mass Media		
No	67.5(255)	5.8(42)
Yes	71.7(2194)	94.2(676)

(Contd...)

1	2	3
Wealth Index		
Poorest	72.9(334)	6.4(46)
Poorer	67.4(448)	12.5(90)
Middle	71.7(518)	15.2(109)
Richer	68.7(559)	26.6(191)
Richest	75.7(590)	39.3(282)
Type of Family		
Nuclear	70.4(988)	43.6(303)
Non-Nuclear	71.7(1340)	56.4(392)
Region		
North	79.2(435)	23.1(166)
Central	75.2(855)	26.0(187)
East	62.6(320)	12.1(87)
North-East	60.7(99)	4.2(30)
West	70.4(420)	22.6(162)
South	66.5(320)	12.0(86)
Residence		
Urban	72.6(942)	53.8(387)
Rural	70.4(1506)	46.2(332)
Total	71.2(2449)	39.4(719)

Those who have completed primary education they are 0.861 less likely indulge in sexual behaviour than the reference group. By religion Muslims are 1.196 more likely to indulge in sexual behaviour than the Hindus. By caste who are in the 'Others' category they are more likely indulge in sexual behaviour than the reference group. Those who are working class they are 1.175 more likely indulge in sexual behaviour than the non-working class. Those who are consumed alcohol the likelihood of sexual behaviour is higher. Media exposure, type of family, away from home more than one month the likelihood of sexual behaviour is higher. In region all the regions sexual behaviour is less than the reference group.

When we look at the condom use in the last sexual intercourse, the present research work found that those who have completed primary, secondary and higher education shows positive results in case of condom use. Muslims are more likely to use condom than the reference group.

Table 13.4: The odds ratio for sexual experience and use of Condom use in last twelve months, 2005-06

Variables	*Exp (B) PMS*	*Exp (B) Condom*
1	*2*	*3*
Age in years		
15-19 ®		
20-24	0.680*	1.337
25+	0.379**	1.209
Education		
No Education ®		
Primary	0.861*	1.166
Secondary	1.027	1.686*
Higher	0.855	1.902*
Religion		
Hindu ®		
Muslim	1.196*	0.911
Christian	1.022	1.595
Sikh	1.175	0.539
Others	1.056	0.931
Caste		
SC ®		
ST	1.391	0.579*
OBC	1.015	0.984
Others	1.203*	1.079
Occupation		
Working	1.175*	0.843
Drink Alcohol		
No ®		
Yes	1.810**	1.378*
Exposure to Mass Media		
No ®		
Yes	1.304	1.098*

(Contd...)

1	2	3
Wealth Index		
Poorest ®		
Poorer	0.736*	1.445
Middle	0.868*	1.669
Richer	0.829*	3.007**
Richest	1.029	4.184**
Type of Family		
Nuclear ®		
Non-Nuclear	1.092	1.055
Type of Residence		
Urban ®		
Rural	0.986	0.818
Region		
North ®		
Central	0.817	0.516*
East	0.634*	0.793*
North-East	0.501*	0.629
West	0.667*	1.110
South	0.589*	0.634
Away for more than one month	1.052	0.840

Note: *p<0.05 and **p<0.01.

By caste, among STs Condom use is 0.579 less likely than the SCs. And among the 'Others' condom use is higher than the reference group. Drinking alcohol and exposure to mass media shows positive results in case of condom use. The condom use is higher in the richer and richest category than the poorer. Those who are away from home more than one month the condom use is less, so they are vulnerable to RTI/STI.

Table 13.5 shows that percentage of last condom used with the last sexual partner. Overall it shows that only 39% had used condom with the last sexual partner, still 60% are vulnerable to RTI/STI. Those who had sex with spouse the percentage is very less, so it indicates that vulnerable towards RTI/STI. Those who have sex with commercial sex worker and the stranger condom use are nearly 62%. Less than one third populations did not use condom when they had sex with relatives and other friends, and less than half populations have not used condom with their girl friend. So here we conclude that the major portion of people have not used condom with their last sexual partner.

Table 13.5: Percentage of Condom used with Last Sexual Partner

Categories	*Last intercourse used condom*		*Percentage of condom used*
	No	*Yes*	
Spouse	60	9	13.0
Girl friend	542	395	42.2
Relative and other friends	413	173	29.4
CSW and Stranger	86	142	62.3
Total	**1103**	**719**	**39.5**

CONCLUSION

The present research work has been done based on the sample population of unmarried men based on the data NFHS, 2005-06. From the sample population 13.5% who have had pre marital sexual experience and among them only about one third have used condom at their first sexual intercourse. So the major chunk of population is vulnerable towards RTI/STI and HIV/AIDS. Sexual behaviour is higher in the rural areas but use of condom is low among the rural people. Sexual behaviour is higher in the central region but condom use is low in the central region than the other regions of India. Among those who are consumed alcohol Sexual behaviour is higher but use of condom is also higher than those who do not consume. Exposure to mass media has clearly shows its impact on the use of condom. Only 40% have used condom with their last sexual partner. Those who are away from home among them sexual experience is higher but condom use is less, so this leads to RTI/STI among the unmarried men. A very large group of young people are being left off unattended in the health sectors. The adolescent behaviour is becoming a matter of concern due to rapid change effected as a result of urbanization, modernization, industrialization and westernization. There is high risk of pre marital and unprotected sexual activity among unmarried men.

POLICY IMPLICATIONS

Youth are the backbone of society and they are the foundation of strong nation which may lead towards progress and prosperity. So there is need for policies aimed exclusively for the youth. On the basis of the findings of the present study, following suggestions are made.

- Information, Education and Communication (IEC) channels should be improved so that it makes the youths aware about the pros and cons of pre marital sex.
- The NGOs and Governmental bodies should take necessary steps to address the vulnerable groups so that the youth are aware of safe sex.
- Condom use as a barrier against RTI/STI and HIV/AIDS should be promoted.

REFERENCES

Bhende, 1993, *A Study of Sexuality of Adolescents Boys and Girls in Under Privileged Groups in Mumbai.*

Chauhan, S.L., and Beena Joshi, 2005, *Adolescents Reproductive Health.*

Chitale, 1992, *A Study of the Knowledge, Attitudes, Beliefs and Practices on AIDS in Four Locals in Maharashtra.*

Family Planning Association of India (FPAI), 1993-94. *Youth Sexuality: A Study of Knowledge, Attitudes, Beliefs and Practices Among Urban Educated Indian Youth.*

Goparaju, Lakshmi,1993, *Unplanned Unsafe: Male Students Sexual Behaviour.*

Gupta, Veena, 1978, Adolescents and Knowledge on Population Dynamics and Family Planning. *Journal of Family Welfare*, pp. 33-40.

Jain, Kalpana, 1994, *Survey Shows on Delhi School Kids Sexually Active*: AIMS, New Delhi.

Jejeebhoy, 1994, *Adolescents Sexual and Reproductive Behaviour: A Review of the Evidence from India.*

Leena, Abraham, 2001, *Understanding Youth Sexuality: A Study of College Students in Mumbai City.*

Lhungdim, Hemkhothang and Verma. K.Ravi, 2002. *Sexual Behaviour of Male Youth in Rural India.* Population Council.

Nag, Moni, 1996, *Sexual Behaviours and AIDS in India.* Vikas Publishing House Pvt. Ltd.

National Family Health Survey, 2005-06, *International Institute for Population Sciences.*

Ram, F., R.K. Sinha, S.K. Mohanty 2006. *Marriage and Motherhood: An Exploratory Study of the Social and Reproductive Health Status of Married,* An Exploratory Study of the Social and Reproductive Health Status of Married Young Women in India, Population Council, New Delhi.

Ramasubbam, Radhika,1992, *Sexual Behaviour and Conditions of Health Care: Potential Risks for HIV Transmission in India.*

Reddy, 1993, *A Report on Selected Urban(Madras) Sexuality with Reference to Sexual Aspects of AIDS/STD.*

Santhya, K.G., Haberland N., F. Ram. R.K. Sinha and Mohanty, S.K., 2007. Consent and Coercion: Examining Unwanted Sex Among Married Young Women in India, *International Family Planning Perspectives,* Vol 33(3). pp. 124-132.

Satihal, D.G.; P.K. Bhargava; Shiva S. Halli; and B.M. Ramesh, 2002, *Sexual Behaviour Pattern and Condom use Among Unmarried Men and Women in Karnataka: Evidence from a Community Based Study.*

Savara, Mira; and C.R. Sridhra, 1994. Sex and the Indian man. *The Debonair Sex Survey.*

Sehgal, Virendra N, 1992, *Study on AIDS Among School Boys.*

Sethi, Geeta, et.al,1995, *AIDS Sexual Behaviour Study.*

Shirur, R. Rajani,2000. *Reproductive and Sexual Health Education for Adolescents: Needs Assessment.* Discovery Publishing House.

Wasta, M.C., 1994, *Sexuality and Sexual Behaviour Among Urban Educated Youth In India.*

14

Health and Sanitation

Subhrabala Behera

HEALTH

A healthy man power is great feature of a developing economy as if leads to greater out put per man. But the health and under nourishment adversely affect the quality of man power. But in underdeveloped countries (UDCs) people are under fed and under nourished which results in poor quality of manpower. There is also deficiency of protein and vitamins in the diet of the people and due to the lack of medical facilities diseases are very common in the people. The best way to improve the quality of man power in under developed countries as to provide adequate food and better nourishment to people, better sanitary facilities and the extension of medical facilities which in turn will raise the health, the efficiency and the productivity of the people.

From *Wikipedia*, the free encyclopaedia—the generally accepted definition of health as "a state of complete physical, mental and social well-being and not merely the absence of disease or infirmity" used by the World Health Organization (WHO) since 1948.

In 1986, the WHO on the Ottawa Charter for Health Promotion said "health is a resource for every day life, not the objective of living. Health is a positive concept emphasizing social and personal resources, as well as physical capacities."

Classification systems such as the alto family of International Classifications (Who-flc), which is composed of the International Classification Functioning, Disability and the Health (ICF) and the International Classification of Diseases (ICD) also define health. Overall health is achieved through combination of physical, mental, emotional and social well-being.

A holistic Approach to development: health and special projects supplementing core programmes

The health status of the communities in healthy remote areas of Orissa where CYSD works as extremely poor, worked by high infant and maternal mortality rates, low immunization coverage a high prevalence of malnutrition among children , and a high incidence of malaria. A substantial number of these villages suffers from scarcity of safe drinking water. Sanitation facilities are generally limited or non-existent only hygienic living conditions are common place and compound the overall health problem. CYSD undertakes a range of preventative and curative activities in the project locations

AWARENESS DRIVES

Efforts on health focus on awareness development through meetings, interfaces and IEC programmes on various health issues including HIV/AIDS among community-based organizations, community health volunteers, traditional birth attendants, and affected sections of the community including adolescents.

HEALTH CAMPS

Regular health camps are run to provide auto and post-natal treatment for women and check ups and basic treatments, such as de-worming medicines for school children.

SANITATION

Work on water and sanitation includes promoting sanitary habits and practices and cost effective and efficient toilet and potable water facilities for households and schools. Communities including youths are trained on low cost toilet construction and tube-well repairing.

Health programme on sanitation and personal hygiene are conducted in primary schools. Work camps and street plays are organised to promote village sanitation.

OTHER HEALTH PROGRAMMES

Community health management systems and linkages with government health programme are strengthened and community health insurance systems are developed. Efforts are made to provide disabled children with certificates and surgical treatment.

SANITATION

Sanitation is the hygienic means of preventing human contact from the hazards of water to promote health. Hazards can be either physical, microbiological, biological or chemical agents of disease. Wastes that can cause health problems are human and animal faces, solid wastes, domestic waste water (sewage, salvage, Gray water) industrial wastes and agricultural wastes. Hygienic means of prevention can be by using engineering solutions [e.g., sewerage and wastewater treatment], simple technologies (e.g., latrines, septic tanks) or even by personal hygiene practices (e.g. simple hand washing with soap).

The term 'sanitation' can be applied to a specific aspect, concept, location or strategy such as:

- **Basic sanitation**

It refers to the management of human faces at the household level. This terminology is the indicator used to describe the target of the Millennium Development Goal on sanitation.

- **On-site sanitation**

  The collection and treatment of waste is done where it is deposited. Examples are the use of pit latrines, septic tanks and Inhofe tanks.

- **Food sanitation**

  It refers to the hygienic measures for ensuring food safety.

- **Environmental sanitation**

  The control of environmental factors that form links in disease transmission. Subsets of this category are solid waste management, water and wastewater treatment, industrial waste treatment and noise and pollution control.

- **Ecological sanitation**

  It is a concept and approach of recycling to nature the nutrients from human and animal wastes.

Proper sanitation is important to stay away from diseases of both personal and community levels. A number of diseases in India occur due to lack of proper sanitary facilities, especially among poor and rural people. By providing proper sanitation facilities to people these diseases can be controlled and a number of health's can be avoided.

While the responsibility of proper sanitation lies with the government, it is equally important that every community and its inhabitants also take steps for personal sanitation

By following the below given sanitation tips a healthy environment can be assured:

- Use adequate toilet and pay attention to proper handling and disposal of excrement.
- Always wash hands before and after eating as well as using toilets.
- Never store water in open containers for long period of time. Water containers should be washed and if possible disinfected on regular basis.

- Food should always be preserved without contact with contaminated water and ground. Preservation of meat and milk products needs special attention especially in regions where cold storage is not an option.

- Avoid lasting certain food items like unbottled drinks and ice cubes, unpacked milk, cream, cold or insufficiently cooked , meat, fish, egg dishes.

National Portal Context Management Team, Reviewed on: 27-05-2008.

SANITATION IS VITAL FOR HUMAN HEALTH

- **Fetch-sheet sanitation is vital for heath**

Sanitation is the most important medical advance since 1840, according to a reader survey in the British Medical Journal. Improved sanitation reduces cholera, worms, diarrhoea, pneumonia and malnutrition among other maladies, that cause disease and death in millions of people. Today 2.6 billon people including almost one billion children live without even basic sanitation. Every 20 seconds, a child dies as a result of poor sanitation. That is 1.5 million preventable deaths each year.

SAFER WATER, BETTER HEALTH

Costs, benefits and sustainability of interventions to protect and promote health. Almost one-tenth of the global disease burden could be prevented by improving water supply, sanitation, hygiene and management of water resources, (WHO, 2008).

- **Healthy villages**

A guide for communities and community health- this guide as intended to provide community leaders with information to assist them in implementing and sustaining a health villages project. It covers topics such as water and sanitation drainage, waste management, housing quality, domestic and community hygienic and provision of health services providing extensive source materials for adoption to local needs and conditions, (WHO/ UNICEF, 2002).

- **Facts for life**

One of the world's most wisely read book with over 15 million copies of previous editions in use in 215 languages life saving knowledge about children's health for parents caregivers, health workers, government officials, journalists and teachers .Includes chapters on hygiene and diarrhoea, (UNICEF WHO, UNESCO, UNFPA, UNDP, UNAIDS, WFP, World Bank, 2002).

- **Health and Sanitation**

Life skills for southern Sudan-mentors' Information and Activity Book provides mentors with life skills to assist with threats to health from living conditions in Southern Suddan.

2008: INTERNATIONAL YEAR OF SANITATION

To put spotlight on sanitation the UN General Assembly declared the year 2008- the International Year of Sanitation. The goal is to raise awareness and to accelerate progress towards the Millennium Development Goal (MDG) target to reduce by half the proportion of the 2.6 billion people without access to basic sanitation by 2015.

The year's purpose is to raise awareness about this crisis and galvanise action to address it. Making the target a reality as critical to economic growth to people's health, to women's empowerment and to environmental sustainability.

The addition, sanitation is one of the best investments a country can make: on average, every Dollar invested yields that can be valued at Nine Dollars.

15

A Study of Child Sex Ratio (0-6 years) in Selected States of India

Satyaban Sahu

ABSTRACT

The emerging pattern of declining child sex ratio (0-6 years) in many of Indian states is a matter of concern. The child sex ratio (0-6) varies by regions, social groups, age group and level of economic conditions. This study mainly uses sex ratio data in 0-6 age group and sex ratio at birth at the district level of some selected states of India to examine the differentials in child sex ratio and by various socio-economic factors. The child sex ratio by major religion, caste, education and economic condition are analyzed. The predictor variables showing negative effects on child sex ratio are percentage of household electrified, percentage of Schedule caste, female literacy rate and urbanization. It suggests that decline in child sex ratios are contributed more by urban, educated and economically better off segment of the population.

INTRODUCTION

India and China, the two most populous countries in the world have lower sex ratios (number of females per 1000 males);

compared to developed Africa which have more balanced sex ratios. Low sex ratios in India indicate lower status of women. In the last three decades, the national level child sex ratio has been declining very sharply. The child sex ratio was 962 in 1981 and 945 in 1991and declined to 927 in 2001. It has also been evident for well over a century that there are pronounced regional differences in India's sex ratio trends. The proportion of women in the population is lowest in northwestern India (especially in Punjab, UP, Rajasthan, Madhya Pradesh and Haryana) and highest in south India (Kerala, Tamilnadu). The greater declines in sex ratios in the northern region clearly suggest the lower position of women in society. Bardhan (1974) writing in the early 1970's saw low sex ratios as a marker of the "general neglect of little girls", the origins of which are to be found in historical, cultural, economical and sociological causes.

The report of the committee on the status of women in India concluded that "an increase in the neglect of female lives as an expendable asset" is "the only reasonable explanation for the declining sex ratio observed to persist over several decades" (Committee on the status of women in India, 1975. Explanations of low child sex ratio (0-6) in India are either the inferior position of women or the discrimination against females in the Indian society (Miller, 1981). Sen (1985) argued that the low Indian sex ratio appears to be the result of differential mortality arising from the neglect of female children. Drawing upon his study of two west Bengal villages, he showed that girls were even more undernourished than boys in both villages were with malnutrition being most severe where landlessness was greatest.

In India, with strong patriarchal and patrilineal norms, there exists strong preference for sons that is determined by socio cultural norms, values of children. Evidence also shows the variation in the son preference between northern to southern parts of India depending on how the above factors play their roles. In the context of fertility decline in India, the desire for at least one son is more prominent and it contributes to unfavourable sex ratio which is tilted towards males. The higher child mortality for girls than that of boys clearly indicates the existence of female disadvantage in the society.

The major components of imbalances in overall and child sex ratio include: (a) sex ratio at birth; (b) sex differentials in mortality; (c) sex differential in migration; and (d) under enumeration of women and girls. Sex ratio varies by region, by social group, age group and level of prosperity. The latest census in 2001 has recorded a significant decrease in the sex ratio of children age 0-6 while registering a marginal rise in the overall female-male ratio at from the previous census in 1991. Many researchers attributed the decline in the child sex ratio to a possible rise in the sex ratio at birth owing to the increasing incidence of sex selective abortion (e.g. as Gupta and Bhat, 1997, Sudha and Rajan, 1999). The decline child sex ratio is both due to discrimination of female child at the age of 1-4 and sex selective abortion practices which is widely prevalent in Punjab, Haryana and Himachal Pradesh. Sex differentials in child mortality in ages 1-5 indicate a huge excess mortality for girls as the result of discriminations against female children in terms of food, nutrition and health care.

Historically low sex ratio in India is mainly attributed to excess female child mortality (Visaria, 1971). However, the accelerated fall in the child sex ratio after 1981 is largely due to the diffusion of parental sex selection techniques in regions with well-entrenched gender bias (Bhat, 2002). Arnold, Kishore and Roy (2002), using NFHS-II data, found evidence of sex selective abortion based on data on use of ultrasound or amniocentesis in India. Biologically sex ratio at birth is always in favour of males, with about 105 boys per 100 girls. A statistical study of registered births in 75 territories with a relatively complete vital registration has confirmed the widely held belief that the masculinity ratio at birth varies generally between 104 and 107(M/F). Sex ratio at birth greater than 107 may suggest evidence of sex selective abortion.

Previous studies also indicated that in India sex-selective abortion is higher among urban women, middle and higher educated women and women living in households with high standard of living (Retherford and Roy, 2003 and Arokiasamy, 2004). In this context, although this study is inspired from the worrying facts of continuously strengthening tendency towards discrimination against women through integration of prevailing traditional gender biased norms and modern technology.

The child sex ratio (0-6 years) is declining steadily during the last five decades and more steeply in northern states of India. In this context, this study aims to examine district wise child sex ratio and sex ratio at birth and study socio economic variations in child sex ratio focusing on Uttar Pradesh, Punjab, Haryana, Rajasthan and Himachal Pradesh, the states with child sex ratios lower than the national average.

Objectives of the study:

- To study the district level child sex ratio (0-6 year age) and sex ratio at birth in selected northern states of India.
- To examine the differentials in child sex ratio and sex ratio at birth by religion and caste.
- To study the effects of socioeconomic factors on child sex ratio and sex ratio at birth.

DATA SOURCE AND METHODOLOGY

The district level data on child sex ratio (0-6 years), sex ratio at birth and socio economic indicators from 2001 census have been used in this analysis.

1. The child sex ratio was calculated at the district level as the number of females per 1000 males and for consistency, sex ratio at birth was also calculated as the number of female births per 1000 male births from census data following the definition in the India census.
2. The differentials in child sex ratio and sex ratio at birth are examined by religious categories such as Hindu, Muslim, Christians and others, social groups i.e. scheduled caste and Scheduled Tribes and women's work status.
3. Multivariate regression analysis is used to study the effect of socio economic factors on child sex ratio and sex ratio at birth. The following predictor variables were used:

(a) Total fertility rate
(b) Percentage of literate women.
(c) Percentage of working women (15-59 years age group).
(d) Percentage of total household electrified.
(e) Percentage of urbanization.
(f) Percentage of Schedule Caste.
(g) Percentage of schedule Tribe.
(h) Percentage of Sikh population.

STATE AND DISTRICT LEVEL CHILD SEX RATIO PATTERNS

Table 15.1 show that Uttar Pradesh has the overall child sex ratio of 916, which is highest among the five states. Punjab occupies lowest position having 798 followed by Haryana (819), Himachal Pradesh (896), and Rajasthan (909). The district level variations in child sex ratios are represented in state wise maps. A few highlights of the districts level sex ratio patterns are as follows:

The overall child sex ratio in Rajasthan is 909 in 2001, which is lower than average child sex ratio of India of 907. Among the districts of Rajasthan, no district has child sex ratio less than 850. In ten districts namely Kota (850) Jhunjhunun (860), Hanumangarh (863), Sikar (869), Baran (872), Alwar (873), Churu (879), Sawai madohpur (885), Bikaner (887), Karauli (899) the child sex ratio range from 850 to 900. Twenty districts have child sex ratio ranging between 900 and 950. Rajsamand (964) and Bhilwara (955) district have the highest child sex ratio in Rajasthan.

The child sex ratio of Himachal Pradesh is 896, it also significantly lower compared to average child sex ratio of the country. There are four districts, which have very low sex ratio. These districts are as Lahul & Pindi (837), Bilaspur (850), and Una (882), Solan (896) .The other districts like Sirmaur (918), Hamirpur (929), kinnaur (934), Shimla (955), Kangra (960), and

Mandi (961) are showing relatively higher child sex ratio. Kullu district found the highest child sex ratio in Himachal Pradesh but apparently more than the country's child sex ratio.

Table 15.1: Child sex ratio (0-6) by state and by religion and caste, 2001

	Rajasthan	*Haryana*	*Punjab*	*Uttar Pradesh*	*Himachal Pradesh*
CSR	909	819	798	916	896
CSR of Hindus	909	816	821	911	895
CSR of Muslims	925	895	879	935	938
CSR of Christian	956	921	870	936	898
CSR of Others	845	745	780	867	871
CSR of SC	919	865	861	930	936
CSR of ST	950	—	—	973	933

CSR: Child Sex Ratio (0-6 year age group).

Punjab (798) has the lowest child sex ratio among the five states. Most districts of the state show low child sex ratio. Extremely low child sex ratio is found in Hosiarpur (769), Amritsar (790), Gurdaspur (789), Kapurtala (785), Fategarh sahib (766), Rupnagar (764), Mansa (786), Muktsar (812), Ludhiana (818), Firozpur (811) and Moga (805) have the lower child sex ratio but higher sex ratio then the state level. The noticeable fact is in the highly urbanized districts also, the child sex ratio is lower.

Haryana has next the lowest child sex ratio of 819 in the country. The district wise child sex ratio ranges from 770 to 858.There are many districts, which have low sex ratios. These districts are such as Hissar (770), Kurukshetra (771), Ambala (782), Sonipat (778), Kaithal (791), Rothak (799).Child sex ratio is higher than the state average is Gurgaon is (858) and followed by Faridabad (850), Bhiwani (841), Panchkula (829), Fatehabad (828), Jind (818), Mahendragarh (818), and sisra (817). Other districts, which have the child, sex ratio range from 800 to 815.

Uttar Pradesh, the biggest state has a total of 70 districts. The overall child sex ratio of Uttar Pradesh is 916, which is relatively higher than Punjab, Haryana and Rajasthan. The districts in order are Baghpat (850), Goutam Budhanagar and Gaziabad (854), Meerut (857), Muzaffernagar (859), Agra (866), Bulandshahar (867), Kanpur Nagar (869), Saharanpur (872). The highest sex ratio is found in Bahraich (970) followed by Siddhartha agar (964). Out of seventy districts in Uttar Pradesh twenty-three districts, the child sex ratio lies ranges from 850 to 900 and in 39 districts child sex ratios ranges between 900 and 950.

CHILD SEX RATIO BY RELIGION AND CASTE

Table 15.1 also shows the child sex ratio by religion and caste for the five states. The lowest child sex ratios are indicated for other religious category other than Hindu, Muslim and Christian. In all the five states, among the major religions, lower child sex ratios are found for Hindus than among Muslims and Christians. The district level child sex ratios followed similar pattern of lower sex ratios among Hindus compared to Muslims and Christians.

By castes, the socially backward scheduled castes are having higher child sex ratios than other caste categories. Moreover, the magnitude of caste-wise differences in sex ratio is quite high in the northern states, namely Punjab, Haryana and Himachal Pradesh compared to the north-central states. Notably, these states also have a significant proportion of scheduled caste population.

In Haryana, across the districts, child sex ratios among Hindus range from 782 to 841. Gurgaon, which has the highest child sex ratio among the total, has comparatively less in this category (Hindu) i.e. 815. Faridabad has the highest child sex ratio of 841 and Kurukshetra has the lowest child sex ratio of 782 among Hindu category. Child sex ratio among Hindus in other districts lies in between these two figures such as Ambala (794), Rattak (798), Karnal (813), and Sisra (834). Among the districts, the highest child sex ratio of 948 is found in Mahendragarh district and Fatehabad district has the lowest child sex ratio of

769 among Muslims. Other districts have ratio between this ranges among Muslims with significant variation among the districts of Haryana. For example Gurgaon (902), Mahendragarh (948), Jhajjar (915), Yamunanagar (817), Panchakulla (855). Child sex ratio by Scheduled caste generally shows that there is a negligible variation of the sex ratios of scheduled caste in the districts of Haryana. Among Scheduled castes, Fatehabad shows the highest child sex ratio of 885 followed by Panchakula and Faridabad where the child sex ratio is (884). In other districts of the state, the sex ratio of Scheduled caste is more than 840 such as Ambala (844), Sonipat (848), Kurukshetra (851) and Panipat (855).

In Uttar Pradesh, the Hindu and Muslim religion have almost same level of child sex ratio across the districts. Christians and other categories show more variation in the child sex ratio among the districts. The total child sex ratio of SC population in Uttar Pradesh is 930 which itself is higher than the countries sex ratio. For Scheduled castes the higher child sex ratio in various districts like Muzaffarnagar (933), Lalitpur and Gorakhapur (965), Balia (952), Kushinagar (949) Basti (956) is showing less discrimination of girls. The ST population of the district occupies less proportion in the total population and they are less in number.

The most unfavorable child sex ratio is found in others category mostly Sikhs in Punjab. Sikh populations, which constitute almost 60 percent of the state's population is a dominating religion in the state, where as Hindu, Muslim and Christians share less proportion in the total population. The districts like Patiala (745), Fatehgarhsahib (744), Gurdaspur (750), Hoshiarpur (769) with more Sikh population has extremely low sex ratio. High child sex ratio is found in Muktsar (1031), Bathainda (1009) for Muslims and Nawansahar (1128) for Christian category. However, it is also noticeable that there are other districts, which have lower child sex ratio. For example Muktsar (720), Faridkot (724) in Hindus, Fatehgarhsahib (746), Patiala (750) among Muslims and sangria (768), Bhandida (782), Mamsa (775) among Christians respectively.

In Himachal Pradesh, for Hindu and Muslim category, the child sex ratio is comparatively in the same range except two districts such as Mandi (1000) and Sirmaur (1153) which is high among Muslim religion.

In Rajasthan, among Hindus highest sex ratio is found in Rajsamand (966) followed by Bhilwara (957), Kota (861) and Jhunjhunun (860) shows the ranges of highest and lowest child sex ratio respectively. Among Muslim, the child sex ratio is higher (more than 900) than Hindus in most districts except one or two districts such as Jhunjhun (851), Hanumannagar (875), Baran (891). In many districts, child sex ratios are higher in comparison to other caste categories. In Barmer district, higher sex ratios are seen for both the categories: 948 for SC and 942 for ST. Chittorgarh 937 in SC and 939 in ST, Ajmeer, 962 in SC and 952 in ST, Nagur, 955 in SC and 945 in ST.

DISTRICT LEVEL VARIATION IN SEX RATIO AT BIRTH

The state wise sex ratios at birth by caste are presented in Table 15.2. Following the pattern in child sex ratios, the lowest sex ratios at birth are indicated for Haryana (786) and Punjab (787). Overall, confirming the state wise pattern of child sex ratio by caste, the sex ratio at birth is also found to be higher among SCs than other castes.

Table 15.2: State level sex ratio at birth by caste wise, 2001

	Rajasthan	*Haryana*	*Punjab*	*Uttar Pradesh*	*Himachal Pradesh*
Sex ratio at birth	864	786	787	901	845
Sex ratio at birth of ST	880	834	845	911	884
Sex ratio at birth of ST	910	—	—	885	884

SRB: Sex ratio at Birth (0-1 year age group).

In Haryana, the overall Sex Ratio at Birth is 786 and 834 for Schedule Caste. Karnal has lowest Sex Ratio at Birth of 713 and Faridabad is 846. For SC the lowest Sex Ratio at Birth again in Sonipat i.e. 788 and highest in 889 observed in Faridabad.

Table 15.3: Socio-economic variables by states

Socio-economic characteristics	*Rajasthan*	*Haryana*	*Punjab*	*Uttar Pradesh*	*Himachal Pradesh*
Total HH electrified (In %)	35	60	85	29.88	95
Percentage of SC (In %)	17.17	19.40	28.94	21.17	24.72
Percentage of ST (In %)	12.57	0.00	0.00	0.07	4.02
Female Work Participation Rate (in %)	17.50	43.60	28.66	27.43	63.44
Female Literacy Rate (In %)	44.34	56.31	63.55	42.98	68.08
Urbanization (In %)	23.38	29.00	33.95	20.78	9.80

In Himachal Pradesh, the overall Sex Ratio at Birth is 845. Una district records the lowest Sex Ratio at Birth i.e. 785 and Lahul and Spiti records high sex ratio at Birth i.e. 929 followed by Shimla (911). For the Schedule caste, Sex Ratio at Birth ranges from 1167 to 833. The district level Sex Ratio at Birth vary for instance for Shimla (923), Sirmaur (907) and Kangra (867), Kullu (876), Solan (858) respectively.

In Punjab, the overall sex ratio at birth is 789. Among all the districts, the sex ratio at birth is lower than 850 but higher than 750. For example, Amritsar and Patiala having 757 and Nawansahar (831) shows the lowest and highest respectively. For example Nawansahar (779) and Hosiarpur (878) shows respectively the lowest and highest sex ratio at birth.

In Rajasthan, the overall sex ratio at birth is 864. Among all the districts, the sex ratio at birth varies between 783 and 978. Kota and Hanumannagar are having lowest sex ratio at birth of 783 and respectively. Rajsamand and Bhilwara occupy highest position in sex ratio at birth having 932 and 978 respectively. Out of 32 districts of Rajasthan in 17 districts Sex Ratio at Birth varies between 850 to 900 and 9 districts lies between 800 to 850 and 6 districts having 900 to 950. Dungarpur occupies highest position with sex ratio at birth of 1111.

Uttar Pradesh's overall sex ratio at birth is 901. Kanpur has the lowest sex ratio at birth having 792 and Khusinagar and

Farrukhabad have the highest sex ratio at birth having1081 and 1038 respectively. The Sex Ratio at Birth ranges from 850 to 900 in 30 districts and it ranges from 900 to 950 in 20 districts. The overall sex ratio at birth of Schedule Castes is 911 higher than overall sex ratio at birth for the state. sex ratio at birth for Scheduled castes is higher than overall sex ratio at birth for the state.

REGRESSION ANALYSIS OF CHILD SEX RATIO AND SEX RATIO AT BIRTH

In order to examine whether socio economic factors influenced child sex ratio and sex ratio at birth, regression analyses was carried out by taking child sex ratio as dependent variable in model-I and II and sex ratio at birth in model-III and socio economic status factors as explanatory variables. Table 15.4 presents the effects of different socio economic determinants on child sex ratio. The explanatory variables in the model include female work participation rate, percentage of total household electrified, percentage of schedule caste population, percentage of urban population, female literacy rate and sex ratio at birth, percentage of sikhs and total fertility rate. The results of regression show that percentage of household electrified, female literacy rate, percentage of urban population and percentage of Sikhs have statistically significant and negative effect on child sex ratio. Total fertility rate and sex ratio at birth show significant and positive effect on child sex ratio of the population. The statistical evidence suggests that low child sex ratio because of sex selective abortion and is contributed to more by urban, educated and economically better off population. Model III represents percentage of sikhs is statistically highly significant and has negative effect on sex ratio at birth but percentage of household electrified, percentage of SC population, percentage of ST population, female work participation rate, female literacy rate has highly statistically significant and positive effect on sex ratio at birth. Percentage of Sikh population shows statistically significant negative effect on sex ratio at birth.

Table 15.4: Regression analysis of child sex ratio and sex ratio at birth with district level socio-economic predictors (all districts of five states combined)

Predictors	*Dependent variable: Child sex ratio (0-6 years)*		*Dependent variable: Sex ratio at birth*
	Model - I	*Model - II*	*Model - III*
	ß	ß	ß
Total fertility rate	12.16** (4.89)	22.67* (4.53)	—
Sex ratio at birth	—	0.11* (0.02)	—
Percentage of household electrified	-0.35** (0.16)	-0.43* (0.14)	1.70** (0.75)
Percentage of SC population	1.15** (0.53)	0.66 (0.47)	4.66*** (2.54)
Percentage of ST population	1.24* (0.29)	0.97* (0.25)	3.360** (1.36)
Female work participation rate	0.25 (0.22)	0.07 (0.19)	1.98*** (1.05)
Female literacy rate	-0.72** (0.32)	-1.08* (0.28)	6.42* (1.33)
Percentage of urban population	-0.97 (0.26)	-0.79* (0.23)	-0.690 (1.23)
Percentage of Sikh population	-0.57 (0.19)	-0.06 (0.18)	-3.71* (0.91)
Constant	878.78	854.60	-404.66*
R^2	0.62	0.71	0.424

* 1 % level of significance.

** 5% level of significance.

CONCLUSION

The falling child sex ratio is a matter of concern. The district wise analysis shows very low child sex ratios in most districts of these five states. Fatehgarh sahib district (766) has the lowest child sex ratio in the state of Punjab. Even though Punjab and Haryana are economically more developed states, the child sex ratio is worse off in most of the districts of these states. In Uttar Pradesh, there is lesser variation between the districts.

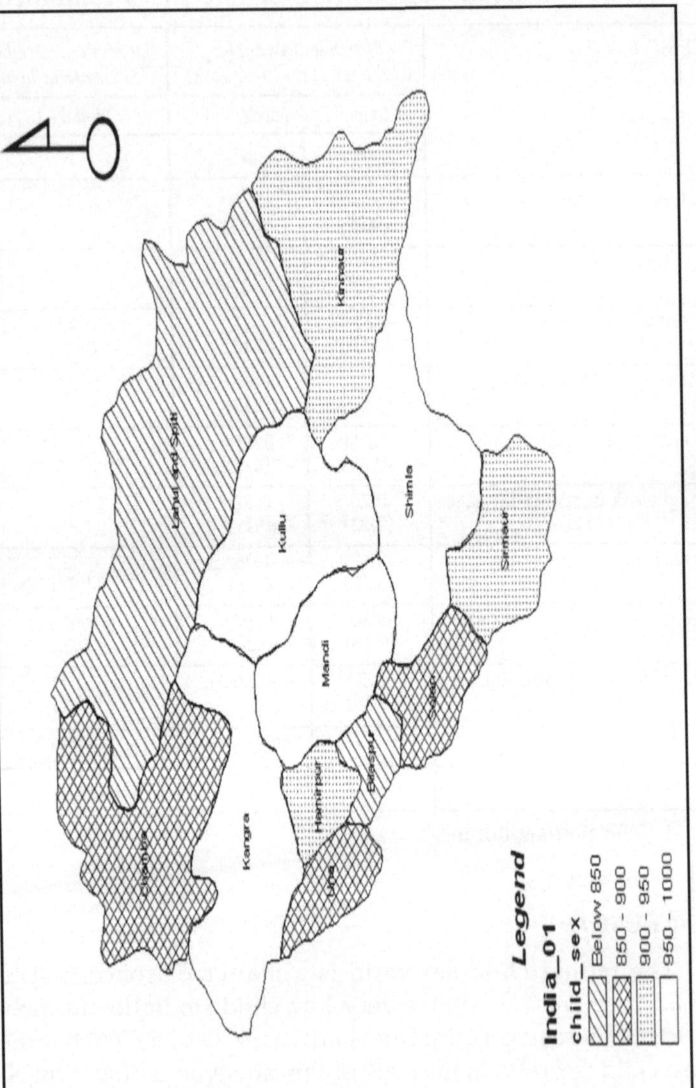

Fig. 15.1: **Child Sex Ratio of Himachal Pradesh**

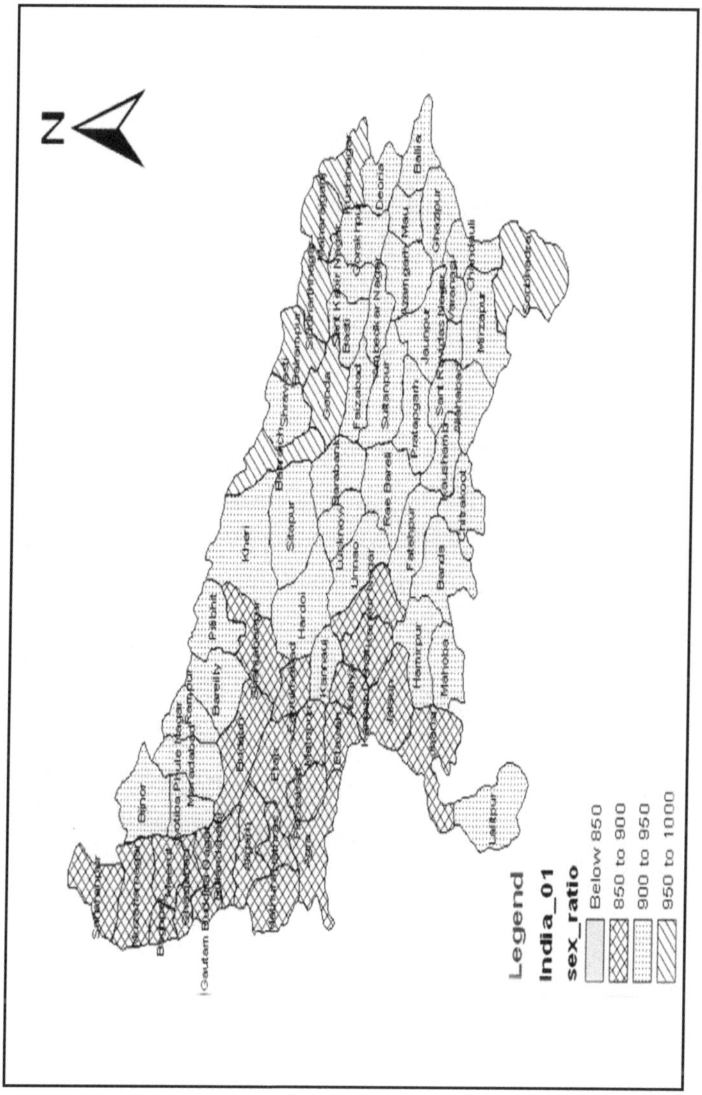

Fig. 15.2: **Child Sex Ratio of Uttar Pradesh**

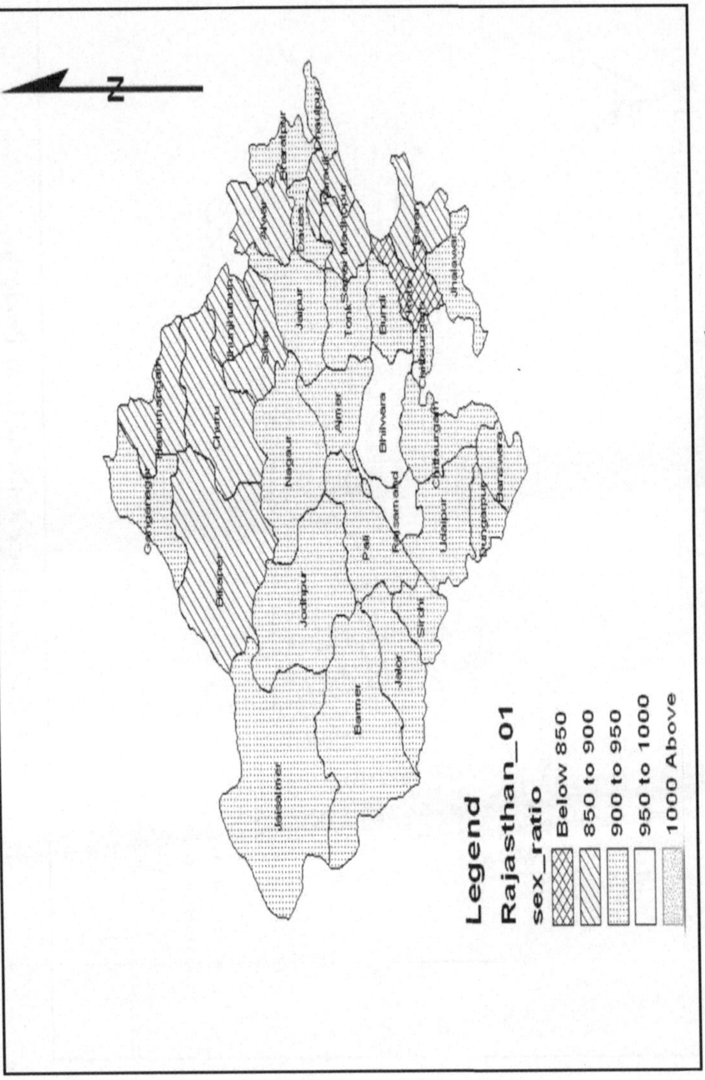

Fig. 15.3: **Child Sex Ratio of Rajasthan**

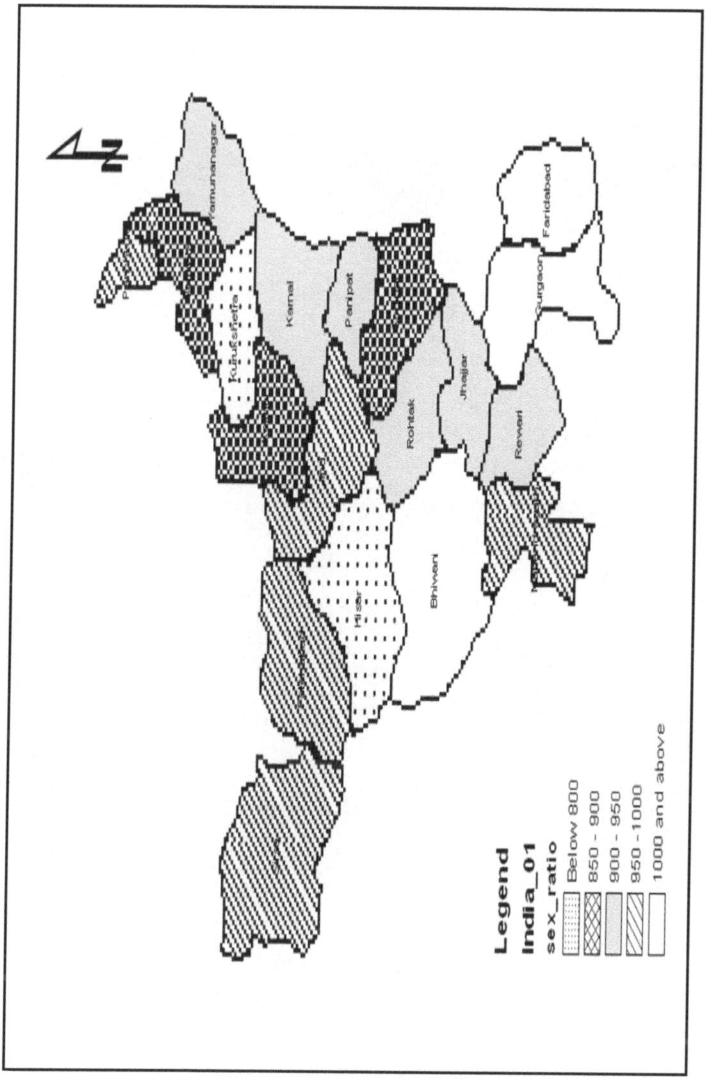

Fig. 15.4: **Child Sex Ratio of Haryana**

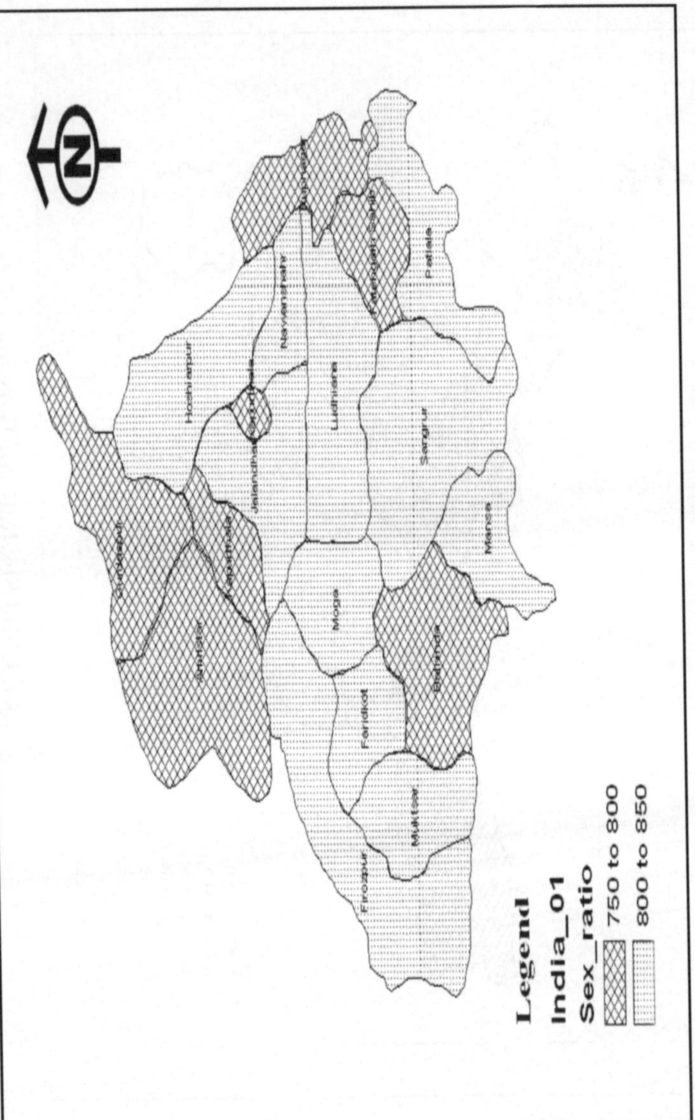

Fig. 15.5: **Child Sex Ratio of Punjab**

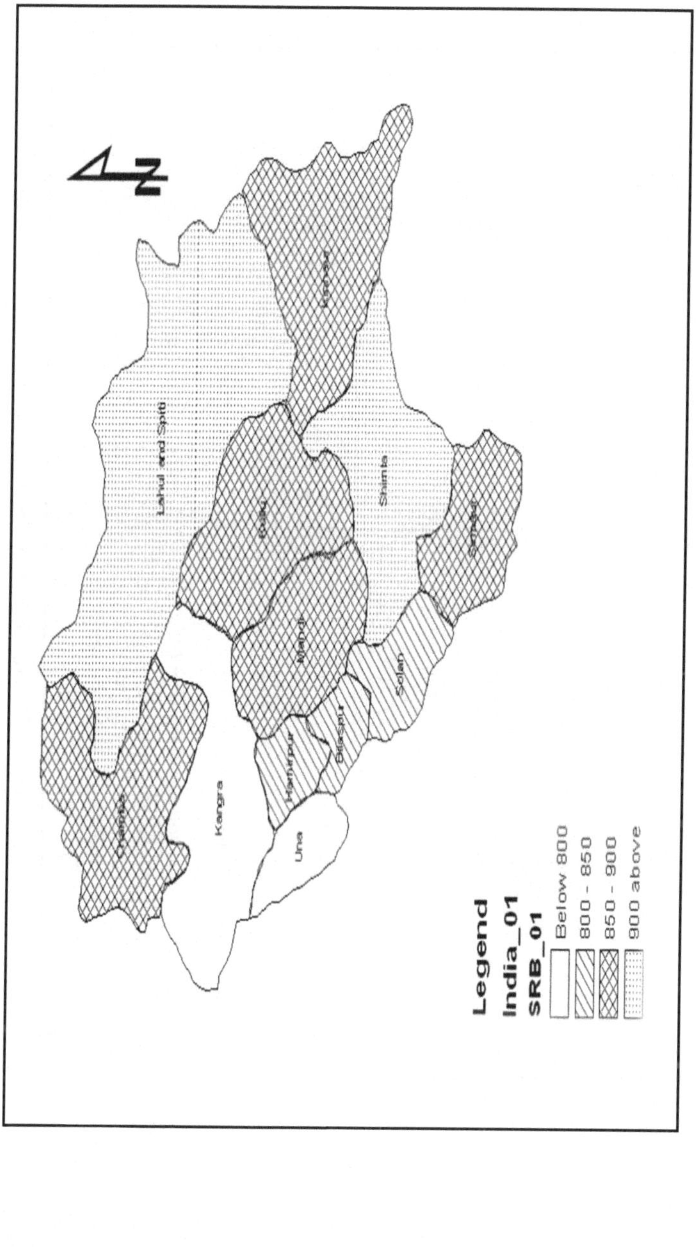

Fig. 15.6: **Sex Ratio at Birth of Himachal Pradesh**

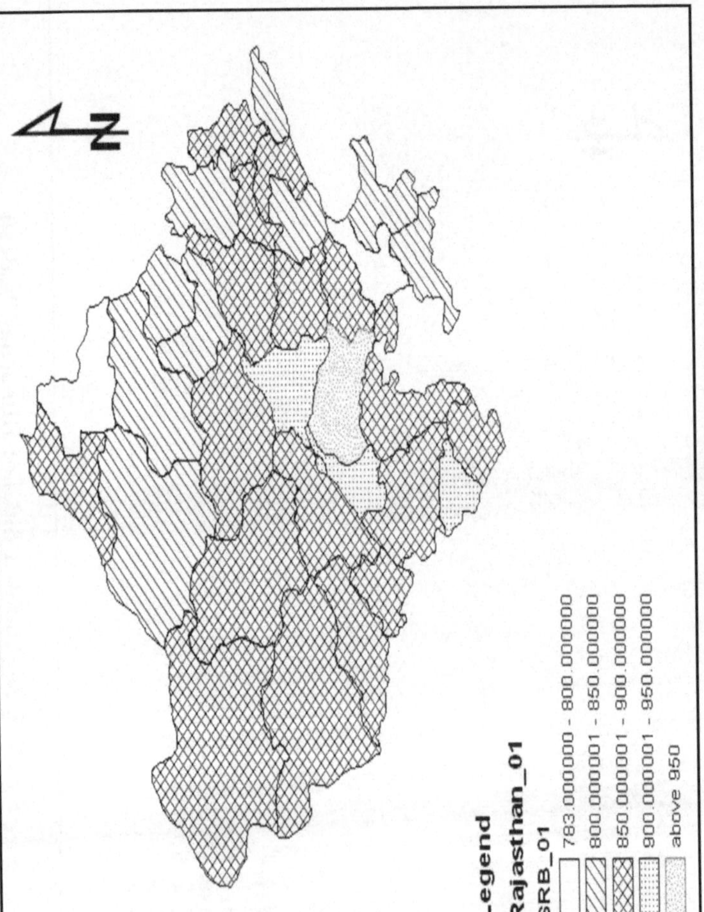

Fig. 15.7: **Sex Ratio at Birth of Rajasthan**

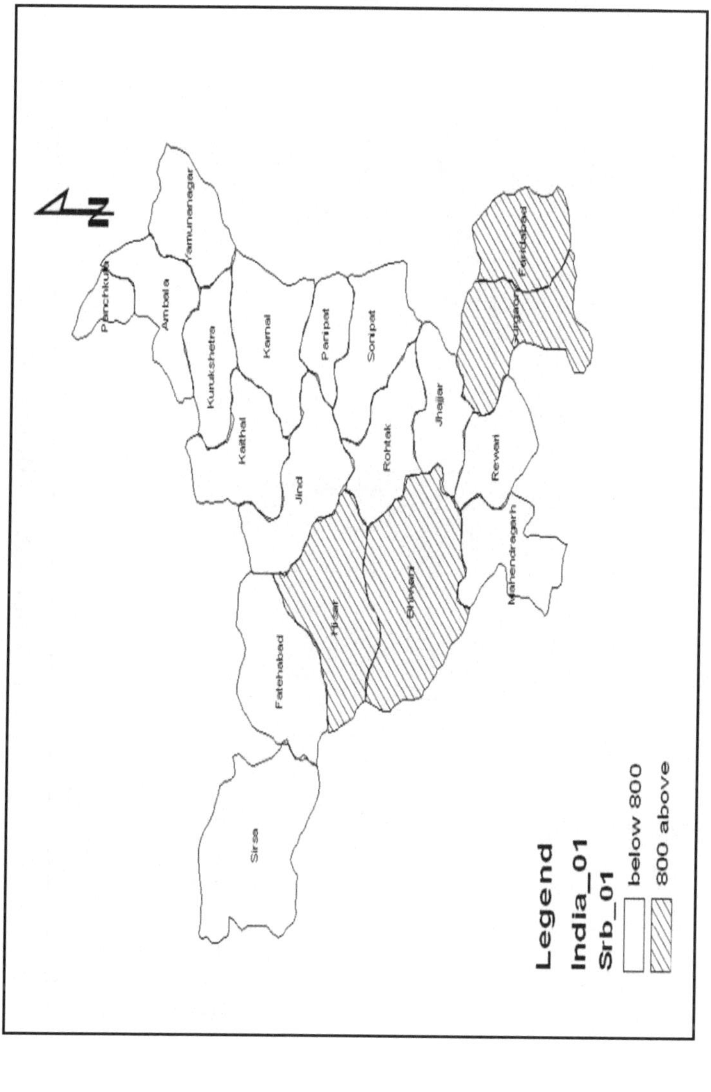

Fig. 15.8: **Sex Ratio of Haryana**

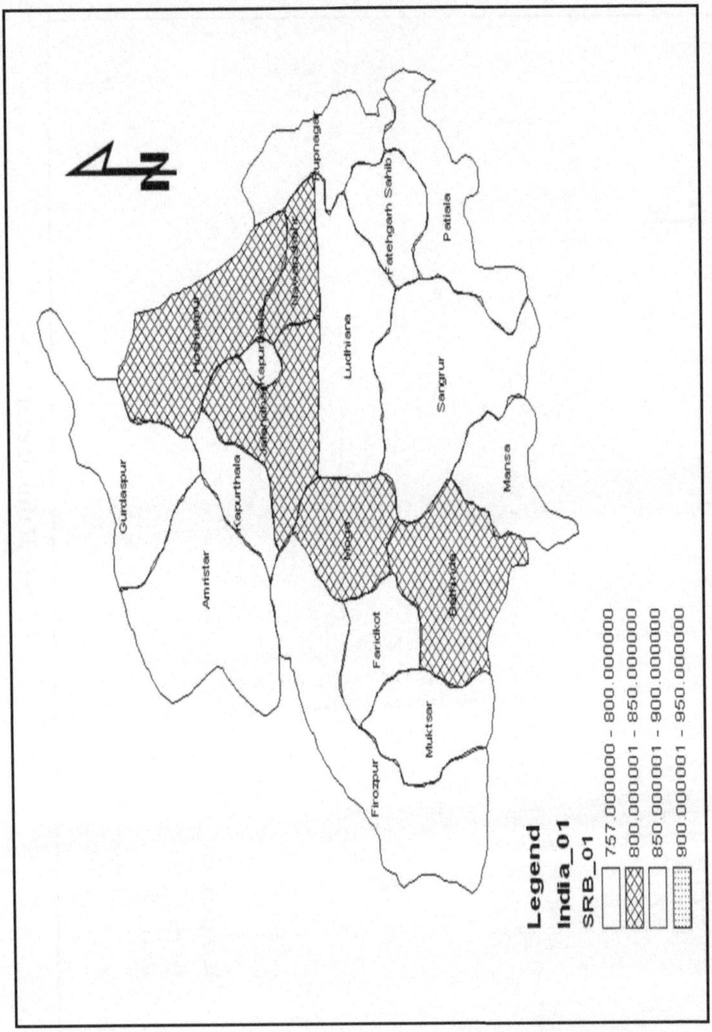

Fig. 15.9: **Sex Ratio at Birth of Punjab**

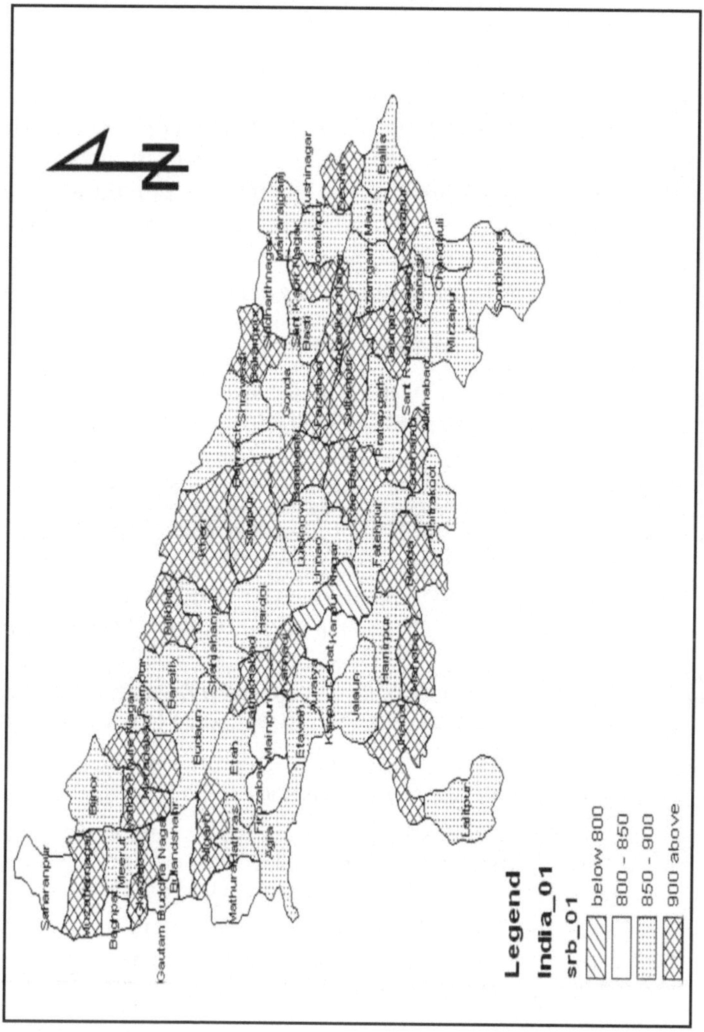

Fig. 15.10: **Sex Ratio at Birth of Uttar Pradesh**

The district wise analysis of child sex ratios in the five states shows that the child sex ratios are lowest among other religious category followed by Hindus, Muslims and then Christians. Child sex ratios are higher among Scheduled castes than the overall child sex ratio of the state. The sex ratio at birth follows a very close pattern of lower child sex ratios for states and districts. Regression analysis shows evidence that lower sex ratio at birth is directly contributing to the declining child sex ratio. The predictor variables showing negative effects on child sex ratio are percentage of household electrified, percentage of Schedule caste, female literacy rate and urbanization. It suggests that decline in child sex ratios are contributed more by urban, educated and economically better off segment of the population.

REFERENCES

Agnihotri, S.B., 2000. "*Sex Ratio Patterns in the Indian Population: A Fresh Exploration*." New Delhi: Sage Publications.

Arokiasamy, P. 2004 "*Regional Patterns of Sex Bias and Excess Female Child Mortality in India*". Population Studies, 59 (6), pp. 833-864.

Bhatt, Mari P.N., 2002. "On the Trail of "Missing" Indian Females (I)." *Economic and Political Weekly*, 37(51 & 52), 5108-118.

Das Gupta, Monica and Bhat, P.N. Mari (1997) "Fertility Decline and Increased Manifestation of Sex Bias in India." *Population Studies*, 51(3). 307-315.

Gulliot, Michel. (2002) "The Dynamics of Population Sex Ratio in India, 1971-96" *Population Studies*, 56(2002), 51-63, Printed in Great Britain.

Guilmoto, C.Z. and S. Irudaya Rajan (2002) "District Level Estimates of Fertility from India's 2001 Census" *Economic and Political Weekly*, Feb. 2002 (672).

Krishnaji, N.1987. "Poverty and Sex Ratio: Some Data and Speculations." *Economic and Political Weekly*, Vol. XXII, No. 23, 892- 897.

Sekher, T.V. and Neelambar Hatti., 2006 "Vulnerable Daughters in a Modernizing Society." Lund Papers in Economic History. No.104, Lund, Sweden: Lund University.

Visaria, Praveen M. (1967). "Sex Ratio at Birth in Territories with a Relatively Complete Registration." *Eugenics Quarterly*, Vol. 14, No. 2 (pp. 132-142).

Index

❑❑❑